CO-OWNERSHIP

AUSTRALIA AND NEW ZEALAND
The Law Book Company Ltd.
Sydney : Melbourne : Perth

CANADA AND U.S.A.
The Carswell Company Ltd.
Agincourt, Ontario

INDIA
N.M. Tripathi Private Ltd.
Bombay
and
Eastern Law House Private Ltd.
Calcutta and Delhi
M.P.P. House
Bangalore

ISRAEL
Steimatzky's Agency Ltd.
Jerusalem : Tel Aviv : Haifa

MALAYSIA : SINGAPORE : BRUNEI
Malayan Law Journal (Pte.) Ltd.
Singapore and Kuala Lumpur

CO-OWNERSHIP

M. P. THOMPSON, LL.B. (Leic.); LL.M. (Keele)
Lecturer in Law, University of Leicester

LONDON   SWEET & MAXWELL   1988

Published in 1988 by
Sweet & Maxwell Limited
11 New Fetter Lane, London
Computerset by Promenade Graphics Ltd., Cheltenham
Printed in Great Britain by
Butler and Tanner Ltd.,
Frome, Somerset.

British Library Cataloguing in Publication Data
Thompson, Mark
  Co-ownership.
  1. England. Real property. Co-ownership.
  Law
  I. Title
  344.2064'32

ISBN 0–421–37500–0

All rights reserved. No part of this publication
may be reproduced or transmitted, in any form or
by any means, electronic, mechanical, photocopying,
recording or otherwise, or stored in any retrieval
system of any nature, without the written permission
of the copyright holder and the publisher, application
for which shall be made to the publisher.

© M. P. Thompson 1988

PREFACE

My principal aim in writing this book is to provide a clear and concise guide, for practitioners, to the law relating to co-ownership. I have sought to have regard to potential practical problems and also to provide a viewpoint on the areas of uncertainty which currently exist in the law. Although primarily aimed at the lawyer in practice, I hope that the book will have some utility for students studying property law subjects for whom the problems associated with co-ownership plays an increasingly important part.

A notable feature in recent litigation involving co-ownership of land is the importance of occupation rights. This is particularly evident from cases, such as *Grant* v. *Edwards*, relating to the establishment of an interest in the home and also from the decisions in *Williams and Glyn's Bank* v. *Boland* and *City of London Building Society* v. *Flegg* concerning the enforcement of those rights against mortgagees. Reflecting the importance of shared occupation rights, I have included a chapter on rights of occupation which do not necessarily derive from beneficial co-ownership of either freehold or leasehold property and their regulation.

One of the pleasant features of working at Leicester is the willingness of colleagues to offer advice and encouragement. I am grateful to Graham Barnsley and Ian Snaith who each commented helpfully on a number of draft chapters and to David Hughes for his considerable assistance on the chapter on leaseholds. I am also indebted to Barbara Goodman and Gladys Hurst for their cheerful and efficient work on the word processor. Finally I am grateful to the staff at Sweet and Maxwell for their encouragement throughout and for their good sense in relieving me of the task of preparing the tables and index. Needless to say, I alone am responsible for all the frailties that remain.

Generally the law is stated as at January 4, 1988, I have, however, been able to make limited reference to subsequent developments, the most important being the decision in *Antoniades* v. *Villiers*, a case which is difficult to reconcile with the almost equally recent case of *A. G. Securities* v. *Vaughan*. At the time of going to press, therefore, the distinction between leases and licences in the context of sharing arrangements is obscure with the law in some disarray. This position can only be clarified in the House of Lords and, it is to be hoped, that this occurs at an early date.

M. P. Thompson
University of Leicester
March 24, 1988

CONTENTS

Preface v
Table of Cases ix
Table of Statutes xxi
Table of Statutory Instruments xxv

1. THE LEGAL FRAMEWORK OF CO-OWNERSHIP   1

    Concurrent and consecutive interests   1
    Strict settlement   2
    Trust for sale   4
    Sales of the property: overreaching   8
    Structure of co-ownership   11
    Co-ownership and trusts for sale   13
    Severance   16
    Acts of severance   19
    Party walls   26

2. THE ACQUISITION OF INTERESTS IN PROPERTY   27

    Personal property   27
    Family home   31
    Acquisition of interests in the family home   33
    Implied, resulting and constructive trusts   35
    Estoppel   46
    Remedies   49
    Valuation and equitable accounting   50

3. PETITIONS FOR SALE BY CO-OWNERS   53

    Section 30 petitions   54
    The underlying purpose   54
    Occupation rent   56
    Orders under the Matrimonial Causes Act 1973   57
    Legal aid   59

4. LEASEHOLD PROPERTY   61

    Joint tenancies or licences?   61
    Co-ownership and the exercise of landlord and tenant rights   64
    Co-ownership and protective legislation   66
    Grounds for possession   70
    Succession   74
    The right to buy   76

5. THE PROTECTION AND REGULATION OF OCCUPATION   79

    Spouse's right of occupation   79
    Regulation of occupation—ouster orders   84
    Criteria for making an order   89
    Interrelation of the statutes   92
    Powers of arrest   95
    Conclusion   97

6. INSOLVENCY   98

Charging orders   **98**
Bankruptcy   **103**
Petitions for sale by the trustee in bankruptcy   **108**
Mortgage possession actions   **112**
Equity of exoneration   **116**

7. PRIORITIES   118

Decision in Williams & Glyn's Bank v. Boland   **118**
Unregistered land   **125**
Undue influence   **128**
Dispositions by two trustees   **129**
Estoppel interests   **136**

TABLE OF CASES

A.G. Securities v. Vaughan (1988) 132 S.J. 301; [1988] 06 E.G. 112; (1988) 138 New L.J. 23 64
Abbott (A Bankrupt), Re [1983] Ch. 45; [1982] 3 W.L.R. 86; (1982) 126 S.J. 345; [1982] 3 All E.R. 181, D.C. 106, 107
Abigail v. Lapin [1934] A.C. 491 124
Adeoso v. Adeoso [1980] 1 W.L.R. 1535; (1980) 124 S.J. 847; [1981] 1 All E.R. 107; (1980) 11 Fam.Law 53, C.A. 89
Ahmed v. Kendrick, The Times, November 12, 1987 134
Ainsbury v. Millington [1986] 1 All E.R. 73; [1986] 1 F.L.R. 331, C.A. 89
Ainscough v. Ainscough (Cedar Holdings Ltd. intervening) (1987) 17 Fam.Law 347 ... 99
Aldrington Garages v. Fielder (1978) 247 E.G. 557; (1978) 37 P. & C.R. 461, C.A. ... 62
Ali v. Hussein (1974) 231 E.G. 372 55
Allen v. Allen [1961] 1 W.L.R. 1186; 105 S.J. 630; [1961] 3 All E.R. 385, C.A. 42
Anderson, Re [1920] 1 Ch. 175 5
—— v. Anderson (1984) 14 H.L.R. 241; (1984) 15 Fam.Law 183, C.A. 91
Ansah v. Ansah [1977] Fam. 138; [1977] 2 W.L.R. 760; (1976) 121 S.J. 118; [1977] 2 All E.R. 638, C.A. 95, 97
Antoniades v. Villiers, The Independent, March 23, 1988 .... 63, 64
Appleton v. Appleton [1965] 1 W.L.R. 25; 108 S.J. 919; [1965] 1 All E.R. 44, C.A. ... 32
Ashburn Anstalt v. W.J. Arnold & Co. (1987) 284 E.G. 1375 138
Atkins' Will Trusts, Re [1974] 1 W.L.R. 761; 118 S.J. 391; [1974] 2 All E.R. 1 6
Att.-Gen. of Hong Kong v. Humphreys Estate (Queen's Gardens) Ltd. [1987] A.C. 114; [1987] 2 W.L.R. 343; 131 S.J. 194; [1987] 2 All E.R. 387 47
Aveling v. Knipe (1815) 19 Ves. 441 .... 15, 19
Avon Finance Co. Ltd. v. Bridger (1979) 123 S.J. 705; [1985] 2 All E.R. 281, C.A. ... 128

B. v. B. (Domestic Violence: Jurisdiction) [1978] Fam. 26; [1978] 2 W.L.R. 160; (1977) 121 S.J. 759; [1978] 1 All E.R. 821 88
Bacon v. Bacon [1947] P. 153; [1948] L.J.R. 530; [1947] 2 All E.R. 327 5
Bagot's Settlement, Re [1894] 1 Ch. 177 120
Bailey (A Bankrupt), Re [1977] 1 W.L.R. 278; [1977] 2 All E.R. 26, D.C. 110, 111
Baker v. Lewis [1947] K.B. 186; [1947] L.J.R. 468; [1946] 2 All E.R. 592, C.A. 71
Bank of Scotland v. Grimes [1985] Q.B. 1179; [1985] 3 W.L.R. 294; 129 S.J. 331; [1985] 2 All E.R. 254; (1985) 15 Fam.Law, C.A. 115
Bannister v. Bannister [1948] 2 All E.R. 133; [1948] W.N. 261; 92 S.J. 377 39
Barclay v. Barclay [1970] 2 Q.B. 677; [1970] 3 W.L.R. 82; 114 S.J. 456; [1970] 2 All E.R. 676; 21 P. & C.R. 908, C.A. 120, 121
Barnett v. Hassett [1981] 1 W.L.R. 1385; [1982] 1 All E.R. 80; (1981) 125 S.J. 376 81
Barton v. Morris [1985] 1 W.L.R. 1257; 51 P. & C.R. 84; [1985] 2 All E.R. 1032 .... 18, 23
Basham, Re [1986] 1 W.L.R. 1498; 130 S.J. 986; [1987] 1 All E.R. 405 .... 48, 49
Beale's Settlement Trusts, Re [1932] Ch. 15 6
Bedson v. Bedson [1965] 2 Q.B. 666; [1965] 3 W.L.R. 891; 109 S.J. 776; [1965] 3 All E.R. 307, C.A. 21, 24
Bendall v. McWhirter [1952] 2 Q.B. 466; [1952] 1 T.L.R. 1332; 96 S.J. 344; [1952] 1 All E.R. 1307 79
Bennet v. Bennet (1879) 10 Ch.D. 474 28
Bernard v. Josephs [1982] Ch. 391; [1982] 2 W.L.R. 1052; 126 S.J. 361; [1982] 3 All E.R. 162; (1983) 4 F.L.R. 178 .... 34, 40, 41, 45, 51
Binions v. Evans [1972] Ch. 359 .... 4, 50, 138
Bishop, Re; National Provincial Bank v. Bishop [1965] Ch. 450; [1965] 2 W.L.R. 188; 109 S.J. 107; [1965] 1 All E.R. 249 30
Blacklocks v. J.B. Developments (Godalming) Ltd. [1982] Ch. 183; [1981] 3 W.L.R. 554; (1981) 125 S.J. 356; [1981] 3 All E.R. 392; (1982) 42 P. & C.R. 27 139
Bostock v. Tacher De la Pagerie (1987) 19 H.L.R. 358; [1987] 1 E.G.L.R. 104; (1987) 282 E.G. 999, C.A. 71

Bothe v. Amos [1976] Fam. 47; [1975] 2 W.L.R. 838; 119 S.J. 150; [1975] 2 All E.R. 321; 5 Fam.Law 86, C.A.	43
Boylan v. Boylan (1981) 11 Fam.Law 76, C.A.	97
Boyle's Claim, Re [1961] 1 W.L.R. 339; 105 S.J. 155; [1961] 1 All E.R. 620	122
Bradshaw v. Toulmin (1784) Dick. 633	11
Brinnand v. Ewens [1987] 19 H.L.R. 415; (1987) 284 E.G. 1052	48
Bristol and West Building Society v. Henning [1985] 1 W.L.R. 778; 129 S.J. 363; [1985] 2 All E.R. 606; 50 P. & C.R. 237; 17 H.L.R. 432, C.A.	123, 124
Brooker Settled Estates Ltd. v. Ayres (1987) 19 H.L.R. 246; (1987) 54 P. & C.R. 165; [1987] 1 E.G.L.R. 50, C.A.	63
Brown v. Brash [1948] 2 K.B. 247; [1948] L.J.R. 1544; [1948] 1 All E.R. 922, C.A.	67, 122
—— v. Brown (1981) 3 F.L.R. 161	58
—— v. Dale (1878) 9 Ch.D. 178	18
—— v. Raindle (1796) 3 Ves. 256	22
—— v. Staniek (1969) 211 E.G. 283	34
Browne v. Pritchard [1975] 1 W.L.R. 1366; 119 S.J. 679; [1975] 3 All E.R. 721, C.A.	57
Brykiert v. Jones (1981) 2 F.L.R. 373; 125 S.J. 323, C.A.	34
Buchanan-Wollaston's Conveyance, Re [1939] Ch. 738	54
Bull v. Bull [1955] 1 Q.B. 234; [1955] 2 W.L.R. 78; 99 S.J. 60; [1955] 1 All E.R. 253, C.A.	15, 16, 54, 119, 120, 121, 129
Burgess v. Rawnsley [1975] Ch. 429; [1975] 3 W.L.R. 99; 119 S.J. 406; [1975] 3 All E.R. 142; 30 P. & C.R. 221, C.A.	18, 22, 23
Burke v. Burke [1974] 1 W.L.R. 1063; (1973) 118 S.J. 98; [1974] 2 All E.R. 944, C.A.	55
—— v. —— (1987) 137 New L.J. 11	91
Burns v. Burns [1984] Ch. 317; [1984] 2 W.L.R. 582; [1984] 1 All E.R. 244; (1984) 14 Fam.Law 244, C.A.	44, 45, 47, 48
Button v. Button [1968] 1 W.L.R. 457; 112 S.J. 112; [1968] 1 All E.R. 1064; 19 P. & C.R. 257, C.A.	36
Caines (dec'd), Re [1978] 1 W.L.R. 540; (1977) 122 S.J. 80; [1978] 2 All E.R. 1	22
Cann v. Ayres (1976) 7 Fam.Law 47, C.A.	30
Cantliff v. Jenkins [1978] Fam. 47; [1978] 2 W.L.R. 177n; (1977) 121 S.J. 849; [1978] 1 All E.R. 836, C.A.	88
Carega Properties S.A. v. Sharratt [1979] 1 W.L.R. 928; (1979) 123 S.J. 505; (1979) 39 P. & C.R. 76; (1979) 252 E.G. 163, H.L.	76
Carne's Settled Estate, Re [1889] 1 Ch. 324	5
Carson v. Carson [1983] 1 W.L.R. 285; (1981) 125 S.J. 513; [1983] 1 All E.R. 478, C.A.	58
Carter and Kenderdine's Contract [1897] 1 Ch. 776	105
Catling, Re [1931] 2 Ch. 359	5
Caunce v. Caunce [1969] 1 W.L.R. 286; (1968) 113 S.J. 204; [1969] 1 All E.R. 722; 20 P. & C.R. 877	119, 125
Cedar Holdings Ltd. v. Green [1981] Ch. 129; [1979] 3 W.L.R. 31; (1979) 123 S.J. 302; [1979] 3 All E.R. 117; (1979) 38 P. & C.R. 673, C.A.	10, 11, 99
Centrax Trustees Ltd. v. Ross [1979] 2 All E.R. 952	115
Chadda v. Chadda (1981) 11 Fam.Law 142	91
Chalmers v. Guthrie (1923) 156 L.T.J. 382	64
Chandler v. Kerley [1978] 1 W.L.R. 693; (1978) 122 S.J. 332; [1978] 2 All E.R. 942; (1978) 8 Fam.Law 108, C.A.	138
Chaplin & Co. Ltd. v. Brammall [1908] 1 K.B. 233	128
Chapman v. Chapman [1969] 1 W.L.R. 1367; 113 S.J. 524; [1969] 3 All E.R. 476; 20 P. & C.R. 1037, C.A.	42
Charlton v. Lester (1976) 238 E.G. 115	54, 55
Chhokar v. Chhokar [1984] F.L.R. 313; (1984) 14 Fam.Law 269, C.A.	56, 122
Chios Property Investment Co. v. Lopez (1987) 138 New L.J. 20	76
Christian v. Christian (1981) 131 New L.J. 43	48
City of London Building Society v. Flegg [1988] A.C. 54; [1987] 2 W.L.R. 1266	9, 10, 34, 121, 130, 131, 132, 133, 135
Coldunell Ltd. v. Gallon [1986] Q.B. 1184; [1986] 2 W.L.R. 466; [1986] 1 All E.R. 429; [1986] F.L.R. 183, C.A.	128

Colin Smith Music Ltd. v. Ridge. *See* Smith (Colin) Music Ltd. v. Ridge.	
Commissioner of Stamp Duties v. Byrnes [1911] A.C. 386	28
Cook v. Cook [1962] P. 235; [1962] 3 W.L.R. 441; 106 S.J. 668; [1962] 2 All E.R. 811, C.A.	120
Cooke v. Head [1972] 1 W.L.R. 518; 116 S.J. 298; [1972] 2 All E.R. 38, C.A.	41, 137
Coombes v. Smith [1986] 1 W.L.R. 808; (1986) 130 S.J. 482	47, 48, 49
Cooper v. Critchley [1955] Ch. 431; [1955] 2 W.L.R. 510; 99 S.J. 148; [1955] 1 All E.R. 520, C.A.	10
—— v. Tait (1984) 128 S.J. 416; (1984) 48 P. & C.R. 410; (1984) 15 H.L.R. 98; (1984) 271 E.G. 105, C.A.	70
Cornish v. Midland Bank plc [1985] 3 All E.R. 513; (1985) F.L.R. 298	128
Cousins v. Dzosens (1984) 81 L.S.Gaz. 2855	56, 57
Cowcher v. Cowcher [1972] 1 W.L.R. 425; (1971) 116 S.J. 142; [1972] 1 All E.R. 943	21, 34, 39
Crabb v. Arun District Council [1976] Ch. 179; [1975] 3 W.L.R. 847; 119 S.J. 711; [1975] 3 All E.R. 865; 32 P. & C.R. 70, C.A.	49, 139
Crancour v. De Silvaesa (1986) 18 H.L.R. 265; (1986) 278 E.G. 618, 733, C.A.	63
Cray v. Willis (1729) P.Wms. 529	19
Crippen, Re [1911] P. 108	23
Crisp v. Mullings (1975) 239 E.G. 119	40, 51
Cronmire, Re [1901] 1 K.B. 480	117
Crutcher v. Crutcher (1978) 128 New L.J. 981	88
Cummins, Re [1972] Ch. 62; [1971] 3 W.L.R. 580; [1971] 3 All E.R. 782, C.A.	43
Cunningham-Reid v. Public Trustee [1944] K.B. 602	74
Curling v. Law Society [1985] 1 W.L.R. 470; [1985] 1 All E.R. 705; (1985) 15 Fam.Law 311, C.A.	60
D.H.N. Food Distributors Ltd. v. Tower Hamlets London Borough Council [1976] 1 W.L.R. 852; 120 S.J. 215; [1976] 3 All E.R. 462; 32 P. & C.R. 251; [1976] J.P.L. 363; 74 L.G.R. 506, Lands Tribunal	138
Darby v. Darby (1856) 3 Drew. 495	18
Davies' Will Trusts, Re [1932] 1 Ch. 530	7
Davis v. Johnson [1979] A.C. 264; [1978] 2 W.L.R. 553; (1978) 122 S.J. 178; [1978] 1 All E.R. 1132, H.L.	88, 89, 94
—— v. Vale [1971] 1 W.L.R. 1021; 115 S.J. 347; [1971] 2 All E.R. 1021, C.A.	46
Dealex Properties Ltd. v. Brooks [1966] 1 Q.B. 542; [1965] 2 W.L.R. 1241; 109 S.J. 253; [1965] 1 All E.R. 1080, C.A.	76
Debtor, A, Re (No. 24 of 1971) [1976] 1 W.L.R. 952; [1976] 2 All E.R. 1010, D.C.	116
Demuren v. Seal Estates (1978) 249 E.G. 440; [1979] J.P.L. 462, C.A.	62, 63, 64
Dennis v. McDonald [1982] Fam. 63; [1982] 2 W.L.R. 275; 126 S.J. 16; [1982] 1 All E.R. 590; (1982) 12 Fam.Law 84, C.A.; affirming [1981] 1 W.L.R. 810; 125 S.J. 308; [1981] 2 All E.R. 632	56, 57
Denny, Re [1947] L.J.R. 1029; 177 L.T. 291	23
Densham (A Bankrupt), Re [1975] 1 W.L.R. 1519; [1975] 3 All E.R. 726; 119 S.J. 774	40, 105, 107, 110, 137
Diligent Finance Co. Ltd. v. Alleyne (1972) 23 P. & C.R. 346	81
Dodsworth v. Dodsworth (1973) 228 E.G. 1115, C.A.	49, 50, 139
Doe d. Aslin v. Summersett (1830) 1 B. & Ad. 135	65
Dorrell v. Dorrell (1986) 16 Fam.Law 15, C.A.	97
Draper's Conveyance, Re [1969] 1 Ch. 486; [1968] 2 W.L.R. 166; 111 S.J. 867; [1967] 3 All E.R. 853; 19 P. & C.R. 71	20, 21, 22
Duke v. Porter (1986) 280 E.G. 633, C.A.	67
Dunn, Re [1916] 1 Ch. 97	17
Dyer v. Dyer (1788) 2 Cox 92	28
Dyson Holdings Ltd. v. Fox [1976] Q.B. 503; [1975] 3 W.L.R. 744; 119 S.J. 744; [1975] 3 All E.R. 1030; 31 P. & C.R. 229; 239 E.G. 39, C.A.	76
Earl Somers, Re (1895) 1 T.L.R. 567	3
88 Berkeley Road, N.W.9, Re [1971] Ch. 648; [1971] 2 W.L.R. 307; [1971] 1 All E.R. 254; 22 P. & C.R. 188	20
Ekyn's Trusts, Re (1877) 6 Ch.D. 115	28

Elias v. Mitchell [1972] Ch. 652; [1972] 2 W.L.R. 740; (1971) 116 S.J. 15; [1972] 2 All E.R. 153; 23 P. & C.R. 159 .... 10, 132
Epps v. Esso Petroleum Ltd. [1973] 1 W.L.R. 1071; 117 S.J. 430; [1973] 2 All E.R. 465; 25 P. & C.R. 402 122
Errington v. Errington [1952] 1 K.B. 290; [1952] 1 T.L.R. 231; [1952] 1 All E.R. 149, C.A. 138
Evers' Trust, Re [1980] 1 W.L.R. 1327; 124 S.J. 562; [1980] 3 All E.R. 399; (1980) 10 Fam.Law 245, C.A. 54, 57
Eves v. Eves [1975] 1 W.L.R. 1338; 119 S.J. 394; [1975] 3 All E.R. 768, C.A. 39, 137

Fairclough (T.M.) & Sons Ltd. v. Berliner [1931] 1 Ch. 60 65
Fairweather v. Kolosine (1984) 11 H.L.R. 61, C.A. 94
Falconer v. Falconer [1970] 1 W.L.R. 1333; 114 S.J. 720; [1970] 3 All E.R. 449; [1971] J.P.L. 111, C.A. 42
Featherstone v. Staples [1986] 1 W.L.R. 861; 130 S.J. 482; [1986] 2 All E.R. 461; 52 P. & C.R. 287; 278 E.G. 867, C.A. 69
Feaver v. Feaver [1977] 5 W.W.R. 271 30
Ferris v. Weaven [1952] W.N. 318; (1952) 96 S.J. 414; [1952] 2 All E.R. 233 83
Figgis, Re [1969] 1 Ch. 123; [1968] 2 W.L.R. 1173; 112 S.J. 156; [1968] 1 All E.R. 999 29
First Middlesbrough Trading Mortgage Co. Ltd. v. Cunningham (1974) 118 S.J. 421; (1974) 28 P. & C.R. 69, C.A. 113
First National Securities Ltd. v. Hegerty [1985] Q.B. 850; [1984] 3 W.L.R. 769; (1984) 128 S.J. 499; [1984] 3 All E.R. 641; (1984) 48 P. & C.R. 200, C.A. 22, 99, 100, 101, 102
Fisher v. Wigg (1700) 1 P.Wms. 14 .... 17, 18
Fowkes v. Pascoe (1875) 10 Ch.App. 343 28
Freeman v. Collins (1983) 13 Fam.Law 113; (1983) 12 H.L.R. 68, 122, C.A. 94
Frewen v. Rolfe (1787) 2 Bro.C.C. 220 17
Fribance v. Fribance [1957] 1 W.L.R. 384; 101 S.J. 188; [1957] 1 All E.R. 357, C.A. ... 42

Gage v. King [1961] 1 Q.B. 188; [1960] 3 W.L.R. 460; 104 S.J. 644; [1960] 3 All E.R. 62 30
Galan v. Galan [1985] F.L.R. 905; (1984) 15 Fam.Law 256, C.A. 94
Gammans v. Elkins [1950] 2 K.B. 328; 66 T.L.R. 1139; [1950] 2 All E.R. 140, C.A. 76
Garnett Orme and Hargreaves' Contract, Re (1884) 25 Ch.D. 595 4
Gee v. Liddell [1913] 2 Ch. 62 116
General Management Ltd. v. Locke (1980) 255 E.G. 155, C.A. 76
Gibbons, Re [1920] 1 Ch. 372 5
Giles, Re [1972] Ch. 544; [1971] 3 W.L.R. 640; 115 S.J. 428; [1971] 3 All E.R. 1141 24
Gissing v. Gissing [1971] A.C. 886; [1970] 3 W.L.R. 255; 114 S.J. 550; [1970] 2 All E.R. 780; 21 P. & C.R. 702, C.A. 32, 35, 37, 38, 41, 43, 44, 124
Goddard v. Lewis (1909) 101 L.T. 528 21
Godwin v. Bedwell, The Times, March 10, 1982 34
Goodman v. Gallant [1986] Fam. 106; [1986] 2 W.L.R. 236; [1986] 1 All E.R. 311; 52 P. & C.R. 180; [1986] 1 F.L.R. 513; 16 Fam.Law 59, C.A. 19, 25, 34
Gordon v. Douce [1983] 1 W.L.R. 563; 127 S.J. 324; [1983] 2 All E.R. 228; 13 Fam.Law 149, C.A. 51
Grace Raymer Investments Ltd. v. Waite [1958] Ch. 831; [1958] 3 W.L.R. 337; 102 S.J. 600; [1958] 2 All E.R. 777, C.A. 131
Grant v. Edwards [1986] Ch. 638; [1986] 3 W.L.R. 114; 130 S.J. 408; [1986] 2 All E.R. 426; 16 Fam.Law 300, C.A. 38, 39, 40, 47, 49, 136, 137
Greasley v. Cooke [1980] 1 W.L.R. 1306; 124 S.J. 629; [1980] 3 All E.R. 710, C.A. 48
Green v. Lewis [1947–51] 1 C.L.C. 8647 73
Greenfield v. Greenfield (1979) 38 P. & C.R. 570 23
Greenwich London Borough Council v. McGrady (1983) 46 P. & C.R. 223; 81 L.G.R. 288; 267 E.G. 515, C.A. 66, 68
Griffiths v. Williams (1977) 248 E.G. 947, C.A. 5, 50, 139
Gross v. French (1974) 232 E.G. 1319 34
Grzeczcowski v. Jedynska (1971) 115 S.J. 126, C.A. 40

Case	Page
Habib Bank v. Habib Bank A.G. Zurich [1981] 1 W.L.R. 1265; (1980) 125 S.J. 512; [1981] 2 All E.R. 650; [1982] R.P.C. 19, C.A.	47
Habib Bank Ltd. v. Tailor [1982] 1 W.L.R. 1218; 126 S.J. 448; [1982] 3 All E.R. 561, C.A.	115
Hadjiloucas v. Crean [1987] 3 All E.R. 1008; (1988) 20 H.L.R. 54, C.A.	63
Halford's Executors v. Boden [1953] 103 L.J. 78h7	75
Halifax Building Society v. Clark [1973] Ch. 307; [1973] 2 W.L.R. 1; 116 S.J. 883; [1973] 2 All E.R. 33; 24 P. & C.R. 339	113
Hall v. Hall [1982] 3 F.L.R. 379	43, 44, 50, 51
—— v. King (1987) 19 H.L.R. 440; (1987) 283 E.G. 1400, C.A.	80
Hanlon v. Hanlon [1978] 1 W.L.R. 592; [1978] 2 All E.R. 889; (1977) 122 S.J. 62, C.A.	58
—— v. The Law Society [1981] A.C. 124; [1980] 2 W.L.R. 756; 124 S.J. 360; [1980] 2 All E.R. 199, H.L.	57, 59, 60
Hanson, Re [1928] Ch. 96	5
Hardwick v. Johnson [1978] 1 W.L.R. 683; (1979) 122 S.J. 162; [1978] 2 All E.R. 935, C.A.	138
Hargrave v. Newton [1971] 1 W.L.R. 1611; [1971] 3 All E.R. 866, C.A.	42
Harman v. Glencross [1986] Fam. 81; [1986] 2 W.L.R. 637; 130 S.J. 224; [1986] 1 All E.R. 545; [1986] 2 F.L.R. 241; (1986) 16 Fam.Law 215, C.A.	58, 100, 101, 102, 106, 112
Harris v. Black (1983) 46 P. & C.R. 366, C.A.	66, 69
—— v. Goddard [1983] 1 W.L.R. 1203; 127 S.J. 617; [1983] 3 All E.R. 242; 46 P. & C.R. 417; 14 Fam.Law 242, C.A.	20, 21, 22
—— v. Harris [1986] F.L.R. 12; (1984) 16 Fam.Law, C.A.	91
Harrison, Re (1920) 90 L.J.Ch. 186	29
Harrogate Borough Council v. Simpson [1986] 2 F.L.R. 91; (1985) 17 H.L.R. 205; 16 Fam.Law 359; 25 R.V.R. 10, C.A.	75
Harvey v. Harvey [1982] Fam. 83; [1982] 2 W.L.R. 283; 126 S.J. 15; [1982] 1 All E.R. 693	58
Hastings & Thanet Building Society v. Goddard [1970] 1 W.L.R. 1544; 114 S.J. 807; [1970] 3 All E.R. 954; 22 P. & C.R. 295, C.A.	114, 116
Hawkesley v. May [1956] 1 Q.B. 304; [1955] 3 W.L.R. 569; 99 S.J. 781; [1955] 3 All E.R. 353	22
Hayes Estate, Re [1921] I.R. 207	22
Hazell v. Hazell [1972] 1 W.L.R. 301; (1971) 116 S.J. 142; [1972] 1 All E.R. 923, C.A.	43
Heathe v. Heathe (1740) 2 A. & R. 121	17
Heglibiston Establishment v. Heyman (1977) 36 P. & C.R. 351; 246 E.G. 567; 121 S.J. 851, C.A.	73
Helby v. Rafferty [1979] 1 W.L.R. 13; (1978) 122 S.J. 418; [1978] 3 All E.R. 1016; 8 Fam.Law 207; 247 E.G. 729; 37 P. & C.R. 376, C.A.	76
Herklots' Will Trust, Re [1964] 1 W.L.R. 583; 108 S.J. 424; [1964] 2 All E.R. 66	5
Heseltine v. Heseltine [1971] 1 W.L.R. 342; (1970) 114 S.J. 972; [1971] 1 All E.R. 952, C.A.	28, 30
Hewett, Re [1894] 1 Ch. 363	22
Heys, Re [1914] P. 192	23
Hine v. Hine [1962] 1 W.L.R. 1124; 106 S.J. 589; [1962] 3 All E.R. 345, C.A.	32, 35
Hoddinott v. Hoddinott [1949] 1 K.B. 406; 65 T.L.R. 266; 93 S.J. 286, C.A.	29
Hodgson v. Marks [1971] Ch. 892; [1971] 2 W.L.R. 1263; 115 S.J. 224; [1971] 2 All E.R. 684; 22 P. & C.R. 586, C.A.	122, 123, 125
Holiday Inns Inc. v. Broadhead (1974) 232 E.G. 951	47, 49
Holliday (A Bankrupt), Re [1981] Ch. 405; [1981] 2 W.L.R. 966; (1980) 125 S.J. 411; [1980] 3 All E.R. 385, C.A.	56, 111
Hopper v. Hopper [1979] 1 W.L.R. 1342; (1978) 122 S.J. 610; [1979] 1 All E.R. 181; (1978) 8 Fam.Law 204, C.A.	94
Horne's Settled Estate (1888) 39 Ch.D. 84	5
Howson v. Buxton (1928) 97 L.J.K.B. 749	66, 69
Hussey v. Palmer [1972] 1 W.L.R. 1286; 116 S.J. 567; [1972] 3 All E.R. 744, C.A.	43
Hyde's Conveyance, Re (1952) 102 L.J. 58	54

Inns, *Re* [1947] 1 Ch. 376; [1947] 2 All E.R. 308; 91 S.J. 468	6
Inwards v. Baker [1965] 2 Q.B. 29; [1965] 2 W.L.R. 212; 109 S.J. 75; [1965] 1 All E.R. 446, C.A.	49, 138
Irani Finance Ltd. v. Singh [1971] Ch. 59; [1970] 3 W.L.R. 330; 114 S.J. 636; [1970] 3 All E.R. 199; 21 P. & C.R. 843, C.A.	10, 98
Ives (E.R.) Investment Ltd. v. High [1967] 2 Q.B. 379; [1967] 2 W.L.R. 789; [1967] 1 All E.R. 504, C.A.	138, 139
Jackson, *Re* (1887) 34 Ch.D. 732	19
—— v. Jackson [1971] 1 W.L.R. 1539; 115 S.J. 723; [1971] 3 All E.R. 774, C.A.	21
Jacobs v. Chaudhuri [1968] 2 Q.B. 470; [1968] 2 W.L.R. 1098; 112 S.J. 135; [1968] 2 All E.R. 124; 19 P. & C.R. 286, C.A.	68
John's Assignment Trusts, *Re* [1970] 1 W.L.R. 955; 114 S.J. 396; [1970] 2 All E.R. 210	34
Johnson v. Agnew [1980] A.C. 367; [1979] 2 W.L.R. 487; 123 S.J. 217; [1979] 1 All E.R. 883; 38 P. & C.R. 424; 251 E.G. 1167, H.L.	82
Jones v. Challenger [1961] 1 Q.B. 176; [1960] 2 W.L.R. 695; 104 S.J. 328; [1960] 1 All E.R. 785, C.A.	54
—— v. Maynard [1951] Ch. 572; [1951] 1 T.L.R. 700; [1951] 1 All E.R. 802	29, 30
Jones (A.E.) v. Jones (F.W.) [1977] 1 W.L.R. 438; (1976) 33 P. & C.R. 147; 242 E.G. 371, C.A.	49, 120
Joyce v. Barker Bros. (Builders) Ltd. (1980) 40 P. & C.R. 512	18
K. (dec'd), *Re* [1986] Fam. 180; [1985] 3 W.L.R. 234; 129 S.J. 364; [1985] 2 All E.R. 833; 16 Fam.Law 19, C.A.	24
Kaur v. Gill, *The Independent*, March 16, 1988	82
Kempthorne, *Re* [1930] 1 Ch. 268	10
Kilvert, *Re* [1957] Ch. 388; [1957] 2 W.L.R. 854; 101 S.J. 372; [1957] 2 All E.R. 196	17
Kings North Trust Ltd. v. Bell [1986] 1 W.L.R. 119; 130 S.J. 88; [1986] 1 All E.R. 423; (1985) 17 H.L.R. 352; 15 Fam.Law 225, C.A.	128
Kingsnorth Finance Co. Ltd. v. Tizard [1986] 1 W.L.R. 783; (1985) 130 S.J. 244; [1986] 1 W.L.R. 783; [1986] 2 All E.R. 54; (1985) 51 P. & C.R. 296	9, 122, 125
Kling v. Keston Properties Ltd. (1984) 49 P. & C.R. 212; (1984) 81 L.S.Gaz. 1683	121, 122
Kowalczuk v. Kowalczuk [1973] 1 W.L.R. 930; 117 S.J. 372; [1973] 2 All E.R. 1042, C.A.	43
Lake v. Craddock (1732) 3 P.Wms. 157	18
—— v. Gibson (1729) 1 Eq.Cas.Ab. 291	15, 16, 19
Landi, *Re* [1939] Ch. 828	120
Leake v. Bruzzi [1974] 1 W.L.R. 1528; 118 S.J. 831; [1974] 2 All E.R. 1196, C.A.	34, 51
Leckhampton Dairies v. Actus Whitefield (1986) 130 S.J. 225; 83 L.S.Gaz. 875	65
Lee v. Lee [1952] 2 Q.B. 489; [1952] 1 T.L.R. 968; [1952] 1 All E.R. 1299, C.A.	79
—— v. —— (1983) 12 H.L.R. 116; (1983) 14 Fam.Law 243, C.A.	91
Leek and Moreland Building Society v. Clark [1952] 2 Q.B. 788; [1952] 2 T.L.R. 401; 96 S.J. 561; [1952] 2 All E.R. 492, C.A.	65
L'Estrange v. L'Estrange [1902] 1 I.R. 467	17
Lever Finance Ltd. v. Needleman's Trustees [1956] Ch. 375	131
Lewen v. Dodd (1595) Cro.Eli. 443h7	17
Lewis v. Lewis [1978] Fam. 60; [1978] 2 W.L.R. 644; (1977) 122 S.J. 161; [1978] 1 All E.R. 729, C.A.	96
Linklater v. Linklater (1987) 137 New L.J. 67	97
Linnett v. Coles [1987] Q.B. 555	97
Lloyd v. Sadler [1978] Q.B. 774; [1978] 2 W.L.R. 721; 122 S.J. 111; [1978] 2 All E.R. 529; 35 P. & C.R. 78; 245 E.G. 479, C.A.	64, 67, 68, 94
Lloyds Bank v. Bundy [1975] Q.B. 326; [1974] 3 W.L.R. 501; 118 S.J. 714; [1974] 3 All E.R. 757; [1974] 2 Lloyd's Rep. 366, C.A.	129
Locobail International Finance Ltd. v. Agroexport [1986] 1 W.L.R. 657; 130 S.J. 245; [1986] 1 All E.R. 901; [1986] 1 Lloyd's Rep. 317, C.A.	69
Lowrie, *Re* [1981] 3 All E.R. 353, D.C.	111, 112
Lyster v. Dolland (1792) 1 Ves.Jun. 431	18

McMahon v. Burchell (1846) 5 Hare 322	56
McIntyre v. Hardcastle [1948] 2 K.B. 82; [1948] L.J.R. 1249; 64 T.L.R. 260; 92 S.J. 181; [1948] 1 All E.R. 696, C.A.	71, 72
McLaren v. McLaren (1978) 9 Fam.Law 153, C.A.	96
McLean v. Nugent [1979] F.L.R. 26; (1979) 123 S.J. 521, C.A.	89
Maharaj (Sheila) v. Chand (Jai) [1986] A.C. 898; [1986] 3 W.L.R. 440; (1986) 130 S.J. 633; [1986] 3 All E.R. 107, P.C.	49, 137
Malayan Credit Ltd. v. Jack Chia-Mph Ltd. [1986] A.C. 549; [1986] 2 W.L.R. 590; 130 S.J. 143; [1986] 1 All E.R. 711, P.C.	18
Marchant v. Charters [1977] 1 W.L.R. 1181; [1977] 3 All E.R. 918; (1976) 34 P. & C.R. 291; 241 E.G. 23, C.A.	63
Marsh v. Von Sternberg [1986] 1 F.L.R. 526; (1986) 16 Fam.Law 160	40, 50, 51
Marshall v. Crutwell (1875) L.R. 20 Eq. 328	29
Martin v. Martin (1987) 54 P. & C.R. 238	18
Masich v. Masich (1977) 121 S.J. 645; (1977) 7 Fam.Law 245, C.A.	95
Mayes v. Mayes (1969) 210 E.G. 925	34
Mayo, Re [1943] Ch. 302	6, 54
Mellish, Re [1929] 2 K.B. 82n	10
Mercier v. Mercier [1903] 2 Ch. 98	28
Mesher v. Mesher [1980] 1 All E.R. 126n, C.A.	57
Metropolitan Properties Co. Ltd. v. Cronan (1982) 126 S.J. 229; 44 P. & C.R. 1; [1983] M.L.R. 47; (1982) 262 E.G. 1077, C.A.	84
Middlemas v. Stevens [1901] 1 Ch. 574	3
Midland Bank Ltd. v. Farmpride Hatcheries Ltd. (1981) 260 E.G. 493, C.A.	124
Midland Bank plc v. Dobson and Dobson [1986] 1 F.L.R. 171; 1985 F.L.R. 314; 16 Fam.Law 55, C.A.	38, 48, 127
Midland Bank Trust Co. Ltd. v. Green [1980] Ch. 590; [1981] A.C. 513; 125 S.J. 33, H.L.	26, 83
Miles v. Bull [1969] 1 Q.B. 258; [1968] 3 W.L.R. 1090; (1968) 112 S.J. 723, 747; [1968] 3 All E.R. 632; 20 P. & C.R. 42	63
Minay v. Sentongo (1982) 126 S.J. 674; (1983) 45 P. & C.R. 190; 266 E.G. 433, C.A.	72
Moate v. Moate (1948) 92 S.J. 484; [1948] 2 All E.R. 486	28
Moodie v. Hosegood [1952] A.C. 61; [1951] 2 T.L.R. 455; 95 S.J. 499; [1951] 2 All E.R. 582, H.L.	75
Morgan v. Marquis (1853) 9 Exch. 145	21
—— v. Morgan (1978) 9 Fam.Law 87, C.A.	95
Morris v. Barrett (1829) 3 Y. & J. 384	18, 22
Mortimer v. Mortimer-Griffin [1986] 2 F.L.R. 315, C.A.	58
Muetzel v. Muetzel [1970] 1 W.L.R. 188; (1969) 114 S.J. 32; [1970] 1 All E.R. 443; 21 P. & C.R. 107, C.A.	43
Munary and Roper's Contract [1899] 1 Ch. 275	2
Myers v. Myers [1982] 1 W.L.R. 247; [1982] 1 All E.R. 776; 12 Fam.Law 117, C.A.	90
National Provincial Bank v. Ainsworth [1965] A.C. 1175; [1965] 3 W.L.R. 1; 109 S.J. 415; [1965] 2 All E.R. 472, H.L.	79, 83, 119
National Westminster Bank v. Morgan [1985] A.C. 686; [1985] 2 W.L.R. 588; 129 S.J. 205; [1985] 1 All E.R. 821; 17 H.L.R. 360; 1985 F.L.R. 266, H.L.	128, 129
National Westminster Bank Ltd. v. Stockman [1981] 1 W.L.R. 67; (1980) 124 S.J. 810; [1981] 1 All E.R. 800	98
Newbould, Re (1913) 110 L.T. 6	4
Newman, Re [1930] 2 Ch. 409	10
—— v. Benesch [1987] F.L.R. 262, C.A.	97
—— v. Keedwell (1978) 35 P. & C.R. 393; 244 E.G. 469	69
Nicholson, Re [1974] 1 W.L.R. 476; (1973) 118 S.J. 133; [1974] 2 All E.R. 386	39, 46
Nielson-Jones v. Fedden [1975] Ch. 222; [1974] 3 W.L.R. 583; 118 S.J. 776; [1974] 3 All E.R. 38	20, 22
Nixon v. Nixon [1969] 1 W.L.R. 1676; 113 S.J. 565; [1969] 3 All E.R. 1133; 20 P. & C.R. 1043, C.A.	43
Oak Co-operative Building Society v. Blackburn [1968] Ch. 370; [1968] 2 W.L.R. 1053; (1968) 112 S.J. 172; [1968] 2 All E.R. 117; 19 P. & C.R. 375, C.A.	81

O'Malley v. Seymour (1978) 250 E.G. 1083; [1979] J.P.L. 675, C.A. 62
O'Neill v. Williams [1984] F.L.P. 1; (1984) 14 Fam.Law 85; 16 H.L.R. 102, C.A. 89
Orakpo v. Manson Investments Ltd. [1978] A.C. 95; [1977] 3 W.L.R. 229; (1977) 121
  S.J. 256; [1977] 1 All E.R. 666, C.A. 130

Paddington Building Society v. Mendelsohn (1985) 50 P. & C.R. 244, C.A. 122, 123,
  124
Palaniappa Chettiar (A.R.P.L.) v. Arunasalam Chettiar (P.L.A.R.) [1962] A.C. 294;
  [1962] 2 W.L.R. 548; 106 S.J. 110; [1962] 1 All E.R. 494, P.C. 28
Pariser v. Wilson (1973) 229 E.G. 786 55
Parker v. Rosenberg [1947] K.B. 371; [1947] L.J.R. 495; 91 S.J. 116; [1947] 1 All E.R.
  87, C.A. 71
Parsons v. Parsons [1983] 1 W.L.R. 1390; 127 S.J. 823; 84 P. & C.R. 494; 269 E.G.
  634 .... 65, 66
Partriche v. Poulet (1740) 2 Atk. 54 22
Pascoe v. Turner [1979] 1 W.L.R. 431; (1978) 123 S.J. 164; [1979] 2 All E.R. 945;
  (1978) 9 Fam.Law 82, C.A. 49, 50, 136, 139
Passee v. Passee (1987) 137 New L.J. 972 51
Pattinson, Re (1885) 1 T.L.R. 216 29
Paul v. Constance [1977] 1 W.L.R. 527; [1977] 1 All E.R. 195; 121 S.J. 320; (1976) 7
  Fam.Law 18, C.A. 27, 29
Payne v. Webb (1874) L.R. 19 Eq. 26 17
Pechar, Re [1969] N.Z.L.R. 574 .... 23, 24
Pettitt v. Pettitt [1970] A.C. 777; [1969] 2 W.L.R. 966; 113 S.J. 344; [1969] 2 All E.R.
  385; 20 P. & C.R. 991, H.L. 28, 29, 30, 31, 32, 34, 35, 36, 40, 45, 46
Petty v. Styward (1632) 1 Ch.Rep. 57 19
Pink v. Lawrence (1977) 36 P. & C.R. 98, C.A. 19
Pittortou (A Bankrupt), Re [1985] 1 W.L.R. 58; (1985) 129 S.J. 42; [1985] 1 All E.R.
  285 117
Plummer, Re [1900] 2 Q.B. 790 105
Pocock v. Steel [1984] 1 W.L.R. 229; 129 S.J. 84; [1985] 1 All E.R. 434; 49 P. & C.R.
  90; 272 E.G. 1218; 17 H.L.R. 181, C.A. 72
Pope, Re [1908] 2 K.B. 169 106
Powell v. Broadhurst [1901] 2 Ch. 160 19
Power's Will Trusts, Re [1947] Ch. 572; 91 S.J. 409; [1947] 2 All E.R. 282 8
Practice Direction (Fam.D.) (Divorce Registry: Injunction) [1972] 1 W.L.R. 1047;
  [1972] 2 All E.R. 400 95
Practice Note (Fam.D.) (Domestic Violence: Power of Arrest) [1981] 1 W.L.R. 27; 125
  S.J. 36; [1981] 1 All E.R. 224 96
Practice Note (Fam.D.) (Matrimonial Cause: Injunction) [1978] 1 W.L.R. 925; 122
  S.J. 460; [1978] 2 All E.R. 919 95
Protheroe v. Protheroe [1970] 1 W.L.R. 1480 81

R. v. Law Society, ex p. Sexton [1984] Q.B. 360; [1983] 3 W.L.R. 830; 127 S.J. 697;
  [1984] 1 All E.R. 92; 14 Fam.Law 149, C.A. 60
——— v. National Insurance Commissioner, ex p. Connor [1981] Q.B. 758; [1981] 2
  W.L.R. 412; (1980) 124 S.J. 478; [1981] 1 All E.R. 769; [1980] Crim.L.R. 579 ... 24
——— v. Seymour (Edward) [1983] 2 A.C. 493; [1983] 3 W.L.R. 349; 148 J.P. 530; 127
  S.J. 522; [1983] 2 All E.R. 1058; (1983) 77 Cr.App.R. 215; [1983] R.T.R. 455;
  [1983] Crim.L.R. 742, H.L. 24
Radziej v. Radziej [1968] 1 W.L.R. 1928; 112 S.J. 822; [1968] 3 All E.R. 624n 21
Rasmanis v. Jurewitsch [1968] 2 N.S.W.R. 166 23
Rawlings v. Rawlings [1964] P. 398; [1964] 3 W.L.R. 294; 108 S.J. 424; [1964] 2 All
  E.R. 804, C.A. 55
Reid v. Reid, *The Times*, July 30, 1984 91
Rennell v. I.R.C. [1964] A.C. 173; [1963] 2 W.L.R. 745; 107 S.J. 232; [1963] 1 All
  E.R. 803, H.L. 105
Rey's Settled Estate, Re (1884) 25 Ch.D. 464 3
Richards v. Dove [1974] 1 All E.R. 888 .... 34, 38
——— v. Richards [1984] A.C. 174; [1983] 3 W.L.R. 173; [1983] 2 All E.R. 807; 12
  H.L.R. 68, 73; 15 Fam.Law 256, H.L. 85, 89, 90, 91, 92, 93

Roberts Petroleum Ltd. v. Bernard Kenny Ltd. [1982] 1 W.L.R. 301 (reversed on the facts [1983] 2 A.C. 192)	99
Robertshaw v. Fraser (1871) 6 Ch.App. 696	17
Robinson v. Donovan [1946] 2 All E.R. 731	71
—— v. Hofman (1828) 4 Bing. 562	65
—— v. Robinson (1977) 241 E.G. 153	34
Rochefoucauld v. Boustead [1897] 1 Ch. 196	39
Rogers' Question, Re [1948] 1 All E.R. 328, C.A.	41
Rooke, Re [1953] Ch. 716; [1953] 2 W.L.R. 1176; 97 S.J. 388; [1953] 2 All E.R. 110	5
Royal Trust Co. of Canada v. Markham [1975] 1 W.L.R. 1416; 119 S.J. 643; [1975] 3 All E.R. 433; 30 P. & C.R. 317, C.A.	116
Ryves v. Ryves (1871) 11 Eq. 539	17
Samson v. Samson [1982] 1 W.L.R. 252; [1982] 1 All E.R. 780; 12 Fam.Law 118, C.A.	90
Savage v. Dunningham [1974] Ch. 181; [1973] 3 W.L.R. 471; 117 S.J. 697; [1973] 3 All E.R. 429; 26 P. & C.R. 177	43
Schobelt v. Barber (1967) 60 D.L.R.(2d) 519	23
Schwab (E.S.) & Co. Ltd. v. McCarthy (1975) 31 P. & C.R. 196, D.C.	122
Sefton Holdings Ltd. v. Cairns (1987) 138 New L.J. 19	76
Sharpe, Re [1980] 1 W.L.R. 219; (1979) 124 S.J. 147; 39 P. & C.R. 459; [1980] 1 All E.R. 198	38, 49, 138, 139
Shephard v. Cartwright [1955] A.C. 431; [1954] 3 W.L.R. 967; 98 S.J. 868; [1954] 3 All E.R. 649, H.L.	28
—— v. Midland Bank plc [1987] 2 F.L.R. 175; 17 Fam.Law 309, C.A.	128
Shinh v. Shinh [1977] 1 All E.R. 97; (1976) 6 Fam.Law 245	32
Simmons v. Simmons [1984] Fam. 17; (1983) 127 S.J. 393; [1984] 1 All E.R. 83; (1983) 13 Fam.Law 179, C.A.	60
Simpson v. Law Society [1987] 2 W.L.R. 1390; [1987] 2 All E.R. 481; [1987] 2 F.L.R. 497; (1988) 18 Fam.Law 19, H.L.	60
Singer v. Sharegin [1984] F.L.R. 114; 14 Fam.Law 58, C.A.	60
Siskinia, The [1979] A.C. 210; [1977] 3 W.L.R. 818; 121 S.J. 744; [1977] 3 All E.R. 803; [1978] 1 C.M.L.R. 190, C.A.	87
Slingsby's Case (1587) 5 Co.Rep. 186	18
Smith v. Smith [1945] 1 All E.R. 584	21
—— v. Smith and Smith (1976) 120 S.J. 100	55
—— v. Smith (1987) 137 New L.J. 767	97
Smith (Colin) Music Ltd. v. Ridge [1975] 1 W.L.R. 463; (1974) 119 S.J. 83; [1975] 1 All E.R. 290; (1974) 29 P. & C.R. 97; 5 Fam.Law 128, C.A.	67, 94
Snook v. London and West Riding Investment Co. Ltd. [1967] 2 Q.B. 786; [1967] 2 W.L.R. 1020; 111 S.J. 71; [1967] 1 All E.R. 518, C.A.	63
Solomon (A Bankrupt), Re [1967] Ch. 573; [1967] 2 W.L.R. 172; 110 S.J. 978; [1966] 3 All E.R. 255	110
Somma v. Hazlehurst [1978] 1 W.L.R. 1014; 37 P. & C.R. 391; [1978] 2 All E.R. 1011; [1978] J.P.L. 554, C.A.	62, 63, 64
Sorochan v. Sorochan (1986) 29 D.L.R. (4th) 1	44
Spencer v. Camacho (1983) 127 S.J. 155; 12 H.L.R. 68, 130; 13 Fam.Law 114, C.A.	94
Spindlow v. Spindlow [1979] Fam. 52; [1978] 3 W.L.R. 777; 122 S.J. 556; [1979] 1 All E.R. 169; (1978) 9 Fam.Law 22, C.A.	91
Spiro v. Lintern [1973] 1 W.L.R. 1002; 117 S.J. 584; [1973] 3 All E.R. 319, C.A.	124
Standard Property Investment plc v. British Plastics Federation (1987) 53 P. & C.R. 25	81
Steadman v. Steadman [1976] A.C. 536; [1974] 3 W.L.R. 56; 118 S.J. 480; [1974] 2 All E.R. 977; 29 P. & C.R. 46, H.L.	10
Steeds v. Steeds (1889) 22 Q.B.D. 537	19
Stevens v. Hutchinson [1953] Ch. 299; [1953] 2 W.L.R. 545; 97 S.J. 171; [1953] 1 All E.R. 699	10, 100
Stott v. Ratcliffe (1982) 126 S.J. 310; (1982) 79 L.S.Gaz. 643, C.A.	57
Strafford v. Syrrett [1958] 1 Q.B. 507; [1957] 3 W.L.R. 733; 101 S.J. 850; [1957] 3 All E.R. 363, C.A.	71
Street v. Denham [1954] 1 W.L.R. 624; 98 S.J. 253; [1954] 1 All E.R. 532	79

Street v. Mountford [1985] A.C. 809; [1985] 2 W.L.R. 877; 129 S.J. 348; [1985] 2 All E.R. 289; 50 P. & C.R. 258; 274 E.G. 821; 17 H.L.R. 402, H.L.	62, 63
Sturolson Co. v. Weniz (1984) 17 H.L.R. 140; 272 E.G. 326, C.A.	62
Summers v. Summers [1986] 1 F.L.R. 343; (1985) 16 Fam.Law 56, C.A.	91
Surtees v. Surtees (1871) 12 Eq. 400	17
Suttill v. Graham [1977] 1 W.L.R. 819; 121 S.J. 408; [1977] 3 All E.R. 1117, C.A.	51
Sykes v. Land (1984) 271 E.G. 1264, C.A.	69
Szczpanski v. Szczpanski [1985] F.L.R. 468; 15 Fam.Law 120, C.A.	97
T. v. T. (1986) 136 New L.J. 391	90
Tanner v. Tanner [1975] 1 W.L.R. 1346; 119 S.J. 391; [1975] 3 All E.R. 776; 5 Fam.Law 193, C.A.	49, 137, 138
Tapp and London and India Docks Co.'s Contract (1905) 74 L.J.Ch. 523	4
Taylors Fashions Ltd. v. Liverpool Victoria Trustee Co. [1981] Q.B. 133; [1981] 2 W.L.R. 576; [1981] 1 All E.R. 897; [1981] Com.L.R. 34; (1979) 251 E.G. 159	47
Thames Guarantee Ltd. v. Campbell [1985] Q.B. 210; [1984] 3 W.L.R. 109; 128 S.J. 301; [1984] 2 All E.R. 583; 47 P. & C.R. 575, C.A.	25, 34, 99, 112
Thompson v. Thompson [1986] Fam. 38; [1985] 3 W.L.R. 17; 129 S.J. 284; [1985] 2 All E.R. 243; 15 Fam.Law 195, C.A.	58
Thurley v. Smith [1984] F.L.R. 875; 15 Fam.Law 31, C.A.	92
Tilling v. Whiteman [1980] A.C. 1; [1979] 2 W.L.R. 401; 123 S.J. 202; [1979] 1 All E.R. 737; 38 P. & C.R. 341; 250 E.G. 51; [1979] J.P.L. 834, H.L.	72
Tinker v. Tinker [1970] P. 136; [1970] 2 W.L.R. 331; (1969) 114 S.J. 32; [1970] 1 All E.R. 540; 21 P. & C.R. 102	23, 28
Turley v. Panton (1975) 119 S.J. 236; 29 P. & C.R. 397, D.C.	66
Turnbull & Co. v. Duvall [1902] A.C. 499	128
Turner, Re [1974] 1 W.L.R. 1556; 118 S.J. 849; [1975] 1 All E.R. 5	56, 110
Turton v. Turton [1987] 3 W.L.R. 622; [1987] 2 All E.R. 641; 17 Fam.Law 383; 84 L.S.Gaz. 1492, C.A.	34, 51
Van Hoorn v. Law Society [1985] Q.B. 106; [1984] 3 W.L.R. 199; [1984] 3 All E.R. 136; [1984] F.L.R. 203	60
Vickers v. Cavell (1839) 1 Beav. 529	19
Viola's Indenture of Lease, Re [1909] 1 Ch. 244	65
Wakeman, Re [1945] Ch. 177	7, 8
Walia v. Naughton (Michael) Ltd. [1985] 1 W.L.R. 1115; 129 S.J. 701; [1985] 3 All E.R. 673; 51 P. & C.R. 11	16, 135
Walker v. Hall [1984] F.L.R. 126; (1984) 14 Fam.Law 21, C.A.	34, 41, 46, 51
Waller v. Waller [1967] 1 W.L.R. 451; 111 S.J. 94; [1967] 1 All E.R. 305	53
Walsh v. Griffiths-Jones [1978] 2 All E.R. 1002	62
Ward, Re [1920] 1 Ch. 334	17
—— v. Ward (1871) 9 Ch.App. 789	12, 18
—— v. Ward and Greene [1980] 1 W.L.R. 4n; (1979) 123 S.J. 838; [1980] 1 All E.R. 176; (1979) 10 Fam.Law 22, C.A.	57
Warren, Re [1932] 1 Ch. 42	120
Watkinson v. Hudson (1826) L.J.(o.s.) Ch. 213	22
Watson v. Gray (1880) 24 Ch.D. 192	26
—— v. Lucas [1980] 1 W.L.R. 1493; 124 S.J. 513; [1980] 3 All E.R. 647; 40 P. & C.R. 531; 256 E.G. 1171, C.A.	76
Watts v. Spence [1976] Ch. 115; [1975] 2 W.L.R. 1039; 119 S.J. 168; [1975] 2 All E.R. 528; 29 P. & C.R. 501	124
—— v. Waller [1973] Q.B. 153; [1972] 3 W.L.R. 365; 116 S.J. 599; [1972] 3 All E.R. 257; 24 P. & C.R. 39, C.A.	82
Webb v. Pollmount [1966] Ch. 584; [1966] 2 W.L.R. 543; 109 S.J. 1029; [1966] 1 All E.R. 481	121
Weldon v. Weldon (1883) 9 P.O. 52	79
Wellsted's Will Trusts, Re [1949] 1 Ch. 296; [1949] L.J.R. 1153; 93 S.J. 216; [1949] 1 All E.R. 577, C.A.	7, 8
Western Bank Ltd. v. Shindler [1977] Ch. 1; (1976) 32 P. & C.R. 352, C.A.	114

Westminster Bank Ltd. v. Lee [1956] Ch. 7; [1955] 3 W.L.R. 376; 99 S.J. 562; [1955] 2 All E.R. 883	79
Wetherall & Co. Ltd. v. Stone [1950] 2 All E.R. 1029	71
Wheelwright v. Walker (No. 2) (1883) W.N. 154	3
White v. White [1983] Fam. 54; [1983] 2 W.L.R. 872; [1983] 2 All E.R. 51; 13 Fam.Law 149, C.A.	89
White's Settlement, Re [1930] 1 Ch. 179	4
Widdowson v. Widdowson [1983] 4 F.L.R. 121; (1982) 126 S.J. 328; (1982) 12 Fam.Law 153, D.C.	96
Wilde v. Wilde, *The Independent*, December 2, 1987	89, 90
Wilford's Estate, Re (1879) 1 Ch.D. 267	23
Wilks, Re [1891] 3 Ch. 59	23
Williams v. Hensman (1861) 1 J. & H. 546	19, 21, 22, 23, 25
—— v. Fawcett [1986] Q.B. 604	97
—— v. Staite [1979] 2 Ch. 291; [1978] 2 W.L.R. 825; 122 S.J. 333; [1978] 2 All E.R. 928; 36 P. & C.R. 103, C.A.	138
—— v. Williams [1970] 1 W.L.R. 1530; 114 S.J. 826; [1970] 3 All E.R. 988; 21 P. & C.R. 915, C.A.	76
Williams & Glyn's Bank v. Boland [1981] A.C. 487; [1950] 3 W.L.R. 138; 124 S.J. 433; [1980] 2 All E.R. 408; 40 P. & C.R. 451, H.L.	9, 10, 16, 33, 99, 118, 119, 121, 122, 123, 124, 125, 127, 129, 131, 132
Willmott v. Barber (1880) 15 Ch.D. 96	47
Windle, Re [1975] 1 W.L.R. 1628; [1975] 3 All E.R. 987	106
Winkworth v. Edward Baron Development Co. Ltd. [1986] 1 W.L.R. 1512; 130 S.J. 954; 84 L.S.Gaz. 340, H.L.	44, 124, 127
Wiscot's Case (1599) 2 Ch.Rep. 606	12
Wiseman v. Simpson [1988] 1 W.L.R. 35	91
Woolley, Re [1903] 2 Ch. 206	17
Wooton v. Wooton [1984] F.L.R. 871; 15 Fam.Law 31, C.A.	92
Wright v. Jess [1987] 1 W.L.R. 1077	97
Wroth v. Tyler [1974] Ch. 30; [1973] 2 W.L.R. 405; 117 S.J. 90; [1973] 1 All E.R. 897; 25 P. & C.R. 138	32, 124
Young, Re (1885) 28 Ch.D. 705	30
—— v. Young [1984] F.L.R. 77; 14 Fam.Law 271, C.A.	40, 51

TABLE OF STATUTES

1882	Married Women's Property Act (45 & 46 Vict. c. 75)—	
	s. 1 (1)	31
	s. 17	31, 32, 35, 36
1889	Interpretation Act (52 & 53 Vict. c. 63)—	
	s. 1	71
1890	Partnership Act (53 & 54 Vict. c. 39)—	
	ss. 1, 2	18
1914	Bankruptcy Act (4 & 5 Geo. 5, c. 59)—	
	s. 42	103, 105, 106
	s. 42 (1)	104
	(2)	105
1925	Settled Land Act (15 & 16 Geo. 5, c. 18)—	
	s. 1 (1) (i)	2
	(ii)	2
	(d)	2
	(7)	4
	s. 3	3
	s. 4 (1)	2
	s. 5 (1)	2
	s. 6 (a)	2
	s. 13	3
	s. 18 (1) (b) (c)	3
	s. 19 (2) (3)	16
	s. 30 (3)	16
	s. 36 (1)	16
	(4)	15, 16
	s. 38 (1)	2
	s. 71 (1)	119
	s. 72	3
	s. 73 (1) (xi)	7
	s. 101	3
	(2)	3
	s. 106	3, 7
	s. 110 (2)	4
	Trustee Act (15 & 16 Geo. 5, c. 19)—	
	s. 14 (2) (a)	8
	s. 17	119
	s. 25	134
	s. 34	9
	s. 36 (6)	135
	s. 40 (1) (2)	135
	Law of Property Act (15 & 16 Geo. 5, c. 20)—	
	s. 1 (6)	13
	s. 2	129, 131
	(1)	8
	s. 14	7, 120, 130, 131
	s. 19 (2)	15
	s. 25 (1)	5
1925	Law of Property Act—cont. s. 25—cont.	
	(4)	4
	s. 26	6
	(1)	6
	(2)	7
	(3)	6, 7, 129, 132
	s. 27	131
	(1)	8, 129
	(2)	8
	s. 28	7
	(1)	7, 8, 119
	s. 29 (1) (2) (3)	8
	s. 30	6, 53, 57, 58, 59, 100, 101, 103, 108, 109, 110, 111, 120, 134
	s. 31	58
	s. 34	15
	(2)	9, 14
	(3)	14, 16
	s. 35	14, 15
	s. 36	61
	(1)	15
	(2)	13, 15, 20, 25, 108
	s. 38 (1)	26
	(2)	26
	s. 40 (1)	10
	s. 53	27
	(1) (b)	33, 34, 35, 38, 39, 47, 105, 137
	(c)	33
	(2)	35
	s. 63	99, 134
	(1)	10
	s. 137	98
	s. 146 (2)	65
	s. 149 (6)	5
	s. 172	103, 104
	s. 184	12
	s. 187 (2)	26
	s. 196 (4)	20
	s. 199 (1) (ii) (b)	125
	ss. 203, 204	26
	s. 205 (1) (ii)	129
	(xxix)	4
	Sched. 1, Pt. VI	11
	Pt. I	120, 129
	Land Registration Act (15 & 16 Geo. 5, c. 21)	81
	s. 3 (xv) (a)	121
	s. 5	4
	s. 19 (1)	123
	(2)	131
	s. 20	9, 83
	(1)	123

Year	Statute	Pages
1925	Land Registration Act—*cont.*	
	s. 26 (1)	123, 130
	s. 27 (3)	131
	s. 47	135
	ss. 54, 55	132
	s. 56	26
	s. 58 (1)	132
	(3)	17
	s. 70	121
	(1)	10
	(g)	118, 121, 122, 125
	s. 82 (1) (*d*)	134
	(3)	134
	s. 83 (2) (ii)	134
	(4)	134
	s. 101 (3)	132
	Land Charges Act (15 & 16 Geo. 5, c. 22)	9, 81
	Administration of Estates Act (15 & 16 Geo. 5, c. 23)—	
	s. 22	3
	s. 33 (1)	10
	Matrimonial Causes Act (15 & 16 Geo. 5, c. 49)—	
	s. 24	43
1926	Law of Property (Amendment) Act (16 & 17 Geo. 5, c. 11)—	
	Sched.	4, 8
1939	London Building Acts (Amendment) Act (2 & 3 Geo. 6, c. 97)—	
	s. 44 (1)	26
	Pt. V	26
1954	Landlord and Tenant Act (2 & 3 Eliz. 2, c. 56)	66, 70
	s. 24	68
	s. 26	68, 69
	s. 30	68
	(1) (g)	71
	s. 41A	68
	Pt. II	68
1956	Administration of Justice Act (4 & 5 Eliz. 2, c. 46)—	
	s. 35	10
	(3)	98
1957	Homicide Act (5 & 6 Eliz. 2, c. 11)—	
	s. 2	24
1964	Law of Property (Joint Tenants) Act (c. 63)	135
	ss. 1–3	25
	s. 2	26
	Criminal Procedure (Insanity) Act (c. 84)	24
1967	Matrimonial Homes Act (c. 75)	80, 90
	s. 2 (7)	114
1969	Family Law Reform Act (c. 46)—	
	s. 12	2
1969	Law of Property Act (c. 59)—	
	s. 9	68, 69
1970	Administration of Justice Act (c. 31)—	
	s. 36	113, 114
	Law Reform (Miscellaneous Provisions) Act (c. 33)—	
	s. 2 (2)	32
	Matrimonial Proceedings and Property Act (c. 45)—	
	s. 4	32
	s. 20	79
	s. 37	37, 45, 46, 127
1971	Guardianship of Minors Act (c. 3)—	
	s. 1	90
	Powers of Attorney Act (c. 27)—	
	s. 1 (1) (2)	135
	s. 9	134
1972	Land Charges Act (c. 61)	9, 25
	s. 2 (7)	81
	s. 3 (1)	81
	s. 4 (8)	83
1973	Administration of Justice Act (c. 15)—	
	s. 8	113, 114, 115
	s. 8 (1)	113
	(2)	114
	Matrimonial Causes Act (c. 18)	84
	s. 24	21, 53, 57, 58, 102, 106
	(A)	57
	(1)	59
	s. 25	32
	s. 39	106
	Pt. II	100
	Guardianship Act (c. 29)	90
1974	Legal Aid Act (c. 4)—	
	s. 9 (6)	59
1975	Inheritance (Provision for Family and Dependants) Act (c. 63)	33
	s. 1	32
1976	Domestic Violence and Matrimonial Proceedings Act (c. 50)	12, 85, 87, 88, 89, 91, 93
	s. 1	87, 93
	(1) (*d*)	94
	s. 2	87
	(1)	95
	(4) (5)	96
1977	Rent Act (c. 42)	61, 66, 70, 73, 74, 76, 79
	s. 1	61, 66, 83
	s. 2	67, 122
	(1) (*a*)	84
	(*b*)	74
	s. 5	5
	s. 12	70
	s. 20	70

1977	Rent Act—*cont.*		1983	Matrimonial Homes Act—*cont*	
	s. 22	64		s. 1	80, 92, 93, 108
	s. 67	66		(*a*)	85
	s. 70	56		(1)(*b*)	81
	s. 98	67		(2)	82, 85, 86, 90
	(1)(*a*)(*b*)	70		(*a*)	94
	Sched. 1, Pt. I	74		(3)	82, 90
	para. 2	74		(*b*)(*c*)	86
	para. 3	74, 76		(5)	82, 112
	paras. 5–6	74		(6)	84, 94
	para. 7	74, 76		(7)	113
	Sched. 15	67		(10)	80
	Pt. I	70, 73		(11)	80
	Cases 1–4	73		s. 2(1)	80
	Case 5	74		(4)	80
	Case 8	71		(5)	81
	Case 9	70, 71, 72		(6)	84
	Case 11	71, 72		(8)	114
	Case 12	72		(*b*)	81
	Pt. III, para. 1	71		s. 3	82
	Pt. V, para. 2	71		(*a*)	85
	(*b*)–(*f*)	72		s. 6	82
	Criminal Law Act (c. 45)—			s. 8 (2)	83, 114
	s. 50	24		(3)	82, 114
1978	Domestic Proceedings and Magistrates' Courts Act (c. 22)	85		s. 9	80, 85, 92, 93
				s. 10(2)	80
				s. 11	81
	s. 16(2)	86		Sched. 1	84
	(3)	86, 95		County Court (Penalties for Contempt) Act (c. 45)—	
	(4)	86			
	(5)	95		s. 1	96
	(6)	95	1984	Matrimonial and Family Proceedings Act (c. 42)—	
	(8)	95			
	s. 18	96		s. 3	32, 57
	(1)(2)	86		s. 12	32
	Sched. 2, para. 53	96		s. 22	84
	Interpretation Act (c. 30)—			Sched. 1	84
	s. 6(*c*)	71	1985	Rent (Amendment) Act (c. 24)—	
1979	Charging Orders Act (c. 53)	98, 134			
				s. 1(1)	72
	s. 1	98		Enduring Powers of Attorney Act (c. 29)—	
	(5)	99			
	(*a*)	101		s. 3(3)	135
	s. 2	98		Housing Act (c. 68)	66, 67, 70, 73, 74, 76, 91
	(1)(*a*)	10			
	s. 3(5)	100		s. 79	67, 84
1980	Housing Act (c. 51)	76		s. 81	67, 84
	s. 65(1)	70		s. 82	67, 84
	s. 72	66		ss. 83–84	67
1981	Matrimonial Homes and Property Act (c. 24)—			s. 86	67
				s. 87	74
	s. 7	57		s. 88(1)(*b*)	75
	Contempt of Court Act (c. 49)—			s. 89(1)(*b*)	76
				s. 113	75
	s. 14	96		s. 118(1)	77
1982	Forfeiture Act (c. 34)—			(2)	77
	s. 2(4)(*b*)	24		s. 119(1)(2)	77
	(5)	23		s. 122	77
	s. 5	24		s. 123(1)	77
1983	Matrimonial Homes Act (c. 19)	80, 85, 93		(2)(3)	77
				s. 129	77

1985	Housing Act—cont.		1986	Insolvency Act—cont.	
	s. 129—cont.			s. 336	109
	(3)	77		(2)	81, 108
	s. 130(1)(3)(4)	78		(3)	108
	s. 132(1)(*a*)(3)	78		(4)(5)	109
	s. 133	78		s. 337(2)(3)(5)	109
	(2)(*b*)	78		(6)	110
	s. 154	77		s. 338	112
	Sched. 2	67, 73		s. 339	104, 106, 108
	Sched. 4, para. 9	77		(3)(*a*)	107
	Housing (Consequential Provisions) Act (c. 71)—			s. 340	104
				s. 341	104, 106
	s. 2	78		(2)	107
1986	Agricultural Holdings Act (c. 5)	66, 70		(3)	107
				s. 342	104
	s. 1	69		s. 346(2)	107
	s. 3(1)	69		s. 423	104
	s. 26(1)	69		(3)	104
	s. 60	69		s. 424	104
	Sched. 3, Pt. I	69		s. 435	107
	Insolvency Act (c. 45)	106		Sched. 11, paras. 17, 20	103
	s. 305(2)	103		Chap. IV	103
	s. 306	108		Housing and Planning Act (c. 63)—	
	(1)(2)	103			
	s. 313	112		s. 2(2)	77
	s. 331	112		(*b*)	78
	s. 332	112		(3)	78

TABLE OF STATUTORY INSTRUMENTS

Year	Instrument	Page
1925	Land Registration Rules (S.R. & O. 1925 No. 1093)—	
	r. 83(1)	132
	r. 83(2)	123
1965	Rules of the Supreme Court (S.I. 1965 No. 1776)—	
	Ord. 50, r. 1(1)	99
	r. 2(1)	99
	r. 3	99
1977	Matrimonial Causes Rules (S.I. 1977 No. 344)—	
	r. 107(1)	92
1978	Land Registration Rules (S.I. 1978 No. 1601)—	
	r. 8(2)	123
1980	Housing (Right to Buy) Mortgage Limit Regulations (S.I. 1980 No. 1423)	78
1981	Rent Act (County Court Proceedings for Possession) Rules (S.I. 1981 No. 139)	72
	County Court Jurisdiction Order (S.I. 1981 No. 123)	98
	County Court Rules (S.I. 1981 No. 1687)—	
	Ord. 13, r. 1	92
	r. 4(4)	95
	Ord. 29	96
	r. 1(3)	96
	(7)	97
	Ord. 31, r. 1(2)	99
	r. 2(2)	99
	r. 3	99
1981	County Court Rules—*cont.*	
	Ord. 47, r. 4(9)	92
	r. 8	93
	(5)(7)	96
1983	Supplementary Benefit (Requirements) Regulations (S.I. 1983 No. 1399)—	
	reg. 15(1)(ii)	116
1984	County Court (Amendment) Rules (S.I. 1984 No. 576)	92
	Matrimonial Causes Rules (S.I. 1984 No. 1511)—	
	r. 107	92
1986	County Court Amendment Rules (S.I. 1986 No. 636)	92
	Land Registration Fees Order (S.I. 1986 No. 1399)—	
	Sched. 6	135
	Legal Aid (General) Regulations (S.I. 1980 No. 1804)—	
	reg. 86	59
	regs. 88–91	60
	Housing (Right to Buy) (Maximum Discount) Order (S.I. 1986 No. 2193)	77
1987	Supplementary Benefit (Housing Requirements and Resources) Amendment Regulations (S.I. 1987 No. 17)—	
	reg. 2(3)	116

1 LEGAL FRAMEWORK OF CO-OWNERSHIP

Trust for sale

Virtually all types of property are capable of being jointly owned. When it is land which is the subject of co-ownership various problems arise. These problems are caused by various factors. One such factor is the legal framework within which co-ownership must take place. Co-ownership occurs primarily, although not exclusively, behind a trust for sale, a device of some antiquity but one which is increasingly thought of by some as inappropriate to modern conditions.[1] In addition, because land is a valuable asset, disputes regularly occur as to whether or not land actually is jointly owned, and if so, what the sizes of the respective shares are. Coupled with this are the different expectations each co-owner has with regard to the land. One co-owner may wish to realise the capital value of the house, whereas the other may wish to continue to use it as a home. A related problem can then occur when one co-owner has mortgaged the land without the other's knowledge and consent. These are but some of the reasons why joint ownership of land gives rise to more problems than joint ownership of other property and why land will be concentrated upon in this book.

Concurrent and consecutive interests

One of the central features of English land law is its ability to accommodate fragmented ownership. From the outset of its development, land law has recognised that different people can own lesser or greater interests in the property, ranging from a life interest to ownership of a fee simple absolute in possession. These interests can be either consecutive or concurrent; alternatively, the arrangements may display features of both. For example, if a testator leaves his house to his widow for life, remainder to his only son, then the widow and son have consecutive interests. Conversely if the house is left to the children in equal shares this involves simply concurrent interests. Finally, in the not unusual case where a testator leaves the house to his widow for life thereafter to his children, both consecutive and concurrent interests are involved.

This book is primarily concerned with concurrent interests. It is nevertheless necessary to pay some regard to consecutive interests, not least because the two types of interest can co-exist with regard to the same land. In addition, the legal consequences may differ depending on which situation arises and it is important that care is taken to distinguish between them.

---

[1] See Law Commission Working Paper (1986) No. 94 which proposes a new legal structure.

Strict settlement

When more than one person is beneficially entitled to land, the land is either subject to a strict settlement or is held upon trust for sale. Distinguishing one from the other is crucial because depending upon which method is used are such consequences as the location of the legal estate and the identity of the person or persons who make such decisions as to whether or not the land is to be sold.

Strict settlement The strict settlement is defined by section 1(1)(i) of the Settled Land Act 1925 as being any deed, will, agreement for a settlement or other agreement under or by virtue of which land stands limited in trust for any persons by way of succession. Section 1(1)(ii) then enumerates various instances where land is so limited but which add little to the basic definition. In section 1(1)(ii)(d), however, it is enacted that if land is held by an infant[2] for an estate in fee simple or a term of years absolute then that land is also within the definition of a settlement.

Two-deed system If land is subject to the Settled Land Act 1925, then the necessary documentation must be used. Once a settlement has been created, a vesting deed must be executed[3] which operates to vest in the tenant for life the legal estate which is the subject matter of the settlement. In addition, a trust instrument is required which sets out the beneficial interests subsisting under the settlement.[4]

This two-deed structure is mandatory in the case of settled land. The beneficial interests are in almost all cases kept away from a purchaser's gaze by the inviolable curtain of the vesting deed, which tells a purchaser all that he needs to know. The vesting deed contains a description of the settled land, the name of the tenant for life or statutory owner, the names of the trustees of the settlement, any powers conferred on the tenant for life additional to those conferred by the Act and the name of the person entitled to appoint new trustees.[5]

The scheme of the Settled Land Act The object of the Settled Land Act 1925 was to enable land which was subject to a succession of interests to become freely alienable.[6] To this end, the tenant for life is invested with the legal estate in addition to his own beneficial interest under the settlement. The role of the trustees of the settlement is to act as watchdogs of the settlement; an essential role given that the tenant for life is statutorily given an interest in the land far greater than the settlement envisaged.

Power of sale Having bestowed on the tenant for life a legal estate, the Act does not then confer upon him all the rights of an estate owner. Rather it confers upon him various powers with regard to the land, of which the most important is the power of sale.[7] It is not

---

[2] The correct expression is now a minor. See Family Law Reform Act 1969, s.12.
[3] Settled Land Act 1925, s.4(1).
[4] In the case of settlements created by will, the will operates as the trust instrument: *ibid.* s.6(a).
[5] *Ibid.*, s.5(1).
[6] See *Re Munday and Roper's Contract* [1899] 1 Ch. 275 at 288–289, *per* Lindley M.R. and Chitty L.J.
[7] Settled Land Act 1925, s.38(1). For a full account of the powers, see Megarry and Wade, *The Law of Real Property* (5th ed., 1984) pp. 358–377.

possible to fetter these powers, any attempts so to do being rendered inoperative by section 106 of the Act. The only safeguards for the other beneficiaries under the settlement are provided by the trustees of the settlement. The tenant for life is required by section 101 of the Act to notify them prior to exercising his powers. This is not a particularly strong safeguard, as this requirement, in the case of a sale, is satisfied simply by the tenant for life giving a general notice that from time to time he intends to exercise his powers under the Settled Land Act.[8] The trustees can intervene, however, to prevent an improper sale.[9]

Subject to these rather limited safeguards, the tenant for life has complete control over the settled land. The purchaser pays the purchase money to the trustees of the settlement and takes a conveyance or transfer from the tenant for life.[10] The conveyance then operates to overreach the beneficial rights under the settlement which take effect in the capital money raised by the sale.[11]

Drawbacks of a settlement   This necessarily thumbnail sketch of the Settled Land Act 1925 presents a fairly straightforward picture. This masks some of the problems which can arise. First, the very existence of the panoply of powers conferred on the tenant for life may defeat the intention of the settlor and, at times, seem inappropriate.[12] Thus in the example given previously where a testator leaves his house to his widow for life thereafter to his children, the widow could not be prevented from selling the property as and when she wishes.

A perhaps more formidable objection is that the Settled Land Act imposes a cumbersome structure. This is particularly marked when the tenant for life dies but the settlement

Succession   subsists.[13] Instead of the land following the normal course of devolution with the rest of the deceased's estate, it vests, by virtue of section 22 of the Administration of Estates Act 1925, in the trustees of the settlement in their capacity of special personal representatives. They then assent to the passing of the legal title to the next tenant for life. Where part of the deceased's estate consists of settled land and part does not, different personal representatives are needed for the different property.[14]

Imperfect settlements   An additional complication arises if the settlement is originally created imperfectly. This may occur when, perhaps through an informal arrangement, a settlement is created unbeknown to the parties and no vesting deed employed. When this occurs section 13 of the Settled Land Act 1925 provides that no disposition of the legal estate can be made until a vesting deed is executed. In this situation, any purported disposition of the

---

[8] Settled Land Act 1925, s.101(2); *Re Rey's Settled Estate* (1884) 25 Ch.D. 464.
[9] *Wheelwright* v. *Walker (No. 2)* (1883) W.N. 154; *Re Earl Somers* (1895) 1 T.L.R. 567; *Middlemas* v. *Stevens* [1901] 1 Ch. 574.
[10] Settled Land Act 1925, s.18(1)(*b*)(*c*).
[11] *Ibid.*, s.72.
[12] *Cf.* H. Potter (1944) 8 Conv. (N.S.) 145.
[13] This may include where the person beneficially entitled is a minor or where any limitation, charge or power of charging under the settlement still subsists: Settled Land Act 1925, s.3.
[14] See further Megarry and Wade, *The Law of Real Property* (5th ed., 1984) pp. 337–338.

land *inter vivos* operates merely as a contract to convey the legal estate.[15] In addition, once this omission has been rectified and the tenant for life comes to sell the land, the purchaser is entitled to inspect the trust instrument to ascertain that the vesting deed is correct.[16]

Trust for sale

The strict settlement is now widely regarded as unnecessarily cumbersome and few such settlements are deliberately created today. This is largely due to the existence of the alternative means of settling land, the trust for sale: an institution which is considerably more flexible, being able to accommodate simultaneously both consecutive and concurrent interests in land.

Definition

If land is held upon trust for sale, it is excluded from the definition of settled land.[17] A trust for sale is defined by section 205(1)(xxix) of the L.P.A. 1925 as meaning an immediate binding trust for sale, whether or not exercisable at the request or with the consent of any person, and with or without a power at discretion to postpone the sale.

Legal title in trustees

If a trust for sale is employed, the legal title is vested in the trustees. Unless the trustees are holding on trust for themselves, the beneficiaries do not hold the legal title: an important distinction between the trust for sale and the strict settlement. From this it follows that the managerial decisions relating to the land are vested in the trustees rather than, as is the case with settled land, in the hands of the beneficial owners.

Because of these factors, it is essential to distinguish between the trust for sale and the strict settlement. Failure to do so will cause the conveyance to be executed by the wrong party.[18] This distinction is, unfortunately, not always easy to make when consecutive interests are involved: a fact which has led many commentators to advocate the repeal of the Settled Land Act to enable the trust for sale to hold exclusive sway.[19]

Creation of a trust for sale

For a trust for sale to be created, it is essential that all the components of the definition are satisfied. At the outset, there must be an imperative duty on the trustees to sell the property. If only a power to sell the land is granted to the trustees, a strict settlement will be created. This used to give rise to difficult questions of construction as to whether there was a trust to sell coupled with a power to postpone sale or whether the position was the other way around.[20] Happily, this problem is now resolved by section 25(4) of the L.P.A. 1925 which provides that when a settlement contains a trust either to sell or retain land, the

Power to postpone sale

---

[15] *Cf. Binions* v. *Evans* [1972] Ch. 359 where this was overlooked.
[16] Settled Land Act 1925, s.110(2); Megarry and Wade, above n. 14, pp. 333–334.
[17] *Ibid.*, s.1(7) added by the Law of Property (Amendment) Act 1926, Sched.
[18] In registered land this on registration is not a problem because the legal estate will be vested in the registered proprietor: Land Registration Act 1925, s.5.
[19] See, *e.g.* Cheshire and Burn, *The Modern Law of Real Property* (13th ed., 1982) p. 205; G.A. Grove (1961) 24 M.L.R. 123.
[20] *Re Garnett Orme and Hargreaves' Contract* (1884) 25 Ch.D. 595; *Re Tapp and London and India Docks Co.'s Contract* (1905) 74 L.J. Ch. 523; *Re Newbould* (1913) 110 L.T. 6; *Re White's Settlement* [1930] 1 Ch. 179.

trust shall be construed as a trust to sell it coupled with a power to postpone the sale.

Residence provisions The requirement that the trust both be for sale and immediate for the arrangement to be a trust for sale does still cause difficulty in cases where it is intended to provide a residence for someone. In *Re Hanson*[21] a testator directed his trustees to buy a house as a residence for his wife until his son attained 25 years, on which event it was to be held upon trust for sale. It was held that there was no trust for sale imposed by the will and consequently the widow was a tenant for life within the Settled Land Act. By contrast, in *Re Herklots' Will Trusts*[22] a will provided that a house was to be held upon trust for sale but that G was to have permission to reside in it during her life or for so long as she wished. *Re Hanson* was distinguished and it was held that a trust for sale was created but that the house was not to be sold without G's consent.

Although correct on the facts, *Re Herklots' Will Trusts* is slightly unusual, in that attempts to give someone an indefinite right of residence in the property have generally caused a strict settlement to be created.[23] This is inconvenient and can be avoided in two ways. The first is to employ a trust for sale but make the execution of it subject to the consent of a person unlikely to give it. Thus land could be conveyed to trustees for sale on trust for a widow for life remainder to the children with the sale subject to the consent of the widow. Such an arrangement will not necessarily give her a right of residence, unless this is conferred expressly by the testator.

Lease An alternative, more satisfactory, method is to convey the land directly to the children but give the widow a non-assignable lease for life at a low rent. This will be converted into a 90-year lease determinable on death by section 149(6) of the L.P.A. 1925. By keeping the rent sufficiently low, the arrangement will also be excluded from Rent Act protection.[24] In this way a right of residence can be granted without the complications caused by either the Settled Land Act 1925 or trusts for sale.

Postponement of sale It is evident from the preceding paragraphs that because land is held upon trust for sale, it does not follow that it must be sold as soon as is practicably possible. It was quite usual when a trust for sale was created to give the trustees power to postpone a sale. It is now unnecessary to do this because under section 25(1) of the L.P.A. 1925, a power to postpone sale shall, in the case of every trust for sale of land, be **Contrary intention** implied unless a contrary intention appears. Whether or not a contrary intention appears is a question of construction. In *Re Rooke*[25] it was held that a testator's direction to his trustees to sell

---

[21] [1928] Ch. 96; *Re Horne's Settled Estate* (1888) 39 Ch.D. 84; *Bacon v. Bacon* [1947] P. 153; P. Smith [1978] Conv. 229.
[22] 1964 1 W.L.R. 583.
[23] *Re Carne's Settled Estate* [1899] 1 Ch. 324; *Re Gibbons* [1920] 1 Ch. 372; *Re Anderson* [1920] 1 Ch. 175. See further Harvey, *Settlements of Land* (1973), pp. 82–88.
[24] Rent Act 1977, s.5; *Griffiths v. Williams* (1977) 248 E.G. 947. *Cf. Re Catling* [1931] 2 Ch. 359.
[25] [1953] Ch. 716.

his farm "as soon as possible after my death" was sufficient to indicate a contrary intention to displace the power to postpone. If the power to postpone is excluded in a testamentary trust for sale then, by analogy with the executor's year, the trustees have a year in which to effect the sale.[26]

One consequence of the trust being a trust for sale with a concomitant power to postpone sale was that the trustees had to be unanimous in deciding to postpone sale. If one of them wished to sell the property, the orthodox view was that the prime objective of the trust should then operate and the land should be sold.[27] In the residential context, this principle has now been substantially modified. The current prevailing principles regarding this matter will be fully considered in Chapter 3.

Consents When a trust for sale is created, it is by no means uncommon for provision to be made that the sale is not to take place unless certain interested persons consent to it. Such clauses are probably more common in wills than in *inter vivos* trusts. If the trust for sale arises by operation of statute,[28] then it is specifically provided by section 26(3) of the L.P.A. 1925 that, subject to the expression of a contrary intention, the trustees for sale should consult the persons of full age beneficially entitled in possession and, so far as is consistent with the general interest of the trust, give effect to their wishes.

Hindering a sale

In the case of express trusts for sale, making the exercise of the sale subject to consents can, paradoxically, be used as a means of making it unlikely that the property will be sold at all. Thus in *Re Inns*[29] a house was devised upon trust for sale, such sale only to be effected with the consent of the testator's widow who was given a right of residence. The provisions of the will were such that it was not in her interest to give such consent and as a consequence the land was virtually unmarketable for her lifetime.

It might be thought that such a situation would run counter to the definition of a trust for sale; in reality, it being most

Petition to the court

unlikely that the land will be sold. This objection is met by the consideration that if the requisite consent cannot be obtained, other persons interested in the property can petition the court for the consent to be dispensed with and the property sold.[30]

Protection of purchasers In theory, any number of consents to a sale can be stipulated for by the creator of the trust. In principle, a purchaser would need to ascertain that all such consents had been obtained, otherwise he would be fixed with notice that the sale was in breach of trust. This would cause practical conveyancing problems. Such problems are obviated by

L.P.A. 1925, s.26

section 26(1) of the L.P.A. 1925, which provides that, in favour of a purchaser, if the consent of more than two persons is made requisite to the execution of a trust for sale of land, the consent of any two such persons is sufficient. In cases where the person whose consent is required is subject to a disability or is not *sui*

---

[26] *Re Atkins' Will Trusts* [1974] 1 W.L.R. 761.
[27] *Re Mayo* [1943] Ch. 302.
[28] See pp. 13–16 below.
[29] [1947] 1 Ch. 576.
[30] L.P.A. 1925, s.30; *Re Beale's Settlement Trusts* [1932] Ch. 15.

juris then by dint of section 26(2) the consent of that person's guardian or, in cases of mental disorder, his receiver should be obtained.

When a trust for sale is implied by law, as opposed to being expressly created, then, as has been seen, section 26(3) places the trustees under a duty to consult the persons of full age beneficially entitled to the rents and profits and to give effect to their wishes. The subsection expressly provides that a purchaser shall not be concerned to see that this requirement has been satisfied. Owing to the operation of section 14 of the L.P.A. 1925, however, this protection for the purchaser may be illusory if the person beneficially entitled to the rents and profits is in actual occupation of the land. The impact of section 14 will be fully considered in Chapter 7.

Powers of trustees for sale A fundamental distinction between the strict settlement and the trust for sale is the location of the legal estate. In the case of the settlement, the legal estate is vested in the tenant for life whereas, when a trust for sale is created, it is possessed by the trustees, regardless of whether or not they are also beneficially entitled. Because the legal estate is vested in the trustees for sale, the power of dealing with it is vested in them as well. The trustees for sale have conferred upon them by section 28(1) of the L.P.A. 1925 all the powers granted to the tenant for life and trustees for sale by the Settled Land Act 1925.

This somewhat laconic method of defining the powers of trustees for sale leaves certain aspects of the position unclear.

Restricting trustees' powers First, it is unclear whether it is permissible for a settlor creating a trust for sale to cut down the powers conferred by statute upon the trustees. The generally accepted view is that this cannot be done because section 106 of the Settled Land Act 1925, which prohibits attempts to cut down the tenant for life's powers, is incorporated into the trust for sale by section 28[31]: an argument which appeared to find some support in *Re Davies' Will Trusts*.[32]

Proceeds of sale A second difficulty arises as to whether land can be purchased with the proceeds of sale of the original property. Under section 73(1)(xi) of the Settled Land Act 1925 capital money may be spent on the purchase of land in fee simple. If the trustees for sale sell part of the property held on trust for sale but retain the rest, then they retain the capacity of trustees for sale and, it is clear, can then use the money to buy land.[33] The difficulty arises when the trustees for sale have sold all the property held under the trust and are not themselves beneficially entitled to the proceeds of sale.

Purchasing more land This issue arose in *Re Wakeman*[34] where Uthwatt J. held that as the trustees no longer retained any of the original property, they were no longer trustees for sale and thus no longer had the power conferred upon trustees for sale by section 28. Consequently they could not purchase land with the proceeds of sale. This result is highly inconvenient and its correctness has

---

[31] Megarry and Wade, *The Law of Real Property* (5th ed., 1984) p. 395.
[32] [1932] 1 Ch. 530.
[33] *Re Wellsted's Will Trusts* [1949] 1 Ch. 296.
[34] [1945] Ch. 177.

been doubted.[35] It could be avoided by adopting the suggestion that section 28(1) should be construed to include persons who have held land upon trust for sale.[36] In the absence of a decision overruling *Re Wakeman*, a settlor should confer upon the trustees for sale power to apply[37] the proceeds of sale for the purchase of land.

Delegation It is provided by section 29(1) of the L.P.A. 1925 that the trustees may, in writing, revocably delegate to a person beneficially entitled in possession to the rents and profits the powers of and incidental to leasing. If such a delegation takes place, the power shall be exercised only in the names and on behalf of the trustees who shall not be liable in relation to the exercise or purported exercise of the power.[38] This limited right to delegate powers does not extend, it will be observed, to the power of sale. The timing of that, subject to the court's jurisdiction to intervene, is a matter for the trustees.

Sales of the property: overreaching

As in the case of settlements, the device of the trust for sale enables transactions to be effected so that the interests subsisting behind the trust are cleared off the title. In the case of the strict settlement, provided that the correct procedure is adhered to, the beneficial interests existing behind the settlement are overreached: they are transferred from the land to the purchase money generated by its sale. A similar transformation occurs when land is held upon trust for sale save that, owing to the doctrine of conversion, it is thought by some to be more accurate to say that overreaching in the strict sense does not occur as the beneficial interests should throughout be regarded as interests in money. The scope of the doctrine of conversion will be assessed shortly. First regard must be had to the conveyancing machinery employed to effect a sale.

Doctrine of conversion

Unlike the position when land is settled, the legal estate is vested in the trustees and it is from them that the purchaser must take the conveyance. It is provided by section 2(1) of the L.P.A. 1925 that a conveyance to a purchaser of a legal estate in land shall overreach any equitable interest or power affecting that estate provided that the conveyance is made by trustees for sale. It is further provided by section 27(1) that a purchaser shall not be concerned with the trusts affecting the proceeds of sale of land subject to a trust for sale, provided that the "capital money . . . shall not be paid to or applied by the direction of fewer than two persons as trustees of the disposition, except where the trustee is a trust corporation . . . "[39]

Two trustees

---

[35] Wolstenholme and Cherry, *Conveyancing Statutes* (13th ed., 1972), Vol. 1, p. 84. *Cf. Re Wellsted's Will Trusts* [1949] 1 Ch. 296 at 319, *per* Cohen L.J. who reserved his opinion on the decision.
[36] D. Pollock (1953) 17 Conv. (N.S.) 134 at 137.
[37] The word "invest" should be avoided here as otherwise the trustees could not purchase a house as a residence for one of the beneficiaries: *Re Power's Will Trusts* [1947] Ch. 572.
[38] L.P.A. 1925, s.29(2)(3).
[39] *Ibid.*, s.27(2) as added by Law of Property (Amendment) Act 1926, Sched. See also Trustee Act 1925, s.14(2)(*a*).

On the face of it, the procedure appears to be simple. In the case of unregistered land, the purchaser need only be concerned to see that the legal title is vested in the trustees for sale, of whom the maximum number is four.[40] He need only concern himself with the devolution of the legal estate which will be investigated in the normal manner and with those interests, such as matters registered under the Land Charges Acts 1925 and 1972, which will not be overreached by the conveyance. He need not concern himself with the nature of the interests under the trust for sale. Similarly, if title to the land is registered, he need not be concerned with the devolution of title; subject to compliance with any restrictions noted on the register, he can deal solely with the registered proprietors.[41]

Implied trusts for sale Matters are not, however, as simple as they might seem. As will be seen, it is by no means the case that all trusts for sale are express: many are created by implication of law. In these circumstances, the existence of the trust for sale and the need to comply with the overreaching provisions may be unknown to a purchaser. Therefore, although the legal title passes, purchasers have been held to take subject to the rights of the beneficiaries behind the trust for sale.[42] In such a situation, the difficulties in so far as a purchaser is concerned can be overcome, provided that the statutory overreaching machinery is operated. Any beneficial interests, even if owned by people in actual occupation will then be overreached.[43] A full analysis of these problems will be made in Chapter 7.

Conversion In pointing out that purchasers can be adversely affected by the rights of beneficiaries under a trust for sale, some attention must be paid to what those rights are. The orthodox view is that the beneficiaries can only be interested in the proceeds of sale, rather than in the land itself. This is because the trust is a trust for sale and as a consequence of the maxim, equity looks upon that as done which ought to be done, the beneficiaries' rights can only be in the proceeds of sale.[44] The judicial attitude to this doctrine, although slightly chequered, has generally been more pragmatic than a strict application of doctrine would suggest.[45]

Succession The context in which the doctrine of conversion has always had the greatest scope is succession. For this purpose, the interest of a beneficiary under a trust for sale has always been regarded as personalty. This view was originally highly significant as prior to 1925 the devolution of realty and personalty differed on intestacy. After that date, upon an intestacy both real

---

[40] L.P.A. 1925, s.34(2); Trustee Act 1925, s.34.
[41] Land Registration Act 1925, s.20.
[42] *Williams & Glyn's Bank* v. *Boland* [1981] A.C. 497; *Kingsnorth Trust Ltd.* v. *Tizard* [1986] 1 W.L.R. 783.
[43] *City of London Building Society* v. *Flegg* [1988] A.C. 54.
[44] Megarry and Wade, above n. 31, p. 315 but see also pp. 404, 443–444; Cheshire & Burn, *The Modern Law of Real Property* (13 ed., 1982) p. 79.
[45] See generally S. Anderson (1984) 100 L.Q.R. 46; H. Forrest [1978] Conv. 194; J. Warburton [1986] Conv. 415.

and personal property is held upon trust for sale[46] and devolves in the same way.

Real and personal property Much of the vitality has gone from the doctrine because of this, but it nevertheless remains applicable should a testator differentiate between his real and personal property in his will. Thus if a beneficiary under a trust for sale dies leaving his real property to A and his personal property to B, B will take his interest under the trust.[47] Indeed any testamentary reference to personalty will operate to pass the beneficial interest under the trust for sale, unless the context of the will makes it clear that this particular interest is not intended so to pass.[48]

Other contexts In the context of succession, the doctrine serves a useful purpose. Were it not to apply, the destination of a testator's beneficial interest might depend on the fortuitous circumstance of the timing of the execution of the trust for sale. By treating his interest as personalty throughout, this inconvenience is avoided. In different contexts, this approach is less appropriate. A good example of this is the attitude taken to contracts to sell beneficial interests behind trust for sale. These contracts have consistently been held to be concerned with the sale of interests in land for the purpose of section 40(1) of the L.P.A. 1925.[49]

Rather more difficulty has been experienced with regard to the doctrine of conversion when dealing with other statutory provisions as is demonstrated by conflicting Court of Appeal decisions. Perhaps the most trenchant judicial endorsement of the doctrine of conversion was in *Irani Finance Ltd. v. Singh*,[50] where it was held that a tenant in common under a trust for sale had no interest in land which could be charged under section 35 of the Administration of Justice Act 1956.[51] Cross L.J. expressed the view that it was essential to the operation of trusts for sale that the beneficial interests be regarded as subsisting only against the proceeds of sale.[52] Similarly in *Cedar Holdings Ltd. v. Green*[53] **Interest in money, not land** it was held that the "all estate" clause in section 63(1) of the L.P.A. 1925 did not operate to convey a beneficial interest behind a trust for sale as it was an interest in money rather than in land.

Restricting conversion These cases represent the high points of the application of conversion.[54] Although recently endorsed in principle,[55] the general trend of recent authority is against deciding disputes on the basis of the technical doctrine of conversion. In *Williams & Glyn's Bank v. Boland*[56] one of the issues was whether such an interest was a right subsisting in reference to land within the meaning of section 70(1) of the Land Registration Act 1925. In

---

[46] Administration of Estates Act 1925, s.33(1).
[47] *Re Kempthorne* [1930] 1 Ch. 268.
[48] *Re Newman* [1930] 2 Ch. 409; *Re Mellish* [1929] 2 K.B. 82n.
[49] *Cooper v. Critchley* [1955] Ch. 431; *Steadman v. Steadman* [1976] A.C. 536.
[50] [1971] Ch. 59; *Stevens v. Hutchinson* [1953] Ch. 299.
[51] See now Charging Orders Act 1979, s.2(1)(*a*) and Chap. 6 below.
[52] [1971] Ch. 59 at 80.
[53] [1981] Ch. 129.
[54] For a different approach, see *Elias v. Mitchell* [1972] Ch. 652.
[55] *City of London Building Society v. Flegg* [1988] A.C. 54 at 82–83.
[56] [1981] A.C. 487.

holding that it was, it was not strictly necessary to hold the right to be an interest in land. Nevertheless, Lord Wilberforce expressed the view that to describe a beneficiary's interest behind a trust for sale as simply being in the proceeds of sale was "just a little unreal."[57] This must now be taken to be the better view so that when property held upon trust for sale is used as a residence,[58] the rights of the beneficiaries will be unaffected by the doctrine of conversion, except in limited cases of succession.

Structure of co-ownership

The trust for sale is a flexible device, quite able to accommodate both consecutive and concurrent interests in property. It is, however, principally with concurrent interests that the trust for sale is concerned in practice. As will be seen, the intention of the legislature in 1925 appears to have been to ensure that all forms of co-ownership of land involved the creation of a trust for sale. To appreciate how the law operates in this area, it is first necessary to have regard to the two principal forms of co-ownership that currently exist.

Joint tenancies and tenancies in common To all intents and purposes, the only forms of co-ownership that exist are joint tenancies and tenancies in common. Tenancies by entireties were abolished in 1925[59] and coparceny is now virtually obsolete. Attention will be focussed exclusively, therefore, on the forms of co-ownership in current use.

Joint tenancy The essential nature of a joint tenancy is that the joint tenants as a group own the entire interest in the property but as individuals they own nothing. The joint tenants together constitute one person in the eye of the law. The significance of this is seen when one joint tenant dies. Because, as an individual the deceased did not own a share in the property, he has nothing to pass on under his will or upon intestacy. The consequence of this is what is termed the *jus accrescendi*—the right of survivorship.

Jus accrescendi

The right of survivorship is one of the most significant features of the concept of the joint tenancy. On the death of one joint tenant, he simply drops out of the picture. Thus if A, B and C are joint tenants and C dies, the position is simply that A and B are joint tenants of the property. No one else becomes involved. Similarly, if B then dies, A becomes the sole owner of the property and co-ownership is at an end.

Contemporaneous deaths

In the light of this doctrine, in the case of contemporaneous deaths, it is essential to know who died first. At common law, if two joint tenants died in circumstances when it could not be ascertained which of them died first, the property would remain in joint tenancy in their respective heirs.[60] The matter is now

---

[57] [1981] A.C. 487 at 507. *Cedar Holdings Ltd.* v. *Green* [1981] Ch. 129 was overruled.
[58] For the right of residence, see Chap. 7 below.
[59] L.P.A. 1925, Sched. 1, Part VI. See Generally, Megarry and Wade, *The Law of Real Property* (5th ed., 1984) pp. 457–462.
[60] *Bradshaw* v. *Toulmin* (1784) Dick. 633.

governed by section 184 of the L.P.A. 1925 which provides that in these circumstances, the younger of the two is deemed to survive the older. Accordingly, the property would devolve with the younger's estate.

The four unities For a joint tenancy to be created, it is essential that what are known as the four unities co-exist. If they do not, a tenancy in common will arise. It should also be observed that the existence of the four unities does not mean that a joint tenancy has necessarily been created; simply, that if one or more is absent, a joint tenancy cannot be in existence.

The four unities are unity of possession, interest, time and title. With regard to unity of possession, this is a feature common to both types of co-ownership. Because the joint tenants are simultaneously entitled to the land, one cannot exclude the other from it. It does nevertheless happen, particularly in the domestic context, that exclusion takes place. In these circumstances, the occupying co-owner can be ordered by a court to pay an occupation rent to the one he has ousted. This matter will be fully explored in Chapter 3. It can also be pointed out that the principle of unity of possession has been modified by statute. The best example is when a person is excluded from a house under the Domestic Violence and Matrimonial Proceedings Act 1976. Again, discussion of this must be postponed until Chapter 5.

Possession

As it is the nature of a joint tenancy that none of the tenants have specific interests in the property, it necessarily follows that one cannot have a larger interest than the other. Hence if one co-owner has a life interest in the property and the other an entailed interest, they cannot be joint tenants.[61] It does not follow from this, however, that the joint tenants cannot have different interests in the property if there is an element of succession involved. Hence, if a devise is made to A and B for life, remainder to B, A and B can be joint tenants of the life interest, despite B owning the fee simple in remainder.[62] If, however, A and B were originally joint tenants for life and B subsequently acquires the remainder, the original joint tenancy is terminated.[63]

Interest

It follows rationally from the theory that no one joint tenant has any interest to call his own, that they all acquired their interest in the same way. This will include a conveyance, an assent under a will or a joint act of adverse possession.[64]

Title

Again it follows from the nature of a joint tenancy that every joint tenant should acquire his interest in the property simultaneously. There are two limited exceptions to this rule[65] which, otherwise, is adhered to.

Time

Tenancies in common The tenancy in common differs fundamentally in nature from the joint tenancy. Each tenant in common has a definite interest in the property. It is not, however, physically demarcated. It is quite permissible, and

---

[61] See Megarry and Wade, above n. 59, p. 420.
[62] *Wiscot's Case* (1599) 2 Co. Rep. 60b.
[63] *Ibid.*
[64] *Ward* v. *Ward* (1871) 9 Ch.App. 789.
[65] A conveyance to uses, or a gift by will, see Megarry and Wade, above n. 59, pp. 423–424.

indeed not uncommon, for land to be owned by two tenants in common in unequal shares, for example A owning one-fifth of the property and B owning four-fifths.

Undivided shares
Various consequences flow from the nature of a tenancy in common. First, although the tenants in common have specific shares in the property, they are undivided. Thus no tenant in common can point to one part of the land as being his own. Unless the land is partitioned, each tenant in common has an equal right to possession of it. Thus the only unity required for a tenancy in common is the unity of possession.

No survivorship
The second important feature of a tenancy in common is that there is no automatic right of survivorship. Again, this follows from the fact that prior to his death, a tenant in common owned a specific share of the property. As such, it passes by will or in accordance with the intestacy rules in the normal way.

Co-ownership after 1925: law and equity From a conveyancing point of view, there is no doubt that a joint tenancy held considerable advantages over the tenancy in common. The problem with the tenancy in common existing at law is that the natural tendency is for the title to become fragmented. Suppose A and B were tenants in common in equal shares. A died leaving his share to C, D and E equally. C then died leaving his share to F and G, again equally. A purchaser of the land would have to ensure that B, D, E, F and G were parties to the conveyance; and yet F and G only held one-twelfth shares in the land.

This simple example shows the drawbacks of legal tenancies in common. Had A and B been joint tenants, then B would have become the sole legal owner by survivorship and as a consequence it would be far easier to convey it.

The abolition of legal tenancies in common In what has been described as "the greatest boon that the . . . statutes could confer,"[66] legal tenancies in common were abolished in 1925. By section 1(6) of the L.P.A. 1925, "A legal estate is not capable of subsisting or of being created in an undivided share . . . "

It is important to realise at the outset that the tenancy in common is only prohibited at law. This is made clear by section 36(2) which prohibits the severance of a legal joint tenancy in order to create a legal tenancy in common but expressly preserves the existence of tenancies in common in equity.[67]

Co-ownership and trusts for sale

The key to understanding the operation of modern co-ownership is to keep separate the legal and equitable positions. The scheme adopted by the framers of the 1925 legislation was to ensure that, unless the land was subject to a strict settlement, all forms of co-ownership should exist behind a trust for sale. The legal estate in the land would be held by a small number of trustees as joint tenants. Because these joint tenants acting together could overreach beneficial interests existing behind the trust for sale, it

---

[66] A. H. Cosway (1929) 15 Conv. (o.s.) 82.
[67] For the meaning of severance, see pp. 16–26 below.

was immaterial, so far as a purchaser was concerned, what the beneficial interests were behind it. This, of course, matters greatly to the beneficiaries themselves but a purchaser could ignore with impunity the fragmentation of the beneficial ownership.

In furtherance of this policy, as has been seen, the maximum number of legal owners of land is four. If there are more than four grantees, section 34(2) of the L.P.A. 1925 operates to vest the legal title in the first four persons named upon the statutory trusts.

Statutory trusts The trust for sale is a convenient device to accommodate both settlements and co-ownership. Provided that the correct machinery is employed, a purchaser is not concerned with the beneficial interests existing behind it. It is therefore desirable, although not mandatory, to keep them off the title. To facilitate this, land can simply be conveyed to the trustees upon the statutory trusts. Alternatively, the conveyance to the co-owners can include a statement that they are beneficially entitled as joint tenants or as tenants in common in specified proportions as is appropriate.[68]

Definition One method of keeping the beneficial interests off the title is to convey the land to the trustees upon the statutory trusts. These are defined as follows by section 35 of the L.P.A. 1925:

> "For the purposes of this Act land held upon the 'statutory trusts' shall be held upon the trusts and subject to the provisions following, namely, upon trust to sell the same and to stand possessed of the net proceeds of sale, after payment of costs, and of the net rents and profits until sale after payment of rates, taxes, costs of insurance, repairs and other outgoings, upon such trusts, and subject to such powers and provisions, as may be requisite for giving effect to the rights of the persons . . . interested in the land."

Imposition of statutory trusts The statutory trusts can be utilised as a shorthand method of creating a trust for sale and keeping the beneficial interests off the title. More significantly they are imposed when certain types of co-ownership occur. If land is conveyed to two or more persons as tenants in common, then section 34(2) of the L.P.A. operates to vest the legal title in them as joint tenants upon the statutory trusts. This means they hold the legal title upon trust for themselves. For example, if land is conveyed to A and B as tenants in common the position is as follows:

Law	A, B	Joint Tenants
	Trust for Sale	
Equity	A + B	Tenants in Common

Devise to tenants in common A similar result occurs if land is devised to A and B as tenants in common. There is a difference, however, in that the legal title vests in the testator's personal representatives, say X and Y, who assume the role of the trustees for sale.[69] The position is:

---

[68] See Encyclopaedia of Forms and Precedents (4th ed., 1969) Vol. 19, p. 1036.
[69] L.P.A. 1925, s.34(3).

Law	X, Y	Joint Tenants

Trust for Sale

Equity	A + B	Tenants in Common

Conveyance to joint tenants If property is conveyed to A and B as joint tenants, again the statutory trusts are imposed but in a slightly more tortuous manner. By section 36(1) the land shall be held upon trust for sale, in like manner as if the persons beneficially entitled were tenants in common, but not so as to sever the joint tenancy in equity. The effect of this is to bring the conveyance within sections 34 and 35, while ensuring that A and B remain as joint tenants in equity. Diagrammatically the position is:

Law	A, B	Joint Tenants

Trust for Sale

Equity	A, B	Joint Tenants

Gaps in the system Unfortunately, not all cases of co-ownership of land have been catered for by the L.P.A.[70] These problem cases occur when there is sole ownership at law but co-ownership involving a tenancy in common. This can occur in the following situations:

(a) Land conveyed to an adult and a minor as tenants in common[71];
(b) Land conveyed to one person, but where two or more people have contributed unequally[72] to the purchase price;
(c) Land owned solely by A who then declares that he holds on trust for himself and another as tenants in common.

Filling the gaps In none of these cases does the legislation provide a clear answer. The answer has now been provided by the courts. In *Bull* v. *Bull*,[73] a house was conveyed into the sole name of a son but his mother had together with him contributed to its purchase. This made them tenants in common in unequal shares in equity. The Court of Appeal relied upon section 36(4) of the Settled Land Act 1925, which provides that an undivided share in land shall not be capable of being created except under a trust instrument or under the L.P.A. 1925, and shall then only take effect behind a trust for sale. It was then held that the effect of this was that the son held the legal estate on trust for sale for himself and his mother.

The weakness in this reasoning is that the case which established that a tenancy in common arises as a result of unequal

---

[70] See (1944) 9 Conv. (N.S.) 27 especially at 46.
[71] If conveyed to them as joint tenants, the adult would hold on the statutory trusts: L.P.A. 1925, s.19(2).
[72] If they contribute in equal shares, they would become joint tenants in equity: *Lake* v. *Gibson* (1729) 1 Eq.Cas.Ab. 291; *Aveling* v. *Knipe* (1815) 19 Ves. 441. This is then governed by L.P.A. 1925, s.36(1).
[73] [1955] 1 Q.B. 234. For criticism, see Bernard Rudden (1963) 17 Conv. (N.S.) 51; William Swadling [1986] Conv. 379; [1987] Conv. 451 at 454–457.

contributions to the purchase of the property also stressed that this fact must be evident from the deed.[74] Applying this reasoning to the facts of *Bull* v. *Bull*, where there was no such indication in the conveyance to the son, would have meant that, because of section 36(4), the mother had no interest in equity at all. Consequently the reasoning in *Bull* is to be welcomed and has been endorsed by the House of Lords.[75] The result is that in all the examples given, the land will be held upon trust for sale.

Co-ownership for life As has been seen, virtually all forms of concurrent ownership now exist behind a trust for sale. An exception to this can occur if land is jointly owned by two people for life with remainders over. If the co-owners of the life interest hold it as beneficial joint tenants then, provided that both are of full age, they together constitute the tenant for life under the Settled Land Act.[76] On the other hand, if they hold as tenants in common, then the land is held upon trust for sale.[77]

Settlement or trust for sale

If, as is likely, such settlements were created by will, the consequences would be as follows. If land were devised to A and B for life as joint tenants remainder to C, then A and B should have the legal title vested in them by means of a vesting assent. Unless other trustees are named, then the testator's personal representatives would assume the role of the trustees of the settlement.[78] If, conversely, A and B took as tenants in common the statutory trusts would be imposed and the legal title would be retained by the personal representatives as trustees for sale.[79] The potential for errors to be made seems clear and is another regrettable consequence of retaining two methods of settling land.

Severance

The joint tenancy and the tenancy in common differ fundamentally in nature. This difference principally affects the beneficiaries but will also concern a purchaser who seeks to purchase the land from the sole survivor of a number of legal joint tenants. It is therefore important to ascertain, first, the circumstances in which the co-owners are regarded as tenants in common from the outset and, secondly, how they can convert what was originally a beneficial joint tenancy into a tenancy in common.

Express tenancies in common The simplest method to establish beyond doubt that the co-owners are tenants in common is to state this expressly in the conveyance of the land to them. By doing this, subsequent disputes are avoided on the death of one of the co-owners as to whether the survivor has become the sole

---

[74] *Lake* v. *Gibson* (1729) 1 Eq.Cas.Ab. 291. See also M. Friend and J. Newton [1982] Conv. 213 at 215.
[75] *Williams & Glyn's Bank* v. *Boland* [1981] A.C. 487; see also *Walia* v. *Michael Naughton Ltd.* [1985] 1 W.L.R. 1115.
[76] Settled Land Act 1925, s.19(2)(3).
[77] *Ibid.*, s.36(1).
[78] *Ibid.*, s.30(3).
[79] L.P.A. 1925, s.34(3). See pp. 14–15 above.

owner by survivorship. In addition, if land is conveyed to A and B as tenants in common and A has died, a purchaser will know that co-ownership may well continue to subsist in equity despite B being the sole owner at law.[80] To ensure a good title he must see that an additional trustee for sale is appointed. If title is unregistered, the purchaser will see the need for this from the conveyance. If title is registered then A and B will originally be registered as joint proprietors but a restriction will be entered on the register preventing the survivor from being able to give a valid receipt for the purchase money.[81]

Words of severance   It is not essential in order to create a tenancy in common in equity that this expression is adopted. While it is preferable so to do if it is intended to create a tenancy in common, other expressions in a conveyance or will have been held to have the same effect. Such expressions are various. The following have been held to have this result:

"in equal shares"[82];

"share and share alike"[83];

"equally"[84];

"to be divided between"[85];

These are but examples of words that have been held to be sufficient to effect a severance. There are many other examples.[86] What should be stressed, however, is that there is no particular magic in these words. Even where an expression such as one of those above is used, it will not necessarily effect the creation of a tenancy in common if it is apparent from the rest of the document that that is not intended,[87] although it will, of course, raise a strong presumption in favour of it.

General intention   The converse is also true. It is not necessary in order to create a tenancy in common to use previously recognised words of severance. Instead, the court will look to the general intention as apparent from the document to see if a tenancy in common is intended. In so doing, a judicial disposition in favour of finding a tenancy in common is evident.[88] If, for example, a will envisages only limited rights of survivorship between the co-owners,[89] or in the slightest degree indicates an intention that the co-owners should have shares in the property,[90] a tenancy in common will arise. Good examples of this are where the trustees are given the power to apply income for the maintenance of the beneficiaries[91] or advance capital to them.[92]

---

[80] It will not do so if A leaves his property by will to B.
[81] Land Registration Act 1925, s.58(3). See further p. 26 below.
[82] *Payne* v. *Webb* (1874) L.R. 19 Eq. 26.
[83] *Heathe* v. *Heathe* (1740) 2 A & R 121.
[84] *Lewen* v. *Dodd* (1595) Cro.Eli. 443. See also *Re Kilvert* [1957] Ch. 388.
[85] *Fisher* v. *Wigg* (1700) 1 P.Wms. 14.
[86] See Megarry and Wade, *The Law of Real Property* (5th ed., 1984) p. 425.
[87] *Frewen* v. *Rolfe* (1787) 2 Bro.C.C. 220.
[88] *Re Woolley* [1903] 2 Ch. 206, 296 at 211, *per* Joyce J.
[89] *Ryves* v. *Ryves* (1871) 11 Eq. 539.
[90] *Robertshaw* v. *Fraser* (1871) 6 Ch.App. 696 at 699, *per* Lord Hatherley L.C. See also *Surtees* v. *Surtees* (1871) 12 Eq. 400.
[91] *Re Ward* [1920] 1 Ch. 334.
[92] *L'Estrange* v. *L'Estrange* [1902] 1 I.R. 467; *Re Dunn* [1916] 1 Ch. 97.

Inconsistent provisions   It may happen that a conveyance to co-owners uses mutually contradictory expressions, such as to A and B as joint tenants in common in equal shares. To resolve such disputes, there is a quaint common law rule that the first words prevailed in a deed but the last in a will.[93] This rule is only to be applied, however, in cases of last resort where it is otherwise impossible to glean the parties' intentions. Where there is any indication of a desire to hold as tenants in common, then despite the use of the term joint tenants, a tenancy in common is likely to have been created.[94]

Implied severance   Fragmentation of title has always been regarded as undesirable at law: "joint tenancies were favoured, for the law loves not fractions of estates, nor to divide and multiply tenures."[95] Equity, however, has always taken a different view because it sees the *jus accrescendi* as being potentially unfair. Accordingly, it has traditionally leaned in favour of a tenancy in common.[96] In particular, there are three situations where equity presumes that a tenancy in common has been created. In these cases, however, it must be remembered that it is only a presumption which is capable of being rebutted.

Partnerships   When two people buy land together as a commercial investment, it is highly improbable that they intend the survivor to become the sole owner by survivorship. They would wish their shares to devolve upon their own families. Equity recognises this by presuming that they originally took the land as tenants in common. A joint tenancy is seen as inappropriate between merchants.[97]

It is not essential that there be a formal partnership within sections 1 and 2 of the Partnership Act 1890 to bring this presumption into play. What does is the joint purchase of land for a commercial venture. Hence if land is bought by a partnership or an unincorporated association for purposes unconnected with trading then, in principle, there is no presumption in favour of a tenancy in common.[98]

Rebuttable presumption   The presumption in favour of a tenancy in common is rebuttable. The most straightforward method of rebutting it is to state in the conveyance or will that there is to be a joint tenancy.[99] For example, in *Barton* v. *Morris*[1] a cohabiting couple purchased a cottage in their joint names to use as a guest house.

---

[93] *Slingsby's Case* (1587) 5 Co.Rep. 186; *Joyce* v. *Barker Bros. (Builders) Ltd.* (1980) 40 P. & C.R. 512. See Megarry and Wade, *The Law of Real Property* (5th ed. 1984) p. 426.
[94] *Martin* v. *Martin* (1987) 54 P. & C.R. 238.
[95] *Fisher* v. *Wigg* (1700) 1 Salk 391 at 392, *per* Holt C.J. (dissenting).
[96] *Burgess* v. *Rawnsley* [1975] Ch. 429 at 438, *per* Lord Denning M.R.
[97] *Lake* v. *Craddock* (1732) 3 P.Wms. 157; *Lyster* v. *Dolland* (1792) 1 Ves.Jun. 431; *Darby* v. *Darby* (1856) 3 Drew. 495; *Malayan Credit Ltd.* v. *Jack Chia-Mph Ltd.* [1986] 1 All E.R. 711.
[98] Lindley, *Partnership* (15th ed., 1984) p. 522. Although the case cited, *Brown* v. *Dale* (1878) 9 Ch.D. 178 provides little support, the proposition nevertheless seems correct in principle.
[99] *Morris* v. *Barrett* (1829) 3 Y. & J. 384. See also *Ward* v. *Ward* (1871) 9 Ch.App. 789 (Joint adverse possession of a farm. Held they took as joint tenants).
[1] [1985] 1 W.L.R. 1257. *Cf.* P. J. Clarke [1985] All E. Rev. 187 at 197 which overlooks this.

As the conveyance declared that they held as joint tenants, the presumption of a tenancy in common was displaced.

Mortgages For the same reason that partners take as tenants in common, there is a strong presumption that the lenders of money take their mortgage security as tenants in common also.[2] Although it has been said that this presumption can be rebutted,[3] a joint account clause in the mortgage has not done so, it being held that this existed solely for the benefit and protection of the purchaser.[4]

Unequal contributions A beneficial interest in land can be acquired by a contribution to its purchase.[5] Where the contributions are unequal in size it is presumed that the contributors take as tenants in common, the size of each person's share being commensurate with the proportion of the purchase price.[6] In the case which established this proposition it was further stated that the fact that there has been unequal contribution should be apparent from the deeds. As explained earlier, however, this requirement has now been discarded, albeit not expressly.[7] Again, this presumption is rebuttable; a statement in the conveyance that the co-owners are to take as joint tenants being the most conclusive way of rebutting it.[8]

Equal contributions Conversely, it has long been accepted that if a house has been purchased by equal contributions, the contributors take as joint tenants.[9] Given the judicial predilection for tenancies in common, this presumption can be fairly easily displaced and frequently this will be the more just result.

Acts of severance

If a joint tenancy has been created at the outset, it is open to the parties to convert it subsequently into a tenancy in common. This process is known as severance. The ability to sever a joint tenancy exists, so it has been said, so that if one joint tenant has an ill opinion of his own life, he can sever the joint tenancy to ensure that survivorship does not work any hardship.[10]

Methods of severance Although severance had long been recognised, the methods of doing so were not assimilated until 1861. In *Williams* v. *Hensman*,[11] Sir William Page-Wood V.-C. delivered the *locus classicus* on the subject. He said:

"A joint tenancy may be severed in three ways: in the first place, an act of any one of the persons interested operating

---

[2] *Petty* v. *Styward* (1632) 1 Ch.Rep. 57; *Vickers* v. *Cowell* (1839) 1 Beav. 529.
[3] *Steeds* v. *Steeds* (1889) 22 Q.B.D. 537 at 541–542, *per* Wills J. instancing trustees: an example clearly only relevant to severance at law.
[4] *Powell* v. *Broadhurst* [1901] 2 Ch. 160; *Re Jackson* (1887) 34 Ch.D. 732.
[5] This is fully discussed in Chap. 2.
[6] *Lake* v. *Gibson* (1729) 1 Eq.Cas.Ab. 391.
[7] See pp. 15–16 above.
[8] *Pink* v. *Lawrence* (1977) 36 P. & C.R. 98; *Goodman* v. *Gallant* [1986] Fam. 106.
[9] *Aveling* v. *Knipe* (1815) 19 Ves. 441; *Lake* v. *Gibson* (1729) 1 Eq.Cas.Ab.391.
[10] *Cray* v. *Willis* (1729) 2 P.Wms. 529.
[11] (1861) 1 J. & H. 546.

on his own share may create a severance as to that share. The right of each joint-tenant is a right by survivorship only in the event of no severance having taken place of the share which is claimed under the *jus accrescendi*. Each one is at liberty to dispose of his own interest in such manner as to sever it from the joint fund—losing, of course at the same time, his own right of survivorship. Secondly a joint tenancy may be severed by mutual agreement. And in the third place, there may be a severance by any course of dealing sufficient to intimate that the interests of all were mutually treated as constituting a tenancy in common. When the severance depends on an inference of this kind without any express act of severance, it will not suffice to rely on an intention, with respect to the particular share, declared only behind the backs of the other persons interested."[12]

Statutory severance The methods of severance stated by Page-Wood V.-C. have been retained by section 36(2) of the L.P.A. 1925 which also states that such severance can only take effect in equity. In addition to these three methods, section 36(2) added a further method, namely the service upon the other joint tenants of a notice indicating the desire to sever. This is a useful method of severance and can be employed by sending the notice by post in a registered letter addressed to the other joint tenant at his address.[13] If this procedure is adopted, then severance is effected irrespective of whether or not the letter is actually received.[14]

Precedent　To sever a joint tenancy by written declaration, it is best to avoid future difficulty by using an appropriate form. A precedent which can be used is as follows:

> I hereby give you notice of my desire to sever as from this day the joint tenancy in equity of and in the property described in the schedule hereto now held by you and me as joint tenants both at law and in equity so that the said property shall henceforth belong to you and me in equal shares.[15]

Unequivocal intention　To sever a joint tenancy, it is desirable to use such a precedent but not essential. What is required is the expression of a clear and unequivocal intention to sever. This can be done by the service of a divorce petition. In *Re Draper's Conveyance*[16] an affidavit in support of the summons asked that the property be sold and the proceeds of sale be distributed equally. This was held to be sufficient to effect a severance. It is important that the summons be unequivocal, as is demonstrated by the cautionary

Harris v. Goddard　tale of *Harris* v. *Goddard*.[17] A married couple held their house as beneficial joint tenants. Upon their marriage foundering, a

---

[12] (1861) 1 J. + H. 546 at 557–558. The Law Commission has provisionally recommended that this be statutorily enacted: Law Commission Working Paper (1986) No. 94, p. 70.
[13] L.P.A. 1925, s.196(4).
[14] *Re 88 Berkeley Rd, N.W.9* [1971] Ch. 648.
[15] Encyclopaedia of Forms and Precedents (4th ed., 1973), Vol. 22, pp. 854–855.
[16] [1969] 1 Ch. 486. The doubts expressed as to the correctness of this decision in *Nielson-Jones* v. *Fedden* [1975] Ch. 222 at 236 have themselves been disapproved: *Harris* v. *Goddard* [1983] 1 W.L.R. 1203 at 1210.
[17] [1983] 1 W.L.R. 1203; S. Coneys [1984] Conv. 148.

divorce petition was submitted which sought relief in the terms of section 24 of the Matrimonial Causes Act 1973 asking that such order might be made by way of transfer of property in respect of the former matrimonial home as may be just. Shortly before the date of the hearing the husband was seriously injured and he died soon afterwards. It was held that as the petition did not assert a present claim to a share in the property, no severance occurred and the wife became sole owner by survivorship.

The case, although correct, illustrates an undesirable feature of the joint tenancy. Upon his death, given that the marriage was on the verge of termination, it is most unlikely that the deceased would have wanted his wife to take the whole property. To avoid such difficulties recurring, if a husband and wife are beneficial joint tenants of the home, it is preferable if the marriage runs into difficulties to serve an express notice of severance, independent from any documents dealing with the divorce, thereby obviating future disputes as to whether severance has occurred.[18]

Husband and wife An additional feature of *Harris* v. *Goddard* is the express acceptance of the proposition that there is no restriction on the right to sever placed upon spouses. This had previously been somewhat uncertain owing to a dictum of Lord Denning M.R. in *Bedson* v. *Bedson*[19] that, if a matrimonial home is used as a dwelling, neither spouse could sever. Although this opinion was described in the same case by Russell L.J. as being "without the slightest foundation in law or in equity,"[20] it was nevertheless repeated six years later.[21] The orthodox view expressed by Russell L.J. has, however, been consistently preferred at first instance[22] and has now been authoritatively endorsed in the Court of Appeal.[23] This is logical because there is no restriction on spouses being tenants in common from the outset.

Unilateral action Although a unilateral form of severance by written notice is now possible by statute, it was already possible for one party acting unilaterally to sever. Under *Williams* v. *Hensman*,[24] the first method of severance was said to be an act of one person operating on his own share.

Alienation

The most clear-cut method of severing a joint tenancy under this head is for one joint tenant to alienate his interest in the property.[25] Any such alienation must be *inter vivos*, a will being

---

[18] For a debate as to whether the couple should take as tenants in common from the outset, see M. P. Thompson [1987] Conv. 29 and 275 and A. M. Prichard [1987] Conv. 273.

[19] [1965] 2 Q.B. 666 at 678. For the opposite view, see *Smith* v. *Smith* [1945] 1 All E.R. 584 at 586, *per* Denning J. For devastating criticism of Lord Denning's later view, see R.E.M. (1966) 82 L.Q.R. 29.

[20] [1965] 2 Q.B. at 690.

[21] *Jackson* v. *Jackson* [1971] 1 W.L.R. 1539 at 1542.

[22] *Radziej* v. *Radziej* [1968] 1 W.L.R. 1928; *Re Draper's Conveyance* [1969] 1 Ch. 486; *Cowcher* v. *Cowcher* [1972] 1 W.L.R. 425.

[23] *Harris* v. *Goddard* [1983] 1 W.L.R. 1203 at 1208, *per* Lawton L.J.

[24] (1861) 1 J. & H. 546.

[25] *Goddard* v. *Lewis* (1909) 101 L.T. 528, where many of the authorities are collected. Involuntary alienation on bankruptcy also causes severance: *Morgan* v. *Marquis* (1853) 9 Exch. 145.

ineffective for this purpose.[26] To come under this head, it is not essential for a formal alienation to occur. Thus if one joint tenant enters into a binding contract to sell his interest, then this will itself effect a severance,[27] such contracts including covenants to settle after-acquired property.[28] Similarly if one joint tenant either pledges or mortgages his interest, this too will sever the joint tenancy in equity.[29]

Oral declarations There is currently some uncertainty as to whether if one joint tenant simply tells the other that he wishes to sever that his words will have this effect. Although it was emphatically said that this was not possible in 1740,[30] this view does not seem currently to hold sway. In *Hawkesley* v. *May*,[31] Havers J. thought that the first head in *Williams* v. *Hensman* obviously included a declaration of an intention to sever and this was accepted in *Re Draper's Conveyance*.[32] In *Nielson-Jones* v. *Fedden*,[33] however, Walton J. expressed the view that Havers J. had totally misapprehended Page-Wood V.-C.'s judgment. The judge pointed out, with force, that if one could sever a joint tenancy by an oral declaration, then the statutory method of severance by a written declaration would be otiose and, indeed, restrictive.[34]

Walton J.'s approach to severance with regard to this matter seems historically correct. The decision itself has since been overruled[35] but this aspect of it nevertheless seems to be right.[36] It is true, however, that the courts have, in recent times, held severance to have taken place by revocable actions[37] such as service of a divorce petition, and rather greater emphasis seems to be placed on the fact of communication of the intent to sever rather than its method. It is therefore possible that if an oral declaration of severance is made to the other joint tenants who do not express dissent an inferred, mutual intent to sever will be found with regard to that share.[38] The better view remains, however, that an oral declaration will be ineffective.

Mutual agreement and course of conduct These two methods of severance are separate but closely related. To sever a joint tenancy by mutual agreement does not necessarily entail that that agreement be enforceable. Hence in the leading case of *Burgess* v.

---

[26] *Re Caines (dec'd.)* [1978] 1 W.L.R. 540 at 555. Query whether showing such a will to the other joint tenant would effect severance under L.P.A. 1925, s.36(2) but *cf. Harris* v. *Goddard* [1983] 1 W.L.R. 1203 at 1209, *per* Lawton L.J. For mutual wills, see p. 23 below.

[27] *Brown* v. *Raindle* (1796) 3 Ves. 256. *Semble* if they all agree to sell, this does not *per se* cause severance, *Re Hayes Estate* [1920] I.R. 207 but an inferred agreement to sever will then be easy to find: *Morris* v. *Barrett* (1829) 3 Y. & J. 384.

[28] *Re Hewett* [1894] 1 Ch. 363.

[29] *Watkinson* v. *Hudson* (1826) L.J. (O.S.) Ch. 213; *First National Securities Ltd.* v. *Hegerty* [1985] Q.B. 850.

[30] *Partriche* v. *Poulet* (1740) 2 Atk. 54 at 55, *per* Lord Hardwicke L.C.

[31] [1956] 1 Q.B. 304 at 313.

[32] [1969] 1 Ch. 486.

[33] [1975] Ch. 222 at 234.

[34] *Ibid.* at 236–237.

[35] *Burgess* v. *Rawnsley* [1975] Ch. 429; *Harris* v. *Goddard* [1983] 1 W.L.R. 203.

[36] *Ibid.* at 448, *per* Sir John Pennycuick. F. R. Crane (1975) 39 Conv. (N.S.) 443; D. J. Hayton [1976] C.L.J. 20 at 22.

[37] *Cf.* J. F. Garner (1976) 40 Conv. (N.S.) 77 at 82.

[38] Megarry's *Manual of The Law of Real Property* (6th ed., 1982) p. 326.

Rawnsley[39] an oral contract between two joint tenants for one to buy the other's interest operated to sever the joint tenancy, despite that contract being unenforceable. Whether negotiations falling short of an agreement over such a sale would have had this effect was left open but it is thought that they would. The very fact of negotiation seems to carry the implication that each regards the other as having a separate interest and should suffice to cause severance. Similarly, if the joint tenants agree to leave mutual wills affecting the jointly owned property, this also effects a severance.[40]

Inferred agreement Where a course of conduct is relied upon to effect severance, one is looking for an inferred agreement between the parties that each should have separate shares. It is necessary that the parties are *sui juris* and therefore have capacity to enter such an agreement.[41] A second point to make is that although the courts assert a tendency to lean in favour of a tenancy in common[42] the onus of proof is nevertheless on the person alleging severance.[43]

Requisite intent In cases where an implied severance is relied upon, the evidence is sifted carefully to assess the intention of the co-owners. In so doing, it may emerge that what appear to be acts of severance were not done with the requisite intent. For example, in *Greenfield* v. *Greenfield*[44] the property was partitioned and yet no severance occurred as it emerged that the joint tenants were happy for the right of survivorship to endure. Similarly in *Barton* v. *Morris*,[45] beneficial joint tenants of a guest house put the proceeds in their separate names solely for tax purposes[46] but without intending to indicate several ownership. It was held on the death of one of them that the other took under the *jus accrescendi*.

Homicide A final method, not mentioned in *Williams* v. *Hensman*, where severance appears to occur is where one joint tenant kills another. The normal common law rule is that a criminal is unable to profit from his own crime. If a murderer inherits under the will of his victim, he holds the legacy upon constructive trust.[47] This principle has now been modified, except in so far as murderers are concerned, so that, in appropriate cases, a killer can be relieved from this equitable jurisdiction under section 2(5) of the Forfeiture Act 1982.

If one joint tenant kills the other, it has long been accepted in the Commonwealth that the survivor cannot take the whole interest but holds one-half of the property on constructive trust.[48] The better view is that the homicide did not effect a

---

[39] [1975] Ch. 429.
[40] *Re Wilford's Estate* (1879) 1 Ch.D. 267; *Re Heys* [1914] P. 192.
[41] *Re Wilks* [1891] 3 Ch. 59 at 61–62 *per* Stirling J.
[42] *Burgess* v. *Rawnsley* [1975] Ch. 429 at 438, *per* Lord Denning M.R.
[43] *Re Denny* [1947] L.J.R. 1029; *Greenfield* v. *Greenfield* (1979) 38 P. & C.R. 570.
[44] *Ibid.*
[45] [1985] 1 W.L.R. 1257.
[46] *Sed quaere* as to whether such evidence was admissible: *Tinker* v. *Tinker* [1970] P. 136; P. J. Clarke [1985] All E. R. Rev. 187 at 198.
[47] See, *e.g. Re Crippen* [1911] P. 108. For valuable surveys of this rather arcane branch of law, see T. G. Youdan (1973) 89 L.Q.R. 235; T. K. Earnshaw & P. J. Pace (1974) 37 M.L.R. 481.
[48] *Schobelt* v. *Barber* (1967) 60 D.L.R. (2d) 519; *Re Pechar* [1969] N.Z.L.R. 574; *Rasmanis* v. *Jurewitsch* [1968] 2 N.S.W.R. 166.

severance but rather the killer took the whole by survivorship, only to hold one-half on constructive trust.[49] In *Re K. (dec'd)*,[50] however, it was conceded that a wife who was guilty of the manslaughter of her husband had thereby severed the joint tenancy which had existed between them, although the court exercised its statutory discretion to relieve against forfeiture in her favour, so that she could take under his will.

Severance or constructive trust? The concession is to be regretted. If correct, the following consequences would ensue. If A, B and C were joint tenants and A murdered B, severance would occur and the destination of B's interest would depend upon his will. C would only then have a one-third share in the property. If the better view was followed, the property would devolve upon A and C by survivorship and A would then be divested of his potential half share by operation of the forfeiture rule leaving C with one-half of the property. Similarly, if E and F were joint tenants and E killed F unlawfully, thereby severing the joint tenancy, again F's share in the property would pass by his will or upon his intestacy. Unless E was a beneficiary under the will or upon intestacy, he would not have been deprived of an interest by the forfeiture rule and the court would not be able to relieve him from the effect of the rule under the Act.[51] To avoid these consequences, it is submitted that homicide does not operate to affect the *jus accrescendi* but causes a constructive trust to be imposed upon the killer.

Types of homicide It is not the case that all forms of homicide bring the forfeiture rule into play. Certainly murder will do so[52] but not all types of manslaughter will. The key to the operation of the forfeiture rule appears to be that it will operate if the killer had caused death after threats of violence,[53] even if there is a partial defence such as diminished responsibility.[54] If the death is caused as a result of a failure to perceive an obvious risk of death or serious injury but where there is no deliberate threat of violence,[55] then it is conceived that the rule will not operate. *A fortiori* if the killer is guilty only of an offence such as causing death by reckless driving.[56]

The effect of severance Before a beneficial joint tenancy is severed, neither party has a quantified interest in the property. Between them the joint tenants own the whole interest and they are regarded as constituting one person. If severance occurs, then in principle each of the tenants in common should have equal shares in the property. This proposition was cast into doubt by dicta in *Bedson* v. *Bedson*[57] which envisaged ownership of unequal shares after a severance. These dicta, which were

---

[49] Youdan, above n.47, at 254–255; Earnshaw & Pace, above n.47, at 488–492.
[50] [1986] Fam. 180.
[51] Unless this case comes within Forfeiture Act 1982, s.2(4)(*b*).
[52] Forfeiture Act 1982, s.5.
[53] R. v. *National Insurance Commissioner, ex p. Connor* [1981] Q.B. 758; *Re K. (dec'd)* [1986] Fam. 180.
[54] Homicide Act 1957, s.2; *Re Giles* [1972] Ch. 544; *Aliter* if the killer is found not guilty by reason of insanity under Criminal Procedure (Insanity) Act 1964: *Re Pechar* [1969] N.Z.L.R. 574 at 581.
[55] See *R.* v. *Seymour (Edward)* [1983] 2 A.C. 493.
[56] Criminal Law Act 1977, s.50.
[57] [1965] 2 Q.B. 666 at 681–682, *per* Lord Denning M.R.; at 685, *per* Davies L.J.

contrary to both principle and precedent and apparently caused considerable difficulties to first instance judges, have now been expressly disapproved in *Goodman* v. *Gallant*.[58] In the absence of a claim to rectification,[59] if there is an express declaration of a beneficial joint tenancy, then upon severance the tenants in common take in equal shares, irrespective of the size of their respective contributions to the purchase price.

If there are only two joint tenants, severance by one necessarily effects total severance. This is not so if there are more than two joint tenants. Thus is A, B, C and D are beneficial joint tenants and A severs, A becomes a tenant in common of a one-quarter share with B, C and D who remain as joint tenants of a three-quarter share.[60]

Procedure on severance A legal joint tenancy cannot be severed, whereas an equitable joint tenancy can. If a house is conveyed to A and B as beneficial joint tenants in 1970 and A has now died, B must be the sole legal owner by survivorship. Prior to his death, however, severance in equity might have occurred with the result that the trust for sale subsists. In this case, in order to comply with the statutory over-reaching requirements, another trustee for sale would be appointed to act with B to execute a conveyance to a purchaser. The difficulty was that whether or not severance had occurred would not be known to a purchaser. If it had not, then B will be solely entitled both at law and in equity but nevertheless a purchaser would insist upon the appointment of a second trustee for sale. To obviate this tedious and cumbersome process, reform was implemented.

Unregistered land The Law of Property (Joint Tenants) Act 1964, which applies only to unregistered land and operates retrospectively,[61] provides by section 1 that, for the purposes of section 36(2) of the L.P.A. 1925, the survivor of two or more joint tenants shall, in favour of a purchaser, be deemed to be solely and beneficially interested if he conveys as beneficial owner or the conveyance includes a statement that he is so interested, for example on a sale by the personal representative of a survivor. A purchaser need not, therefore, insist upon the appointment of a second trustee in the circumstances envisaged above provided:

(a) a memorandum of severance has not been endorsed on or annexed to the conveyance by virtue of which the legal estate was vested in the joint tenants; or
(b) a receiving order in bankruptcy, or a petition for such an order, has not been registered against any of the joint tenants under the Land Charges Act 1972.

Notice of severance One uncertainty exists as to what the position would be if there was no notice of severance endorsed on the conveyance but a purchaser had notice of the fact of severance.[62] Probably the purchaser would get a good title as the deeming provision in

---

[58] [1986] Fam. 106.
[59] *Thames Guarantee Ltd.* v. *Campbell* [1985] Q.B. 210 at 227–229, *per* Slade L.J.
[60] *Williams* v. *Hensman* (1861) 1 J. & H. 546.
[61] Law of Property (Joint Tenants) Act 1964, ss.2, 3.
[62] See P. Jackson (1966) 30 Conv. (N.S.) 27.

section 2 seems sufficiently strong to exclude general equitable principles.[63] Good practice is clearly to ensure that a note of severance is endorsed on or annexed to the conveyance.

Registered land   The 1964 Act does not apply to registered land. If severance has occurred, then the appropriate method of preventing the survivor conveying to a purchaser and receiving the capital money is to enter a restriction on the register prohibiting the survivor from giving a valid receipt for the purchase money.[64]

Party walls

With the great incidence of contiguous housing, problems could occur with regard to party walls. The possible legal positions with regard to them were listed in *Watson* v. *Gray*[65] as being:

(a) a tenancy in common of the wall;
(b) the wall divided longtitudinally, each side owning up to the middle;
(c) the wall belonged to one with the other having an easement or right to have it maintained; or
(d) longitudinal division as in (b) but mutual easements of support.

Mutual easements   The common law favoured (a) but this is now inappropriate as it would cause the wall to be held upon trust for sale. Section 38(1) of the L.P.A. 1925 now provides that party walls erected after 1925 shall be held in accordance with the fourth possibility.[66] Party walls created prior to 1925 which were subject to a tenancy in common are converted by the Act to accord with the above position.[67] Should a dispute occur with regard to a party structure, then any person can apply to the court for an order declaring the rights and interests which exist.[68]

London   In so far as party walls in London are concerned, these are subject to the definition in section 44(1) of the London Building Acts (Amendment) Act 1939. Part V of that Act sets out a complex regime for the service of notices and acquisition of consents with regard to building affecting these structures, the details of which are beyond the scope of this book.[69]

---

[63] *Cf. Midland Bank Trust Co. Ltd.* v. *Green* [1981] A.C. 513. See generally M. P. Thompson [1985] C.L.J. 280. For a different view, see Barnsley, *Conveyancing Law and Practice* (2nd ed., 1982) pp. 329–330.
[64] Land Registration Act 1925, s.56.
[65] (1880) 24 Ch.D. 192 at 194–195, *per* Fry J.
[66] There is no legal bar to the holding of legal easements in common: L.P.A. 1925, s.187(2).
[67] L.P.A. 1925, Sched. 1, Pt. V, para. 1.
[68] *Ibid.*, ss.38(2), 203, 204.
[69] For the fullest account, see D. Wright (1954) 18 Conv. (N.S.) 347. See also K. A. Pollard (1980) 256 E.G. 375; J. Anstey (1986) 83 L.S.Gaz. 2125.

2 THE ACQUISITION OF INTERESTS IN PROPERTY

In recent years, one of the more difficult problems that has exercised the courts has been to determine the beneficial ownership of houses that have been used for cohabitation, either by married or unmarried couples. A separate but related problem then frequently arises as to whether or not that property should be sold; a common situation being where one party has left the home and wishes the investment in the home to be realised whereas the other wishes to remain in it, frequently with children. In this chapter, the problems relating to acquisition of an interest in property will be considered, deferring attention to the issue of sale until Chapter 3.

The methods by which interests are acquired in real property are not, in principle, markedly different from those which apply to personal property. Real property disputes cause greater difficulty, however, for various reasons. First, section 53 of the L.P.A. 1925 imposes formal requirements for the creation of equitable interests in land which are not present in the case of personal property. Secondly, in the case of land the time taken actually to buy the property is much longer and thirdly, there is frequently a conflict between the co-owners as to whether the property should be retained or sold. This problem is far less common in the case of personal property.

Personal property

In the case of personal property, co-ownership can arise in two ways: either by express creation or by implication. In the first method, the property can simply be taken in joint names thereby giving rise to co-ownership at law. Subject then to the possible imposition of a resulting trust,[1] the position in equity will mirror that at common law. Alternatively, there may be a sole legal owner of the property who declares himself a trustee of the property in favour of himself and the co-owner. No formalities are required to do this; simply a manifestation of intention to create a trust. For example, in *Paul* v. *Constance*[2] a bank account was financed almost entirely by Mr. Constance. He had told the plaintiff on many occasions that the money in it was as much hers as his. This, it was held, was sufficient to amount to a declaration of trust in her favour, so that, upon his death, she was entitled to half of the money in the account.

Resulting trusts If an express trust is not created, then it is possible for co-ownership to arise by way of resulting trust. Such trusts have their greatest application in the sphere of real property and will

---
[1] See pp. 36–46 below.
[2] [1977] 1 W.L.R. 527.

be considered in detail in that context. Nevertheless the essential principle can be briefly stated here. This was stated in *Dyer* v. *Dyer*[3] by Eyre L.C.B. as being:

> "The clear result of all the cases, without a single exception is, that the trust of a legal estate . . . whether taken in the names of the purchasers and others jointly, or in the names of others without that of the purchaser; whether in one name or several; whether jointly or successive, results to the man who advances the purchase money."

Presumption of trust

It should be pointed out that this statement embodies only a presumption. The normal inference is that a co-purchaser of, for example, shares would intend to have an interest in them, despite not taking the legal title together with the other purchaser. Such a presumption can be rebutted, however, if the evidence shows that the intention was to make a gift of the property.[4] Conversely, however, the existence of certain relationships gives rise to the rebuttable presumption that a gift or advancement was intended rather than a resulting trust. Such a presumption of advancement would arise when a husband transferred property to his wife[5] but not if the wife transferred property to her husband.[6] Similarly, a transfer by a father to a legitimate child or to one to whom he stands *in loco parentis* will raise a presumption of advancement.[7] This presumption does not apply if the transfer is made by the mother to her child,[8] although only slight evidence will be needed to rebut the presumption of resulting trust.

Gift or advancement

These presumptions have in modern society lost a good deal of force.[9] In particular, this means that as between husband and wife, little evidence is needed to rebut the presumption of advancement in order to give rise to a resulting trust in the husband's favour. Nevertheless, unless evidence of a contrary intention is admissible the presumption will apply and no resulting trust will arise.[10]

Joint bank accounts[11]   Joint bank accounts can give rise to various problems. These relate to the ownership of the account itself, the position on the death of one of the joint owners and, finally, the ownership of items of property bought using funds from the account. These matters will be considered in turn.

When a joint bank account is created by individuals, it will almost always be the case that the two joint owners are a

---

[3] (1788) 2 Cox 92.
[4] See, *e.g. Fowkes* v. *Pascoe* (1875) 10 Ch.App. 343.
[5] *e.g. Moate* v. *Moate* (1948) 92 S.J. 484.
[6] *Mercier* v. *Mercier* [1903] 2 Ch. 98.
[7] *Re Ekyn's Trusts* (1877) 6 Ch.D. 115 at 118; *Commissioner of Stamp Duties* v. *Byrnes* [1911] A.C. 386; *Shephard* v. *Cartwright* [1955] A.C. 431.
[8] *Bennet* v. *Bennet* (1879) 10 Ch.D. 474. Perhaps a different result will occur in the case of a one-parent family.
[9] *Pettitt* v. *Pettitt* [1970] A.C. 777 at 792, *per* Lord Reid; at 811, *per* Lord Hodson; at 813, *per* Lord Upjohn. *Cf.* the scathing remarks of Lord Diplock, *ibid.* at 824.
[10] *Tinker* v. *Tinker* [1970] P. 136; *Palaniappa Chettiar (A.R.P.L.)* v. *Arunasalam Chettiar (P.L.A.R.)* [1962] A.C. 294. *Cf. Heseltine* v. *Heseltine* [1971] 1 W.L.R. 342.
[11] See M. C. Cullity (1969) 85 L.Q.R. 530; Miller, *Family Property and Financial Provision* (2nd ed., 1983) pp. 44–46.

cohabiting couple, usually married to each other. If one partner provides the funds for the account which is put into joint names, the question as to the beneficial ownership of the fund can arise. The presumptions of resulting trust or advancement have little part to play in this situation.[12] Rather the issue is whether the account was put in joint names simply for the convenience of the contributor of the funds or whether joint beneficial ownership was intended.

Co-ownership for convenience

A good example of the former situation is provided by *Marshall v. Crutwell*.[13] The plaintiff's husband, when in failing health, transferred his bank account into their joint names. Thereafter, all the cheques drawn upon the account were signed by her at his direction. It was held after his death that the account was not jointly owned in equity. The transfer of the account into joint names was done merely for convenience to enable him to operate it during his illness.

Beneficial co-ownership

Such a finding, although clearly correct on the facts, is unusual. The normal position is that putting the account into joint names is indicative of an intention to create beneficial co-ownership. This is particularly the case when the account is put into joint names unbeknown to the other partner. In these circumstances, it is untenable to argue that the account was put into joint names simply for convenience.[14] Similarly, if there is a deposit account rather than a current account, it is hard to maintain that this was done merely for operational convenience. The presumption that joint ownership was intended will be difficult to rebut.[15]

Ultimately, the issue is one of fact. It seems clear, however, that the longer the account remains in joint names, the stronger the inference will be that the fund is jointly owned. Putting the account into joint names may at the outset be explicable on the grounds of convenience. Leaving the position unaltered thereafter is indicative of an intention to create joint ownership.[16]

Joint tenancy or tenancy in common

The significance of a joint bank account being found to be jointly owned in equity emerges either on the termination of the relationship between the co-owners or upon the death of one of them. In the former situation, no attempt is made to calculate who contributed what to the account: they share it out equally.[17] This is correct in principle because it is generally accepted that the co-owners of a joint bank account are joint tenants. Thus on the death of one of them, the survivor is solely and beneficially entitled to the funds in the account.[18]

Purchase of investments When a bank account is in joint names and thus jointly owned in equity, problems can arise with regard to the ownership of property bought by only one of the parties using funds from that account. The issue will be whether

---

[12] *Pettitt v. Pettitt* [1970] A.C. 777 at 815, *per* Lord Upjohn.
[13] (1875) L.R. 20 Eq. 328; *Hoddinott v. Hoddinott* [1949] 1 K.B. 406 (it was physically difficult for the husband to get to the bank).
[14] *Re Pattinson* (1885) 1 T.L.R. 216; *Re Harrison* (1920) 90 L.J. Ch. 186.
[15] *Re Figgis* [1969] 1 Ch. 123 at 146, *per* Megarry J.
[16] *Ibid.*
[17] *Jones v. Maynard* [1951] Ch. 572 at 575, *per* Vaisey J.
[18] *Re Pattinson* (1885) 1 T.L.R. 216; *Re Harrison* (1921) 90 L.J. Ch. 186. Cf. *Paul v. Constance* [1977] 1 W.L.R. 527.

that property is solely owned by the purchaser or whether it is, like the account itself, jointly owned.

The traditional view is that such investments are owned by the purchaser of it. Thus in *Re Young*[19] a wealthy wife had opened a joint bank account with her husband. He drew cheques on it to purchase investments in his own name and was held to be the sole owner of them. The basis of this was that, although the account was joint, each party was authorised to draw upon it and consequently any purchases made belonged to the person who had made the withdrawal. This was followed in *Re Bishop*[20] where Stamp J. held that, unless the account is opened for the limited purpose of financing joint investments, then either party was free to use it to buy property for himself or herself.

Joint ownership

This more limited intention was found to exist in *Jones* v. *Maynard*[21] and, indeed, is a likely finding particularly when both parties contribute to the fund.[22] In this case, although the husband made larger contributions to the account than the wife, Vaisey J. found that their intention was to pool their resources and use the resulting fund to buy property jointly. Accordingly, she was held to have a half-share in investments purchased in his name.

Jones v. *Maynard* was approved in *Heseltine* v. *Heseltine*[23] and this led Scarman L.J. to say in *Cann* v. *Ayres*[24] that, in so far as it conflicted with *Re Bishop*, it was to be preferred. The conflict between the authorities is, however, more apparent than real, in that the difference between them is that the result is dictated by the different inferred intention of the parties. Where the property that is bought represents a major investment, particularly if it is their house, then it is thought that the most likely inference is that it is a joint investment.

Cohabitation

Two final observations may be made. First, it has been suggested that the courts may be more likely to find an intention to use a joint account to finance joint investments if the couple are cohabiting rather than being married.[25] Now that non-married cohabitation is a common occurrence, it seems doubtful whether this distinction will be made and that the legal status of the couple will not influence the decision which is made. Secondly, in *Jones* v. *Maynard*, Vaisey J. drew a distinction between the husband purchasing investments in his own name and the wife doing this. In the former case he held that the husband would hold on trust for himself and his wife whereas in the latter situation, owing to the presumption of advancement, he thought that she would be solely entitled.[26] In the light of the decreased weight now given to the presumptions, this must be considered doubtful. If a joint account is established to finance

---

[19] (1885) 28 Ch.D. 705.
[20] [1965] Ch. 450. See also *Gage* v. *King* [1961] 1 Q.B. 188; *Feaver* v. *Feaver* [1977] 5 W.W.R. 271; *Pettitt* v. *Pettitt* [1970] A.C. 777, *per* Lord Upjohn.
[21] [1951] Ch. 572.
[22] It is true that in *Re Bishop* [1965] Ch. 450, both parties did contribute to the account. Some investments were bought in joint names, however, leading to the inference that those which were not were to be solely owned. *Cf.* Cretney, *Principles of Family Law* (4th ed., 1984) p. 659.
[23] [1971] 1 W.L.R. 342.
[24] (1976) 7 Fam. Law 47.
[25] M. C. Cullity (1969) 85 L.Q.R. 530 at 541–542.
[26] [1951] Ch. 572 at 575.

joint investments then, irrespective of whether they are bought by the husband or the wife, any investment bought will itself be jointly owned.[27]

The family home

The task of ascertaining the beneficial interests in the family home is a difficult one which has exercised the courts frequently in recent years. Along with the difficulty of establishing whether co-ownership exists, are the related problems of quantifying the shares, working out the effect of the departure from the home of one of the co-owners and, finally, deciding whether or not the house should be sold. This latter aspect of the problem involves occupation rights in the property which can sometimes arise without beneficial co-ownership existing, through the medium of licences.

Background to the problem[28] In the context of matrimonial property, the job of ascertaining the beneficial ownership really began in 1882. Prior to this date, a husband and wife were legally regarded as one person. That person was regarded as being the husband. The consequence of this was that the wife's property vested in him. The seemingly draconian effects of this doctrine were in fact alleviated, particularly in so far as land was concerned, both by the doctrine of dower and by judicious use of the trust and restraints upon anticipation inserted in many marriage settlements.

Despite these alleviations, pressure for change built up. This pressure came from various sources and was directed to one goal: establishing the principle of separate ownership of property between spouses. Success came with the enactment of the Married Women's Property Act 1882. Section 1(1) provides that:

Separate ownership

"A married woman shall . . . be capable of acquiring, holding, and disposing by will or otherwise, of any real or personal property as her separate property, in the same manner as if she were a feme sole, without the intervention of any trustee."

This statutory provision establishes the principle of separate ownership of matrimonial property. Although the Law Commission have made proposals to effect equal ownership of the matrimonial home,[29] these proposals have not been implemented and the principle enacted above remains the cornerstone of matrimonial property.

Consequences of separate property Under section 17 of the Married Women's Property Act 1882, provision was made for either spouse to apply, in any question as to the title to or possession of property, by summons or in any summary way to the High Court or county court which may make such order with

---

[27] *Pettitt* v. *Pettitt* [1970] A.C. 777 at 815, *per* Lord Upjohn.
[28] See Cretney, above n. 22, pp. 629–634; an account containing a good bibliography.
[29] Law Commission (1978) No. 86, para. 1–1.

respect to the property in dispute as it sees fit.[30] It was initially held in the Court of Appeal that this provision gave the courts the power to reallocate property on divorce: quite literally, the judge could make such order as he saw fit.[31] This view has been decisively rejected in the House of Lords.[32] In any application made under the section, "the question for the court was—'Whose is this' and not—'To whom shall this be given.' "[33] The discretion given by section 17 extended only as to how property rights were to be enforced; not to their existence.

Reallocation of property

This approach meant that there was no separate property law regime in so far as spouses were concerned.[34] The effect of this has now been radically changed, however. Section 4 of the Matrimonial Property and Proceedings Act 1970 gave the court, on granting a decree of divorce, nullity or judicial separation, the power to order one party to the marriage to transfer to the other party, or any child of the family, property to which he is entitled, either in possession or reversion.

This statutory discretion to adjust property rights on divorce was re-enacted by section 24 of the Matrimonial Causes Act 1973. Its existence has eased considerably the task of the courts in dealing with disputes as to matrimonial property. When such matrimonial disputes are before the court little regard need be paid to who owned what prior to the proceedings. The court simply pays regard to the factors to be considered as laid down by section 3 of the Matrimonial and Family Proceedings Act 1984 and then makes whatever order seems appropriate.[35]

Married couples

Relevance of ownership While it is true that the jurisdiction of the courts to alter property rights upon divorce has reduced considerably the need to calculate the ownership of the matrimonial home, that need has by no means disappeared entirely. A number of common situations exist where it will be necessary to determine this issue. In so far as married couples are concerned, the ownership of the matrimonial home will become relevant when proceedings are not instituted under the Matrimonial Causes Act 1973.

This situation can arise for a number of reasons. One of the parties may have religious objections to divorce proceedings.[36] More important, the claim to a beneficial share in the house may arise after one of the spouses has died testate without naming the other as the beneficiary under his will. The survivor would clearly prefer to be able to claim an interest in the property as of right rather than having to rely on a discretionary award under section 1 of the Inheritance (Provisions For Family and

---

[30] Engaged couples may also utilise this summary jurisdiction, if the proceedings are commenced within three years of the termination of the agreement to marry: Law Reform (Miscellaneous Provisions) Act 1970, s.2(2).
[31] *Hine* v. *Hine* [1962] 1 W.L.R. 1125; *Appleton* v. *Appleton* [1965] 1 W.L.R. 25.
[32] *Pettitt* v. *Pettitt* [1970] A.C. 777.
[33] *Ibid.* at 798, *per* Lord Morris of Borth-y-Gest.
[34] *Gissing* v. *Gissing* [1971] A.C. 886 at 899.
[35] The types of co-ownership orders made are discussed in Chap. 3.
[36] See, *e.g. Shinh* v. *Shinh* [1977] 1 All E.R. 97. It used to be the case that if a marriage had been terminated by an overseas decree, then the English courts lacked jurisdiction to make a financial order in favour of the ex-spouse. Such an order is now possible under the Matrimonial and Family Proceedings Act 1984, s.12.

Dependants) Act 1975. A third reason, perhaps most important of all, is if the dispute is not between the spouses but involves a third party. If one spouse has mortgaged the property, the other spouse may be able to resist a possession action brought by the mortgagee by establishing a prior interest in the property.[37] This can only be done if she can establish a proprietary interest in the house.

Unmarried couples

As between spouses, it can be important to determine the beneficial interests in the matrimonial home. This task will assume much greater importance with regard to what might be termed the "quasi-matrimonial" home. In recent years, it has become increasingly common for couples to cohabit without being married, sometimes having children. As such, various legal problems ensue.[38] In some instances their relationship has been treated in a similar way by the law as if they had been married.[39] Ownership of the family home is not such an example. The courts possess no power to reallocate property on the termination of the relationship. Consequently, questions regarding the ownership and occupation of the family home must be answered by reference to the law of property.

Acquisition of interests in the family home[40]

As with co-ownership generally, one is far more concerned with the position in equity than that which pertains at law. The two will frequently diverge. To create an express trust concerning land, writing is required. Section 53(1)(*b*) of the L.P.A. 1925 provides that:

> "a declaration of trust respecting any land or any interest therein must be manifested and proved by some writing signed by some person who is able to declare such trust or by his will."

A similar, but not identical requirement of formality is insisted upon in the case of a disposition of an equitable interest. By section 53(1)(*c*) any such dispositions must be in writing signed by the disposer of the interest or by his agent thereunto lawfully authorised in writing or by will.

The relevance of the latter provision appears if the beneficial ownership in the house is originally solely enjoyed by one person who later agrees that his partner should be a co-owner in equal shares. This would amount to a disposition of an equitable

---

[37] *Williams & Glyn's Bank* v. *Boland* [1981] A.C. 487.
[38] See Freeman and Lyon, *Cohabitation Without Marriage* (1983); Parker, *Cohabitees* (1981); Parry, *Cohabitation* (1981).
[39] *e.g.* Inheritance (Provision for Family and Dependants) Act 1975. See generally D. Pearl [1978] C.L.J. 252. For a discussion of contracts between cohabitees, see J. L. Dwyer (1977) 93 L.Q.R. 386.
[40] The literature on this topic is vast. See *e.g.* Cretney, *Principles of Family Law* (4th ed.) pp. 635–669; Miller, *Family Property and Financial Provision* (2nd ed.) pp. 17–49; Murphy and Clarke, *The Family Home* (1983) pp. 26–80; Hanbury and Maudsley, *Modern Equity* (12th ed., 1985) pp. 252–260; H. Lesser (1973) 23 Univ. of Toronto L.J. 148; A. A. S. Zuckerman (1978) 94 L.Q.R. 26.

interest and would *per se* be void unless this agreement was in writing.[41]

Express trusts Should the parties declare the trusts upon which the family home is to be owned then that declaration is prima facie conclusive.[42] This conclusion can only be avoided if one of the parties can secure rectification of the trust document. This occurred in *Thames Guaranty Ltd. v. Campbell*,[43] where Mrs. Campbell had provided the entire purchase price but the solicitors were instructed to put the property in the joint names of her and her husband out of courtesy to him. Although the Campbells apparently intended the property to belong solely to her in equity, the solicitors wrongly described them as joint tenants in law and equity. As this did not accurately express their intentions as to the beneficial ownership, she succeeded in earlier rectification proceedings in having the words "and equity" deleted. The onus on the person seeking rectification is, however, a heavy one.

Execution of deed A second point to be noted about express declarations is that it appears to be necessary, if they are contained in a deed, that the deed should be executed by both parties if it is to be conclusive. Hence it has been held that a land transfer form declaring the parties to be beneficial joint tenants was not conclusive as it had not been executed by the purchasers.[44] Although this has been cogently criticised,[45] it is nevertheless good practice to ensure that such execution takes place.[46] Further, if the trusts are kept off the title and declared in a separate document then, to comply with section 53(1)(*b*), the signatures of the parties should be appended.

Declaration of interest It should be stressed that it is good practice to ensure that such a declaration should be made when acting for co-owners. This will entail making specific enquiries as to their intentions and then drawing up a document to give effect to them.[47] Adopting this course will preclude complex and expensive litigation thereafter to determine what those shares are. The difficulty caused by this litigation has now prompted Dillon L.J. to express the view that solicitors acting for couples who are buying a house together who fail to adopt this course may well be liable to their clients in negligence for failing to do so.[48]

---

[41] *Richards v. Dove* [1974] 1 All E.R. 888 at 894, *per* Walton J.; *Cowcher v. Cowcher* [1972] 1 W.L.R. 425 at 432, *per* Bagnall J.
[42] *Pettitt v. Pettitt* [1970] A.C. 777 at 813, *per* Lord Upjohn; *Leake v. Bruzzi* [1974] 1 W.L.R. 1528; *Brykiert v. Jones* (1981) 2 F.L.R. 373; *Re John's Assignment Trusts* [1970] 1 W.L.R. 955; *Brown v. Staniek* (1969) 211 E.G. 283; *Godwin v. Bedwell, The Times,* March 10, 1982; *Goodman v. Gallant* [1986] Fam. 106. The comment, seemingly to the contrary in *City of London Building Society v. Flegg* [1987] 2 W.L.R. 1266 at 1268, *per* Lord Templeman is incorrect. See now *Turton v. Turton* [1987] 3 W.L.R. 622.
[43] [1985] Q.B. 210.
[44] *Robinson v. Robinson* (1977) 241 E.G. 153. See also *Gross v. French* (1974) 232 E.G. 1319 at 1321, affirmed without reference to this point at (1976) 238 E.G. 39. *Cf. Mayes v. Mayes* (1969) 210 E.G. 925.
[45] (1977) 41 Conv. (N.S.) 78 at 79; D. G. Barnsley (1983) 127 S.J. 554.
[46] See S. Farren (1977) 41 Conv. (N.S.) 365.
[47] *Cowcher v. Cowcher* [1972] 1 W.L.R. 425 at 442, *per* Bagnall J.; *Bernard v. Josephs* [1982] Ch. 391 at 493, *per* Griffiths L.J.
[48] *Walker v. Hall* [1984] F.L.R. 126 at 129. It is not at all clear what damages would be available should such an action succeed. *Cf.* M. J. Sookias, J. Cole and R. L. Price (1987) 84 L.S.Gaz. 1309.

Interests at acquisition

A final point to make about express declarations of trust is that, subject to what has already been said, they are conclusive, but only as to the position at the time the property is acquired. Subsequent events may cause those interests to vary. In addition, problems of equitable accounting may arise. Nevertheless, declaring the beneficial interests in the home at the time it is acquired will reduce dramatically the scope for subsequent disputes.

Implied, resulting and constructive trusts

Ascertaining the beneficial interest

Despite it being a well-accepted counsel of good practice to declare the beneficial interests in the home at the time it is acquired, it is, unfortunately, common for this not to take place. In this event, the beneficial interests must be calculated by the courts in accordance with the principles of property law. This will generally entail an application of the principles of implied, resulting or constructive trusts which, by dint of section 53(2) of the L.P.A. 1925, are exempt from the formal requirements of writing imposed by section 53(1)(b) in the case of express trusts of land. In addition to acquiring a beneficial interest under one of the types of trust referred to in section 53(2), a claim to an interest in the home may be based on the principles of proprietary estoppel. Finally, rights of occupation, if not ownership, may be acquired through a contractual licence. Unfortunately, establishing what these principles are has not proved easy; neither has their application. The result has been that some of the decisions are difficult to reconcile with House of Lords' authority or, indeed, with each other.

"Family asset"

Background English law has never embraced any principle of community of property. Consequently, disputes as to ownership of the family home should involve the application of the same principles, irrespective of whether or not the parties are married.[49] At one time, however, a different notion appeared to have been at least flirted with. In *Hine* v. *Hine*,[50] Lord Denning M.R. expressed the view that if a house was acquired by joint efforts, which would include a wife looking after the children, then the house became a "family asset" and the court had a discretion under section 17 of the Married Women's Property Act 1882 as to the shares to be awarded in it. The rights arising from law and equity prior to separation were not regarded as being useful in determining the beneficial shares.[51]

This fluid approach to the issue did not survive the analysis of this area of law by the House of Lords. In *Pettitt* v. *Pettitt*[52] and *Gissing* v. *Gissing*[53] the area of family property was subjected to close examination. The resulting judgments form the

---

[49] *Gissing* v. *Gissing* [1971] A.C. 886 at 889, *per* Viscount Dilhorne.
[50] [1962] 1 W.L.R. 1124.
[51] *Ibid.* at 1128.
[52] [1970] A.C. 777. The term "family assets" also failed to find favour, *ibid.* at 817, *per* Lord Upjohn. See, however, the valuable discussion by J. G. Miller (1970) 86 L.Q.R. 98.
[53] [1971] A.C. 886.

cornerstone of this branch of law although, unfortunately, there was some diversity of view apparent in the speeches,[54] which has led to different subsequent approaches to the question of interpreting them.

The House of Lords approach In *Pettitt* v. *Pettitt* a house was conveyed into the wife's name, the purchase price being derived from the sale of a house owned solely by her. Her husband, on an application under section 17 of the 1882 Act, claimed a share in it, that claim being based on decorating work he had done which he said enhanced the value of the property by £1,000. The House of Lords held, unanimously reversing the Court of Appeal, that he was not entitled to any interest in the property.

Intention at acquisition

All the members of the House agreed that what the husband had done was of far too ephemeral a nature to enable him to claim that an interest had been acquired.[55] Opinion was divided as to what the position would have been had his contribution been more substantial. The speech of Lord Upjohn directed attention to establishing the intention of the parties at the time the property was acquired in order to ascertain what the position was to be with regard to the beneficial ownership of it. In approaching this task, regard is first of all had to any documentary declaration as to ownership which, in the absence of a claim to rectification, is conclusive. In the absence of such documentation and, where the conveyance is taken in the names of either one or both of the partners, evidence is admissible of any agreement as to the beneficial ownership which the parties had reached, including inferences drawn from their conduct. In the absence of any such evidence, however, one falls back on the presumptions.

The presumptions

With regard to these presumptions, one looks in the first instance at the ownership of the legal title. If that is shared, then, prima facie, so is the beneficial title. Similarly, if the legal title is in one name (usually the man's) he also owns the beneficial title. This may well not be conclusive. One turns then to resulting trusts and the presumption that a contribution towards the acquisition of the home caused a corresponding share of the beneficial ownership to be acquired. Conduct subsequent to the acquisition of the property could only be relevant either to shed light on their intentions at the time of acquisition or as evidence of a fresh agreement affecting title to the property. In the absence of such an agreement, or any argument based upon estoppel, a spouse who expends money on the property of the other acquires no interest in it.

Agreement as to beneficial interests

The speech of Lord Upjohn, which employed traditional resulting trust reasoning, was in substance agreed with by Lord Morris of Borth-y-Gest and Lord Hodson. Both of these Law Lords stressed the need to find an agreement between the parties as to what the beneficial interests were to be.[56] Lord Reid and Lord Diplock, on the other hand, disagreed. Whereas the majority held that one must infer from the conduct of the parties

---

[54] The result has been described as more delphic than the oracle which at least had the advantage that her ambiguities were uttered in only one voice. J. Tiley [1969] C.L.J. 191 at 196.
[55] See also *Button* v. *Button* [1968] 1 W.L.R. 457.
[56] *Pettitt* v. *Pettitt* [1970] A.C. 777 at 804–805 and 810 respectively.

what they had agreed upon, the minority took a more discretionary approach. According to Lord Diplock, this meant that if the courts could find an inferred intention then effect should be given to it, but if they could not, then an intention should be imputed to them on the basis of what reasonable people would have intended.[57]

Legislative response

The notion of finding an agreement between the partners as to the beneficial shares each should have in the house has caused considerable difficulty. Before considering it further, mention should be made of the legislative response to *Pettitt* in so far as improvements to the home are concerned. It was felt both that *Pettitt* operated to prevent a spouse who had spent substantial sums on improving a house from claiming an interest in it and that this was undesirable. Consequently section 37 of the Matrimonial Property and Proceedings Act 1970 was enacted to cater for this situation. The current position will be explained later in this Chapter.

Intention upon acquisition The emphasis placed by the House of Lords in *Pettitt* on the intention of the parties at the time the property is acquired was repeated shortly afterwards in *Gissing* v.

Gissing v. Gissing

Gissing.[58] In this case a wife unsuccessfully claimed a share in the matrimonial home, having spent some £220 on furnishings and laying a lawn, buying clothes for herself and her son and for some extras around the house. Her husband paid all the mortgage instalments and supplied the deposit.

Resulting or constructive trust

All the members of the House agreed that, for her to succeed, she must establish an interest behind a resulting or constructive trust. In establishing such a trust, it was emphasised that the courts must be able to infer an agreement that she should have such a share. The court cannot impute to the parties an intention to make an agreement which they never had but which, as reasonable people, they ought to have had.[59] Such an intention is inferred from the fact that a financial contribution is made to the acquisition of the property.

Constructive trust A good deal of attention was paid to the role of the resulting trust in *Gissing* v. *Gissing*. In addition, the constructive trust also came to prominence in this context. In an oft-quoted passage. Lord Diplock said:

> "A resulting, implied or constructive trust—and it is unnecessary for present purposes to distinguish between these three classes of trust—is created by a transaction between the trustee and the cestui que trust in connection with the acquisition by the trustee of a legal estate in land, whenever the trustee has so conducted himself that it would be inequitable . . . to deny the cestui que trust a beneficial interest in the land acquired. *And he will be held so to have conducted himself if by his words or conduct he has induced the*

---

[57] *Pettitt* v. *Pettitt* [1970] A.C. 777 at 822–823. See also Lord Reid, *ibid*. at 796.
[58] [1971] A.C. 886.
[59] *Ibid*. at 904, *per* Lord Diplock who expressly recognised that his original view stated in *Pettitt* did not represent the law. Lord Reid adhered to the minority view he expressed in *Pettitt*.

cestui que trust to act to his own detriment in the reasonable belief *that by so acting he was acquiring a beneficial interest in the land.*"[60]

Formalities The context in which Lord Diplock made these remarks was that of the formalities necessary to create a trust of land. Clearly in that context it is unnecessary to distinguish the three types of trust. Equally, it is also true that constructive and resulting trusts both have a role to play in this area. The two concepts are different, however, albeit related. The problem with Lord Diplock's dictum is that it allowed scope for the two types of trust to be equated for all purposes with the result that the essential principles of *Gissing* could become distorted.

This process indeed occurred. In a line of cases involving Lord Denning M.R. this dictum was used as authority to impose a constructive trust whenever the avoidance of an inequitable result demanded it, usually omitting the italicised part of Lord Diplock's speech.[61] The status of these decisions will be reviewed shortly. First, the correct interrelationship of resulting and constructive trusts will be examined.

Inferring an agreement When an equitable interest is claimed under a resulting trust, it is slightly misleading to speak of inferring the intention of the parties. What occurs is that if one partner has contributed to the acquisition of the property, then the court ascribes to the parties an intention that the contributor should receive a commensurate share in the property. This intention is assumed unless the contribution can best be explained as a gift or as a loan.[62] Where there is such a contribution then the existence of an agreement to share the beneficial ownership is assumed; one does not look for an actual meeting of minds.[63] In these cases, the difficulties relate to ascertaining what amounts to a contribution to acquisition and then assessing its value.

Actual agreement In some cases it is not only possible to ascribe intentions as to what the beneficial interests should be because of contributions: there is evidence of an actual agreement. In this case, the agreement *per se* will not be effective to confer an equitable interest on a person who has not contributed to the purchase of the property. Unless the agreement is in writing, section 53(1)(*b*) of the L.P.A. 1925 is not satisfied and no trust is created.[64] If, however, a contribution to the acquisition is made, it then becomes inequitable to insist upon the lack of formality to deny the contributor a beneficial interest. A constructive trust is imposed in her favour.

---

[60] [1971] A.C. 886 at 905. Italics supplied.
[61] See the comments by Sir Nicolas Browne-Wilkinson V.-C. in *Grant* v. *Edwards* [1986] Ch. 638 at 654 and D. J. Hayton in *Lord Denning: The Judge and the Law* (eds. Jowell & McAuslan) (1984) at pp. 79, 83–88.
[62] *Re Sharpe* [1980] 1 W.L.R. 219; *Richards* v. *Dove* [1974] 1 All E.R. 888.
[63] *Gissing* v. *Gissing* [1971] A.C. 886 at 902, *per* Lord Pearson; H. K. Bevan and F. W. Taylor (1966) 30 Conv. (N.S.) 354, 438 at 442–443 and F. Webb (1976) 92 L.Q.R. 489. See also *Grant* v. *Edwards* [1986] Ch. 638 at 647, *per* Nourse L.J.
[64] *Gissing* v. *Gissing*, above n. 63, at 905 *per* Lord Diplock; *Midland Bank plc* v. *Dobson* [1986] 1 F.L.R. 171.

Eves v. Eves   A good example of this situation occurred in *Eves* v. *Eves*.[65] Janet, then aged 19, went to live with Stuart originally intending to marry him. They bought a house which was conveyed into his name alone, he having told her that her name could not go on to the title deeds until she was 21. He provided the finance for the property but she expended a great deal of physical labour on it. Upon her application for a declaration that he held the house on trust for them both, the Court of Appeal held that she had a one-quarter share in it.

Lord Denning M.R. held that Lord Diplock's speech in *Gissing* had brought a new model constructive trust into the world to be imposed when it was fair to do so. This was such a case given the extensive work that she had done. The more orthodox, and preferable, analysis was that of Brightman J., with whom Browne L.J. agreed. Because of Stuart's lie about the legal ownership, he inferred from that that there must have been some agreement that Janet should have a beneficial interest in the house. She expended labour improving the property on the faith of that agreement which consequently became enforceable.

Money consensus and interest consensus   The nature and enforceability of the inferred agreement between the parties was considered in *Cowcher* v. *Cowcher*,[66] where Bagnall J. analysed closely the speeches in *Gissing*. He concluded that a beneficial interest in a house could be obtained either by the actual provision of the purchase price or from a common agreement or intention inferred from the facts. He found the latter concept ambiguous. It could mean that the parties had agreed that each of them should have an interest commensurate with their financial contribution—the money consensus—or they might have agreed that one party should have an interest greater than her financial contribution would warrant—the interest consensus. He concluded that the latter type of agreement would be void for non-compliance with section 53(1)(*b*) and that, consequently, when the House of Lords referred to an inferred agreement between the parties, it was the money consensus which was meant.[67]

Rejection of this distinction   This analysis seems highly impractical, it being hard to imagine a couple contemplating, let alone agreeing upon, any dichotomy between money consensus and interest consensus.[68] With respect, it is also unsound in principle, confusing resulting and constructive trust principles. Where there is an actual agreement that A should have an interest in property conveyed to B and, in consequence of that agreement, B pays less to A than the market price, or A contributes to the purchase of it, then it is fraudulent for B to rely on the lack of formality required by the L.P.A. 1925. Instead a constructive trust is imposed to give effect to that agreement.[69] Where no such agreement is found,

---

[65] [1975] 1 W.L.R. 1338; *Grant* v. *Edwards* [1986] Ch. 638. See M. Richards (1976) 40 Conv. (N.S.) 351.
[66] [1972] 1 W.L.R. 425; see also *Re Nicholson* [1974] 1 W.L.R. 476.
[67] *Cowcher* v. *Cowcher* [1972] 1 W.L.R. 425 at 436.
[68] See A. A. S. Zuckerman (1978) 94 L.Q.R. 26 at 45.
[69] *Bannister* v. *Bannister* [1948] 2 All E.R. 133; *Rochefoucauld* v. *Boustead* [1897] 1 Ch. 196. See M. P. Thompson (1985) 36 N.I.L.Q. 358 at 364–370. Where there is no such contribution but there is reliance, estoppel will be in issue. See below pp. 46–50.

however, and one party has made contributions to the purchase price then a resulting trust is implied, to give effect to the presumed intention that the contributor should have a beneficial share in the property proportionate to the size of the contribution.[70]

Joint names It is rare to find a case where there is a real agreement to share the beneficial interest in the home, whereby one party acquires a greater interest than that which would have been obtained by applying solely resulting trust principles. More commonly the position is that the interest acquired is the same. An illustration of this is where the legal title is conveyed into joint names.

When property is acquired in joint names, there is an inference that it is intended also to share the beneficial interest in it.[71] This inference is rebuttable if the reason for co-ownership at law is that the co-owner is simply a nominee, such as where the Building Society insists upon title being taken in joint names.[72] Similarly, the inference is either rebutted or ineffective if one partner makes no contribution to the purchase price: the two legal co-owners will hold on trust for the sole contributor.[73]

Where the property has been put into joint names, there is an inference that co-ownership in equity is also intended. It does not necessarily follow, however, that because there is a joint tenancy at law that a beneficial joint tenancy in equity will also ensue, although there is an initial presumption to that effect.[74] Instead, regard is had to the proportions in which the purchase price is provided, the size of the beneficial interests corresponding with that.[75] This is because, although there is an inferred agreement that there should be beneficial co-ownership, the size of the contribution is often the only evidence of what the quantum of the shares is to be. If, however, there is evidence that they have agreed to equal beneficial shares then, if both make contributions to the acquisition of the home, that agreement should be enforceable.

Size of contributions

Contributions to acquisition In the absence of an express, written document setting out the beneficial interests in the home, the most common method of acquiring an interest in the house is by way of contribution to its acquisition. This gives rise to a resulting trust in favour of the contributor. The usual situation is when the house is conveyed into the man's name and a woman subsequently claims an interest in it. The following discussion will assume this to be the case. The relevant principles apply *mutatis mutandis* if the roles are reversed.

---

[70] *Re Densham (A Bankrupt)* [1975] 1 W.L.R. 1519 at 1525, *per* Goff J. See also *Grant* v. *Edwards*, above n. 65 where the distinction between resulting and constructive trusts is clearly drawn, a point missed in the critique of this decision by J. Warburton [1986] Conv. 291.
[71] *Crisp* v. *Mullings* (1975) 239 E.G. 119.
[72] *Grzeczcowski* v. *Jedynska* (1971) 115 S.J. 126.
[73] *Young* v. *Young* [1984] F.L.R. 77.
[74] *Pettitt* v. *Pettitt* [1970] A.C. 777 at 813–814, *per* Lord Upjohn.
[75] *Bernard* v. *Josephs* [1982] Ch. 391; *Marsh* v. *Von Sternberg* [1986] 1 F.L.R. 526 at 530, *per* Bush J. Cf. *Crisp* v. *Mullings* (1975) 239 E.G. 119 at 119–121, *per* Russell L.J.

The principle established by *Gissing* v. *Gissing* is that if the woman contributes to the purchase of the property, it is then possible to infer from that the intention that she is to acquire a corresponding beneficial interest in it. It is, however, far easier to state this principle than to apply it.[76] In seeking to apply the principles of resulting trusts, it is helpful to distinguish between direct and indirect contributions.

Direct contributions In the unusual situation where a house is bought outright, the position is simple. One simply calculates the contribution made by each party. In *Re Rogers' Question*[77] a house was bought for £1,000. The wife contributed £100 and her husband paid the balance by meeting the mortgage instalments. The house was in his name. It was held that he held the property on trust for them both, in the proportion of one-tenth for her and nine-tenths for himself.

In cases where the woman contributes to the out and out purchase of the home or contributes only to the deposit, the balance being paid by a mortgage and the instalments are paid only by the man, the assessment of her interest is fairly simple. Where the woman's contribution to the acquisition takes the form of helping to pay the mortgage instalments, the position is more complex.

The basis of the resulting trust is that effect is given to the presumed intention of the parties as to the beneficial ownership at the time of acquisition. Strictly speaking paying mortgage instalments occurs after the property has been acquired and might not therefore seem relevant. Such a view would be unduly legalistic. The true position is that "The conduct of the spouses in relation to the payment of the mortgage instalments may be no less relevant to their common intention as to the beneficial interests in the matrimonial home acquired in this way than their conduct in relation to the payment of the cash deposit."[78]

To ascertain the quantum of the interest one must pay regard to the proportion of the acquisition price contributed. Thus in *Walker* v. *Hall*[79] the money for the house was derived from the proceeds of the sale of his former house over which she had a lien for £139, £195 each from joint savings and £1,000 from a bank loan for which she was jointly liable. Her contribution to the purchase of the new house was £834, which was one-quarter of the price. Hence her beneficial share, subject to equitable accounting, was one-quarter.

Quantification of interest In cases where a direct contribution to the purchase of a house is made, the courts will now take some little trouble to assess the actual financial contribution that has been made.[80] Previously there had been a tendency to apply the maxim equity is equality and award each of the parties a half-

Marginal notes: Mortgage instalments; Proportion of payments

---

[76] *Bernard* v. *Josephs*, above n. 75, at 402 *per* Griffiths L.J.
[77] [1948] 1 All E.R. 328.
[78] *Gissing* v. *Gissing* [1971] A.C. 886 at 906, *per* Lord Diplock. Isolated payments of instalments would not give rise to a resulting trust: *ibid*. at 900, *per* Viscount Dilhorne.
[79] [1984] F.L.R. 126.
[80] This will include the expenditure of labour: *Cooke* v. *Head* [1972] 1 W.L.R. 518.

share in the property.[81] This is no longer the case.[82] Refuge is only taken in the maxim where it proves impossible to quantify the contribution made by each party. Alternatively, a half-share would be awarded if one can infer that this was the intention upon acquisition. Such a finding would be appropriate if the parties completely integrate their finances, so that it is legitimate to see the purchase as being a joint venture. One need not then have too nice a regard to a portion-for-portion approach to quantification.[83]

Indirect contributions   In ascertaining when an interest can be acquired by indirect financial contributions, again, one must turn to *Gissing* v. *Gissing* for the applicable principles. It was accepted in this case that it is not necessary, in order to acquire an interest, that the woman makes direct financial contributions to the purchase price. For example, the payment by her of household expenses which thereby enables him to meet the mortgage instalments would enable the court to infer that there was an intention for her to have some interest in the home.[84] For this inference to be made, it must be shown that her contributions were referable to the acquisition of the house and to establish this, it is necessary to show some adjustment in the way contributions were made to the household budget consequent upon the house being acquired.[85] It is not sufficient if she merely makes some contribution to the household expenditure. Accordingly, in *Gissing* itself, her actions in paying for the laying of a lawn and the purchase of clothes for herself and their child did not suffice to give her an interest in the matrimonial home.[86]

Assistance in business   When indirect contributions to the purchase of a house are relied upon to establish that an interest in it has been acquired, the courts will seek to employ resulting trust principles. The indirect contributions made by the woman allows the inference to be made that she was to have an interest in the property. In order to quantify that interest the courts then perform the difficult task of assessing the value of it. She is then awarded a corresponding beneficial share in the property. In the normal domestic case this will frequently be a somewhat artificial process. Where it works best is where the woman is involved in her partner's business.

The scenario envisaged is where a man acquires a business, the profits of which are used to finance the purchase of the house. If the woman works unpaid in that business, then she makes a real contribution to the accumulation of savings and hence the acquisition of the house. The courts will regard this effort as indistinguishable from a situation where both work and their

---

[81] *Fribance* v. *Fribance* [1957] 1 All E.R. 357.
[82] *Gissing* v. *Gissing* [1971] A.C. 886 at 897, *per* Lord Reid; at 903 *per* Lord Pearson.
[83] *Chapman* v. *Chapman* [1969] 3 All E.R. 476; *Falconer* v. *Falconer* [1970] 1 W.L.R. 1333; *Hargrave* v. *Newton* [1970] 3 All E.R. 866. See A. A. S. Zuckerman (1978) 94 L.Q.R. 26 at 34.
[84] *Gissing* v. *Gissing*, above n. 82, at 903 *per* Lord Pearson.
[85] *Ibid.* at 909, *per* Lord Diplock.
[86] *Ibid.* at 901, *per* Viscount Dilhorne; at 909 *per* Lord Diplock. See also *Allen* v. *Allen* [1961] 3 All E.R. 385 at 387, *per* Lord Evershed M.R.

earnings are pooled to buy the house.[87] A distinction is however drawn between cases when the business belonged to the man before marriage and when it was acquired afterwards. In the latter situation she is likely to acquire a half-share in the house whereas in the former case, she will not, credit being given to the man for his greater contribution.[88]

Household expenditure It is by no means uncommon, when a couple are living together and both are earning, that one salary is used for mortgage payments and the other used for living expenses. As has been seen, in *Gissing*, it was accepted that this type of indirect contribution could suffice to enable an interest in the house to be acquired. The difficulty since then has been to determine the circumstances in which such contributions will suffice.

In *Gissing* itself, emphasis was placed on the need for this type of contribution to be referable to the acquisition of the home so that it is possible to infer some agreement that an interest was to be acquired.[89] This requirement was soon watered down, however, leaving the law somewhat obscure: an obscurity which has recently been clarified.

The flexible approach

In a series of cases, Lord Denning M.R. used the dictum of Lord Diplock cited earlier, concerning implied, resulting and constructive trusts, as providing a warrant to introduce a new flexible constructive trust to be imposed whenever justice and good conscience require it.[90] A typical example is *Hazell* v. *Hazell*[91] where the view was expressed that there was no need to show any inferred agreement that the wife should acquire an interest in order for her to do so. Similarly he also stated his hope that references to contributions made to the acquisition of the home would be heard less frequently.[92]

General discretionary approach

This flexible approach, which is itself at odds with *Gissing* v. *Gissing*, was nevertheless taken even further in *Hall* v. *Hall*.[93] In considering the acquisition of an interest in the home, Lord Denning said that:

> "It depends on all the circumstances and how much she has contributed—not merely in money—but also in keeping up the house, and, if there are children, in looking after them."[94]

Had the application in *Hall* been for a property adjustment order under section 24 of the Matrimonial Causes Act 1925, Lord Denning's approach would have been apposite. Because it was not, it could only lead to difficulties in reconciling it with the law stated by the House of Lords. Perhaps it should occasion little

---

[87] *Nixon* v. *Nixon* [1969] 1 W.L.R. 1676; *Re Cummins* [1972] Ch. 62; *Bothe* v. *Amos* [1976] Fam. 47; *Muetzel* v. *Muetzel* [1970] 1 W.L.R. 188.
[88] *Nixon* v. *Nixon* above, at 1679, *per* Lord Denning M.R.
[89] See also *Savage* v. *Dunningham* [1974] Ch. 181.
[90] *Hussey* v. *Palmer* [1972] 1 W.L.R. 1286 at 1289.
[91] [1972] 1 W.L.R. 301. The orthodox approach of Megaw L.J. who found that the husband could not have paid the mortgage without his wife's financial contribution to household expenditure is much to be preferred.
[92] *Ibid.* at 302–304.
[93] [1982] 3 F.L.R. 379. The couple were unmarried.
[94] *Ibid.* at 381. *Cf. Kowalczuk* v. *Kowalczuk* [1973] 1 W.L.R. 930 at 933, *per* Lord Denning M.R.

surprise that the Court of Appeal has, in the absence of Lord Denning, returned to the orthodox position.

Burns v. Burns **The return to orthodoxy** In *Burns* v. *Burns*[95] the principles enunciated in *Gissing* were applied and the heresy of the recent past expunged. In 1963 the plaintiff moved to a house which was conveyed into the defendant's name. He provided the finance for it. She had a child and did not take employment until 1975, when she got a job as a driving instructor. She used her earnings to pay the rates and telephone bills and also to buy household fixtures and fittings and household chattels. On the breakdown of their relationship, she claimed a beneficial interest in the house. She relied on her work in looking after it and the child over a 17-year period coupled with her financial contribution since 1975. The Court of Appeal held that she had no interest in the house and leave to appeal was refused both by the Court of Appeal and the House of Lords.

In reaching this conclusion, emphasis was placed on the need to be able to infer an agreement that she should acquire an interest in the house and that such an agreement could only be inferred from a financial contribution to its acquisition. Accordingly housework and bringing up children were not relevant: Lord Denning's dictum in *Hall* v. *Hall* was stated to be wrong.[96]

Reference to acquisition In assessing contributions, if she had contributed to the deposit or paid mortgage instalments she would have acquired an interest. As she had not, she had to rely on indirect contributions to the household budget. These have to be substantial and made so as to enable him to be able to meet the mortgage repayments. In the instant case this was not so. Although she had contributed considerable effort in maintaining the home, her financial contributions were not substantial and could not be said to be referable to the acquisition of the property. For example paying the telephone bills was what one would commonly expect to happen when a house is shared, particularly when, as here, she made the majority of calls.

Burns v. *Burns* is the most significant decision in this branch of the law since *Gissing* v. *Gissing*. It re-emphasises the importance of financial contributions towards buying the home and, in cases where indirect contributions are relied upon, restores the position to that pertaining after *Gissing*. For a woman to acquire an interest, it will in practice mean that the situation will be that his earnings are devoted to paying the mortgage and hers used to meet the remaining outgoings, or at least a substantial part of them.

Married and unmarried couples As stated previously, where a married couple are concerned, the court has considerable discretion to reallocate property between the spouses on divorce; a discretion which is not available if the parties are not married.

---

[95] [1984] Ch. 317. See also *Winkworth* v. *Edward Baron Development Co. Ltd.* (1986) 52 P. & C.R. 67 at 74, *per* Nourse L.J. reversed on the facts [1986] 1 W.L.R. 1512. For the very different approach adopted in Canada, see *Sorochan* v. *Sorochan* (1986) 29 D.L.R. (4th) 1.
[96] *Ibid.* at 331, *per* Fox L.J.; at 342, *per* May L.J.

In addition to this distinction, the courts have also indicated that the marital status of the couple may be relevant in assessing the significance of indirect contributions to the purchase of the home. In *Bernard* v. *Josephs*,[97] Griffiths L.J. said that although the principles to be applied were the same, irrespective of the relationship between the parties, that factor might affect the result of their application.

Nature of the relationship Attention was being focussed here on the fact that cohabitation arrangements vary substantially in nature. Whereas if a couple are married, the purchase of a joint house is clearly seen as a long-term project, this is not necessarily true if the two are unmarried. The relationship may be experimental or fairly casual. If so, it is harder to draw an inference that by contributing to the household budget it was intended that she acquire an interest. If, however, the relationship is as stable as a marriage, as in *Burns* itself, this consideration loses its force.

Improvements In applying the law of trusts, considerable emphasis is placed by the courts on the intentions of the parties at the time when the house is acquired. Obvious difficulties are then caused by work done some considerable time later. This situation may occur either because the relationship started when one partner moved into a house owned solely by the other or, simply, when one partner makes no financial contribution for a number of years.

In the light of the decision in *Pettitt* v. *Pettitt*, some concern was felt that the contributor would acquire no interest in the house in these circumstances. This fear was probably not well-founded but, to resolve any doubt on the matter, the position has now been modified by statute. Section 37 of the Matrimonial **Matrimonial Proceedings and Property Act 1970** provides that:

> "It is hereby declared that where a husband or wife contributes in money or money's worth to the improvement of real or personal property in which or in the proceeds of sale of which either or both of them has a beneficial interest, the husband or wife shall, if the contribution is . . . substantial . . . and subject to any agreement between them to the contrary express or implied, be treated as having then acquired by virtue of his or her contribution a share or an enlarged share, as the case may be, in that beneficial interest of such an extent as may have been agreed or, in default of such agreement, as may seem in all the circumstances just . . ."[98]

Limits of the section A number of points can be made about this section. First, it only applies as between husband and wife. The position with regard to unmarried couples is governed by the general law. Secondly, the section makes clear that the acquisition of the interest occurs from the date of the contribution. It is not back-dated to the date of the initial purchase. This is important, as a mortgage granted prior to that date will have priority over an interest acquired by subsequent improvements.[99] A third point is

---

[97] [1982] Ch. 391 at 402–403; *Burns* v. *Burns* [1984] Ch. 317 at 335, *per* May L.J.
[98] For a critique of this section, see R. T. Oerton (1970) 120 New L.J. 1008.
[99] See Chap. 7.

that the section is declaratory in nature, thereby implying that it is simply restating the law. This is partially true,[1] in that if the parties actually agree that an improvement enables the contributor to acquire an interest, equity has always given effect to that agreement.[2] The discretion given to the court to award such a share as seems just is, however, new.

Improvements under the Act   Subject to what has been said, if a spouse spends money on the property and seeks to invoke the Act, she must first establish that what has been done is an improvement. This term is generally used in contradistinction to repairs and maintenance. Activities such as painting and decorating would seem to be outside the scope of the section.

Improvement must be substantial

Secondly, the work done must be of a substantial nature. In *Re Nicholson*,[3] the wife had spent money installing central heating, two gas fires and a gas cooker. Although the latter three items were viewed collectively, together they cost only small amounts. Hence, even if they had been regarded as improvements, they were to be disregarded in exercising the statutory discretion.

Statutory discretion

In deciding how to vary the beneficial shares, *Re Nicholson* also establishes that one takes a mathematical approach. One quantifies each party's beneficial share prior to the improvement and then assesses the value by which the value of the house has been increased. In this case, the spouses initially had equal shares in a house worth £6,000. After she had installed central heating its value rose to £6,150. The extra £150 was added to her share, thereby giving her $\frac{21}{41}$ of the beneficial interest in the house.

Cases outside the Act

If a cohabitee or a spouse, instead of making improvements, pays mortgage instalments, then section 37 will not be in issue. In these circumstances, to acquire an interest, or an enlarged share, in the property, the general law is applicable. If it is sought to apply trust principles, an agreement to share the beneficial interest must be proved. This may be difficult even when mortgage instalments are paid, in that where there is no evidence of an actual agreement, the courts are quite likely to hold that the contributor has simply a right to be reimbursed, without acquiring a proportionate share in the house.[4] A greater chance of acquiring an interest in these circumstances exists in utilising the doctrine of estoppel.

Estoppel

The principal methods by which an interest can be acquired are either under a resulting or a constructive trust. For a resulting trust to arise, an intention to create a beneficial interest is inferred from financial contribution to its acquisition. In the case of a constructive trust, there is an oral agreement that the woman should have an interest in the property. This in turn leads her to

---

[1] *Davis* v. *Vale* [1971] 1 W.L.R. 1021; Hanbury and Maudsley, *Modern Equity* (12th ed., 1985) p. 258.
[2] *Pettitt* v. *Pettitt* [1970] A.C. 777 at 816, *per* Lord Upjohn.
[3] [1974] 1 W.L.R. 476.
[4] *Walker* v. *Hall* [1984] F.L.R. 126.

contribute in money or money's worth to its acquisition with the consequence that the oral agreement is enforced.

Limitation of trusts
The application of the law of trusts, which is based on the actual or implied intention of the parties at the time when the property is acquired, can cause harsh results. For example, although the reasoning in *Burns* v. *Burns* seems impeccable, it has been said of the result that "even the most lukewarm feminist can see the injustice of [it]."[5] To an extent this is true, given the high level of commitment towards the home which she had put in. In some cases where it is not possible to establish either a constructive or a resulting trust, some rights may nevertheless be acquired through the closely related doctrine of proprietary estoppel.[6]

Proprietary estoppel
Establishing an estoppel[7] Proprietary estoppel is an equitable concept which bears a close proximity to the constructive trust. There are however differences. A constructive trust arises when there is an oral agreement that A should have an interest in land to be bought by B and, as a result of that agreement, A contributes to the purchase of that land. Despite the declaration of trust not complying with section 53(1)(*b*) of the L.P.A. 1925, the oral testimony is admitted and the agreement enforced. Not to do so would enable B to be unjustly enriched. Estoppel differs in that an agreement is not necessary; it is sufficient but not essential that money is spent on the house: detrimental action in reliance on the expectation will cause the estoppel to arise. Finally, whereas in the case of a constructive trust the actual agreement is enforced, in the case of estoppel the court possesses considerable discretion as to what remedy should be given.[8]

It used to be thought that to establish an estoppel, five *probanda* needed to be satisfied. These *probanda* were enumerated in *Willmott* v. *Barber*[9] and have occasionally been used as a checklist to be gone through in any estoppel case. Such an approach is now regarded as obsolete.[10] In *Taylors Fashions Ltd.* v. *Liverpool Victoria Trustee Co.*[11] Oliver J., after a lengthy review of the authorities, concluded that the basis of estoppel is

Unconscionability
unconscionability; one must simply consider whether A has behaved in such a way towards B as to make it inequitable for him to insist upon his strict legal rights.

This may at first sight seem a somewhat vague formula, but in practice it is not used to confer some general discretion to achieve results which simply seem to be fair. The essence of estoppel is that one party has an expectation of gaining rights in another's property. That expectation must be encouraged, or at

Acquiescence and reliance
least acquiesced in, by the other party. In addition to the existence of the expectation, the party relying on estoppel must

---

[5] (1984) 14 Fam. 4. See also N. V. Lowe and A. Smith (1984) 47 M.L.R. 341. *Cf.* J. K. Dewar, *ibid.* at 735 where the reasoning is criticised.
[6] See *Grant* v. *Edwards* [1986] Ch. 638 at 656, *per* Browne-Wilkinson V.-C.
[7] See generally M. P. Thompson [1983] C.L.J. 257.
[8] *Holiday Inns Inc.* v. *Broadhead* (1974) 232 E.G. 951 at 1087, *per* Goff J.
[9] (1880) 15 Ch.D. 96 at 105–106, *per* Fry J.
[10] Despite their use in *Coombes* v. *Smith* [1986] 1 W.L.R. 808.
[11] [1981] Q.B. 133. See also *Habib Bank* v. *Habib Bank A.G. Zurich* [1981] 1 W.L.R. 1265; *Att.-Gen. of Hong Kong* v. *Humphreys Estate (Queen's Gardens) Ltd.* [1987] A.C. 114.

also have acted in reliance and, again, that reliance must be acquiesced in by the other party.[12] If these requirements are satisfied, then an estoppel is created and the court has discretion as to how it should be satisfied.

Finding the existence of an expectation of gaining rights should present few problems. If a couple embark on long-term cohabitation in a house owned by the man, a normal expectation on the woman's part will be that she has a right of permanent occupation.[13] The difficulty which she then faces is to establish reliance. This is true despite the much criticised decision in *Greasley* v. *Cooke*[14] to the effect that when A causes B to have an expectation of an indefinite right to remain in a house, the onus is on him to prove that this has not induced B to act in reliance.

Proving reliance

In *Coombes* v. *Smith*[15] the plaintiff and defendant, who were each married to other partners, became lovers. He bought a house and when the plaintiff became pregnant, she moved into it. He did not, but instead visited her regularly. He also paid all the bills. Later he bought a different house nearer his work where she continued to live with her child. She redecorated this house several times and installed central heating, although this was unknown to the defendant. When after 10 years the relationship foundered, she claimed that he should be ordered to convey the house to her or, alternatively, that a declaration should be made that she was entitled to live in the house indefinitely.

Changed conduct necessary

Mr. Jonathan Parker, Q.C., sitting as a Deputy High Court judge, rejected her claims which were based on estoppel.[16] While it was true that he had assured her that she would always have a roof over her head, he was able to establish that she had not relied on this expectation. The various acts of reliance claimed; getting pregnant; leaving her husband; giving birth; housekeeping; looking after their daughter and redecorating the house were all regarded as insufficient. All of these things she would have done anyway; it was inherent in their relationship. Neither was the installation of central heating of any utility as he was unaware that she had done it. Consequently her action failed; indeed to have held otherwise would, as the judge recognised, have caused virtually all cohabitees to have interests in the house, thereby making *Burns* v. *Burns* a broken-backed authority.

Moving house

To establish an estoppel it is necessary for the woman to act more in reliance on her expectation of permanent accommodation in the house than occurred in *Coombes* v. *Smith*. This it seems will be satisfied if she moved out of secure accommodation of her own to move into his house. Here she would clearly be prejudicially affected if he was permitted to renege on his assurance that she would be secure in the new house. Formerly the courts would seek to construct a type of contractual licence in

---

[12] See *Re Basham* [1986] 1 W.L.R. 1498. *Brinnand* v. *Ewens* (1987) 284 E.G. 1052.

[13] Not necessarily in the house currently occupied: *Re Basham* [1986] 1 W.L.R. 1498.

[14] [1980] 1 W.L.R. 1306, cf. *Christian* v. *Christian* (1981) 131 New L.J. 43. See M. P. Thompson (1981) 125 S.J. 539; R. E. Annand [1981] Conv. 54.

[15] [1986] 1 W.L.R. 808; *Midland Bank plc* v. *Dobson and Dobson* [1986] 1 F.L.R. 171.

[16] Interestingly, it was conceded that she could stay until her daughter attained 17. In the light of the judgment, this concession seems wrong.

these circumstances.[17] The modern approach is to regard such cases as being governed by estoppel.[18]

Giving up employment
An alternative act of reliance which might suffice is the giving up of employment to look after the house and children. Although this occurred in *Coombes* v. *Smith* she gave up her job well into her pregnancy. If, however, this is part of an arrangement for their future life together, it may be possible to place more stress on this,[19] particularly if the children are his from a previous relationship.

Remedies

Once an estoppel has been established, it is a matter for the court's discretion as to how the equity that has arisen should be satisfied. This discretion may extend to enforcing the expectation in full. Thus in *Pascoe* v. *Turner*[20] a female cohabitee had been told by her male partner that he would give her the house and its contents. In reliance on this assurance, she spent some £230 on repairs and improvements. When he sought a possession order, she counterclaimed that he held the house on trust for her. This counterclaim succeeded and he was ordered to convey the house to her. This decision has been criticised on the basis that it enabled the woman to gain a considerable windfall, having performed only relatively minor acts of reliance.[21]

Perfecting an imperfect gift?
On the other hand, the case has been defended as demonstrating the true role of estoppel, that of perfecting an imperfect gift.[22] This argument is, however, inconsistent with both the explanations of the doctrine by judges and also the result in a number of other decisions.[23] The courts have consistently stressed that once an estoppel has arisen, it is a matter for discretion as to how it should be satisfied.[24] Equity is seen at its most flexible.[25]

Discretion
There are many examples of the different ways in which the courts have exercised their discretion. The starting point is to ascertain what the full expectation was, this being the most extensive order that can be made.[26] This is not by any means the universal solution, however. A court can simply dismiss a possession action, thereby conferring on the licensee an indefinite right to remain.[27] Alternatively, the right to remain may be limited in time until the licensee is compensated for the action taken in reliance.[28] A further option available is to order the

---

[17] *Tanner* v. *Tanner* [1975] 1 W.L.R. 1346.
[18] *Maharaj (Sheila)* v. *Chand (Jai)* [1986] A.C. 898. See also *Grant* v. *Edwards* [1986] Ch. 638 at 656, *per* Browne-Wilkinson V.-C.
[19] See *Jones (A.E.)* v. *Jones (F.W.)* [1977] 1 W.L.R. 438.
[20] [1979] 1 W.L.R. 431; *Re Basham* [1986] 1 W.L.R. 1498.
[21] Hanbury and Maudsley, *Modern Equity* (12th ed., 1985) pp. 865–866.
[22] S. Moriarty (1984) 100 L.Q.R. 376.
[23] See M. P. Thompson [1986] Conv. 406.
[24] *Holiday Inns Inc.* v. *Broadhead* (1974) 232 E.G. 951; *Crabb* v. *Arun District Council* [1976] Ch. 179.
[25] Snell's, *Principles of Equity* (28th ed., 1982) p. 562.
[26] *Dodsworth* v. *Dodsworth* (1973) 228 E.G. 1115.
[27] *Inwards* v. *Baker* [1965] 2 Q.B. 29.
[28] *Dodsworth* v. *Dodsworth* (1973) 228 E.G. 1115; *Re Sharpe* [1980] 1 W.L.R. 219.

house-owner to grant a long non-assignable lease at a rent sufficiently low to take the tenancy outside Rent Act protection.[29]

Given the wide discretion that exists in estoppel cases, one cannot be too dogmatic in predicting the result of different factual situations. Nevertheless certain trends have emerged. First, the courts are reluctant to confer a life interest to satisfy the equity, as to do so would involve the complexities of the Settled Land Act 1925.[30] Secondly, the courts are willing to pay regard to family law considerations in exercising their discretion. Thus, in *Pascoe* v. *Turner*, although the remedy seemed extreme, it was the type of case where, had the proceedings been for divorce, the court may well have ordered him to transfer the house to her. It would seem likely that the courts will exercise their discretion in estoppel cases, so far as possible, as they would with regard to the matrimonial home under the Matrimonial Causes Act 1973.

Family law considerations

Valuation and equitable accounting

It is quite common when a house is jointly owned for one of the co-owners to stop living there leaving the other in the house paying the mortgage and the other bills. The question which then arises is as to what credit should be given for this when the house is ultimately sold.

Proportions and valuation

In approaching this task care must be taken to distinguish between ascertaining the proportionate shares each co-owner has in the house and calculating the actual amount in cash that each party receives on a sale. This was spelled out in *Marsh* v. *Von Sternberg*[31] where Bush J., said:

> "The practitioner must be on guard not to confuse the proportion of the contributions (which is assessed at the date of the agreement and which does not change unless there is an express or implied variation of the agreement) and the assessment of the value, which occurs on the dissolution of the trust."

Date of assessment The dictum of Bush J. emphasised, correctly, that the proportionate share that each party has in the property stays constant throughout the period of joint ownership. Doubt was cast on this, however, in *Hall* v. *Hall*[32] where the equity in the house was worth £15,000 when the couple separated and £25,000 at the date of the hearing. The county court judge assessed the value of her one-fifth share at the date of separation and was upheld in the Court of Appeal on the basis that, as the trust ended at separation, this was a proper exercise of his discretion.

This reasoning is extremely obscure with regard to the trust ending upon separation. The trust for sale upon which the land is

---

[29] *Griffiths* v. *Williams* (1977) 248 E.G. 947.
[30] *Dodsworth* v. *Dodsworth*, above n. 28; *Griffiths* v. *Williams*, above n. 29. *Cf. Binions* v. *Evans* [1972] 3 Ch. 359.
[31] [1986] 1 F.L.R. 526 at 533.
[32] [1982] 3 F.L.R. 379, cogently criticised by G. K. Pople [1981] Conv. 389.

Time of sale held must continue until the house is sold.[33] Consequently the value of the share should rise proportionately with the value of the house. Thus, if the house is owned in equal shares and, when separation occurs, the equity is worth £10,000 the value of the share of the one who leaves should not be fixed at £5,000. Rather it should increase with the value of the equity, so that if when the house is sold, the equity is worth £20,000, then the shares should each be worth £10,000.

This result now seems to be accepted as correct, in principle, by the courts. Thus in *Gordon* v. *Douce*[34] it was stated that there was no rule that valuation is to occur at the date of separation. Indeed Lord Denning M.R., who gave the leading judgment in *Hall*, gave a judgment of rather a different tenor in *Bernard* v. *Josephs*.[35] It is now clear that *Hall* v. *Hall* was wrongly decided.[36]

Increases in value The date of valuation is an important matter in dividing up the proceeds of sale. Over the years, it is likely that the value of the house will appreciate, thereby causing the value of the equity to rise. One factor which causes the value of the equity to rise is inflation. Ordinarily, when a house is sold, the owner of it will expect to make a profit having discharged the mortgage. The other factor that will cause the value of the equity to rise is, of course, repayment of the mortgage loan. If one party has been paying this off alone, then it is unfair not to give credit for this in the division of the proceeds of sale. On the other hand, regard must also be had to the fact that that party has enjoyed the occupation of the house, whereas the other has not.

The approach that has been consistently taken is to differentiate between payments of interest and payments of **Interest and** capital. Credit is then given for the amount of capital that has **capital** been repaid which is over and above that which he would expect to pay having regard to his share in the property. The payment of interest is disregarded as being proper payment for exclusive use of the property.[37] An example may assist.

Examples of In *Crisp* v. *Mullings*[38] it was held that the beneficial **accounting** ownership in the house was shared in the proportions $\frac{3400}{6250}$ and $\frac{2850}{6250}$. The owner of the larger share continued in occupation after separation and paid all the mortgage instalments. It was held that on a sale of the property, he should be credited with $\frac{2850}{6250}$ of the repayments of capital made after separation: *i.e.* he was entitled to be refunded the amount of capital that she should have paid to the mortgagee having regard to the size of her beneficial interest.

The Court of Appeal decision in *Young* v. *Young*[39] appears inconsistent with this. A couple assumed joint liability for the mortgage but the woman made virtually all the repayments. She was held to be solely entitled in equity and not merely entitled to

---

[33] See *Walker* v. *Hall* [1984] F.L.R. 126.
[34] [1983] 1 W.L.R. 563; *Walker* v. *Hall*, above n. 33; *Marsh* v. *Von Sternberg*, above n. 31.
[35] [1982] Ch. 391, 400.
[36] *Turton* v. *Turton* [1987] 3 W.L.R. 622; *Passee* v. *Passee* (1987) 137 New L.J. 972.
[37] *Leake* v. *Bruzzi* [1974] 1 W.L.R. 1528; *Suttill* v. *Graham* [1977] 1 W.L.R. 819; *Walker* v. *Hall* [1984] F.L.R. 126.
[38] (1975) 239 E.G. 119.
[39] (1984) 14 Fam. Law 271. See also *Walker* v. *Hall*, above n. 33; *Marsh* v. *Von Sternberg*, above n. 31.

be reimbursed for her outlay. The case is best seen as one where the man had made no contribution to the purchase of the property thereby making ineffective their agreement to share the beneficial ownership. Ordinarily, extra capital payments by one party should be relevant to accounting; the size of the shares should be determined by their agreement to share liability for repayments.[40]

Endowment mortgages The method of accounting outlined above will not work in the case of an endowment mortgage because there are no capital repayments as such towards the acquisition of the house. Interest payments are made to the mortgagee for the period of the loan and premiums paid on an assurance policy which will mature at the end of the loan period providing funds sufficient to repay the mortgage loan together, in some cases, with an additional sum as profit.

The courts do not appear to have grappled with this problem but it is suggested that the principles articulated above should produce the following results:

Initial contributions to deposit

(1) A and B buy a house for £50,000, each contributing £10,000 and the remaining £30,000 provided by an endowment mortgage financed solely by A. B has a 20 per cent. interest in the house but no interest in the policy.

Joint payments of policy

(2) Both contribute to the original cash payment and A and B pool their resources to pay both interest payments and the policy premiums, the policy being taken against A's life. B should now get an interest in the policy as well as in the house, so that when the policy matures, they should share the profits.

Sale prior to policy maturing

(3) The position is as in (2) but the house is sold prior to the maturation of the assurance policy. First they should share in the balance of the sale price after the mortgage has been redeemed. Secondly B should also have an interest in the policy which should be realised either by A buying B out or surrendering the policy and sharing the proceeds.

Accounting

(4) The position is again as in (2) but B leaves the premises and A meets all the repayments on the house for a period before it is sold. To effect accounting, it is suggested that the payments under the policy should be treated as payments of capital. Hence the interest payments to the mortgagee should be discounted but he should be credited with capital payments under the policy. Thus if they contributed equally to the purchase of the house but A alone makes all the payments for a period, B is entitled to a half-share in the house and the policy but liable to account for one-half of the premium payments made after separation.

---

[40] *Re Rogers' Question* [1948] 1 All E.R. 328.

3 PETITIONS FOR SALE BY CO-OWNERS

It is not at all uncommon for there to be a disagreement between co-owners of property as to when it should be sold. Such disagreements will usually occur when a relationship has broken down and one of the co-owners has left the property and is anxious to realise his capital share in it. Conversely those remaining in occupation of the house wish to retain it to continue its present use as a home. In this chapter, the judicial attitude to such disputes will be considered, deferring until Chapter 6 discussion of the position when a sale is sought as a result of the insolvency of one of the co-owners.

Disputes as to sale

If the co-owners cannot agree as to whether the property is to be sold, it will be important whether or not there exists legal co-ownership or merely equitable co-ownership. If legal co-ownership exists, then one co-owner cannot transfer the legal estate without the other's co-operation and, if this is not forthcoming, a petition to the court will be essential. If there is sole ownership at law but co-ownership in equity, then the legal owner can pass a good legal title without the other's consent, although prior to the sale taking place, the equitable co-owner can restrain it by applying for an injunction.[1] If the sale takes place when no injunction has been obtained, the purchaser runs a substantial risk of not getting a good title, in that he may be bound by prior equitable interests.[2]

When the co-owners cannot agree on whether the property should be sold, then an application can be made for an order that a sale should take place under section 30 of the L.P.A. 1925. This provides that:

L.P.A. 1925, s.30

> "If the trustees for sale refuse to sell or to exercise any of the powers conferred by either of the last two sections, or any requisite consent cannot be obtained, any person interested may apply to the court for a vesting order or other order for giving effect to the proposed transaction or for an order directing the trustees for sale to give effect thereto, and the court may make such order as it thinks fit."

In this chapter, the approach of the courts to petitions brought under this section will be considered, together with the related question of the disposal of property when a co-ownership order is made under section 24 of the Matrimonial Causes Act 1973. Finally the consequences of either party being legally aided will be examined.

---

[1] *Waller* v. *Waller* [1967] 1 W.L.R. 451.
[2] See Chap. 7.

Section 30 petitions[3]

Originally, the fact that land subject to co-ownership was necessarily held upon a trust for sale was of almost decisive importance. The prime duty of the trustees is to sell the property, subject to a discretion to postpone the sale. For the power to take precedence over the duty, the trustees should be unanimous. Accordingly if one of the trustees wished to sell, his wishes would be acceded to.[4]

Although this decision did recognise that an order for sale would not be automatically granted, great stress was laid upon the trust being a trust for sale. It has since been recognised that an immediate sale may not always be desirable, particularly if young children are living in the house. In such cases, the courts have developed the concept that if there is an underlying purpose to the trust for sale, then an order for sale should not be made if the effect of a sale would be to defeat that purpose.

The underlying purpose

The idea of considering the underlying purpose of the trust for sale has been developed from *Re Buchanan-Wollaston's Conveyance*,[5] where four people bought land and expressly contracted that it should not be sold except by unanimous agreement. A sale was sought against the wishes of one of the co-owners and the application was refused.

In *Re Buchanan-Wollaston's Conveyance*, there was an express agreement between the co-owners as to when the land should be sold. The reasoning has been extended to cases where

Implied agreement   there was no express agreement but an implied underlying purpose to the trust. In *Re Evers' Trust*[6] a couple had been cohabiting in a house with three children, two of whom were the defendant's from an earlier marriage, while the third was a child of both parties. The parties, who were joint tenants, separated and the plaintiff sought an order for the sale of the house which was resisted by the defendant who was living there with the three children. This petition was rejected by the Court of Appeal, who held that the underlying purpose of the trust for sale was to provide a home for the family and that this purpose continued to subsist. Accordingly it was ordered that the sale be postponed indefinitely, with liberty to either party to apply for a sale at a later date.

Underlying purpose test   The underlying purpose test is most useful in terms of a co-owner resisting an application for a sale when dependent children are living in the house. When there are no children involved, a sale is more likely to be ordered. This is particularly the case when the co-owners have not bought the house as a

---

[3] See generally R. Schuz (1982) 12 Fam.Law 108; M. P. Thompson [1984] Conv. 103.
[4] *Re Mayo* [1943] Ch. 302.
[5] [1939] Ch. 738; *Re Hyde's Conveyance* (1952) 102 L.J. 58. See also *Charlton v. Lester* (1976) 238 E.G. 115.
[6] [1980] 1 W.L.R. 1327. See also *Bull v. Bull* [1955] 1 Q.B. 234; *Jones v. Challenger* [1961] 1 Q.B. 176.

Joint occupation

"quasi-matrimonial home" but, instead have simply bought the property for joint occupation. In *Smith* v. *Smith and Smith*,[7] the plaintiff bought a house with the defendants, her brother and sister-in-law, to be used as a joint family home. When they fell out and the plaintiff left, it was held on her petition for a sale that the underlying purpose of the trust had ended and that there was nothing inequitable in ordering a sale.

Such a result is quite likely when a house is bought for joint occupation and one of the co-owners leaves. The court may well be prepared to offer the co-owner in occupation the chance to buy out the share of the other but, subject to that, in most cases a sale will be ordered.[8] In unusual cases, however, a sale will be refused. In *Charlton* v. *Lester*[9] a sitting, protected tenant had bought a house with her son and daughter-in-law on the clear understanding that she could always remain in the house as her home. Despite the couple having moved out, Oliver J. refused to order a sale, thereby giving effect to the prior understanding.

Children If a couple have been cohabiting and also have dependent children, the courts are often reluctant to order a sale if to do so would cause housing problems to the parent who is remaining in the house looking after the children. At one time, the needs of the children were regarded as simply an incidental factor to which regard should be had. In no way, however, were their needs decisive.[10] That attitude was not, however, typical. Thus in *Rawlings* v. *Rawlings*,[11] Salmon L.J. said when ordering a sale of the property "if there were young children, the position would be different. One of the purposes of the trust would no doubt have been to provide a home for them, and whilst that purpose still existed a sale would not generally be ordered."

Rawlings v. Rawlings

It is quite clear that while there are young children in the house, the co-owner who has left the property and who is seeking a sale of it can be refused the order sought by relying on the underlying purpose test. The courts will regard the provision of a home for the children as part of the underlying purpose of the trust. The problems with this approach are, first there may have been no intention to have children when the property was acquired, with the consequence that it is somewhat artificial to speak of them as being within any underlying purpose of the trust. Secondly, as was recognised in *Rawlings* itself, once the children have left home, the underlying purpose no longer subsists. Consequently the property should be sold, although this might not be the most desirable social result.

Limitations of the underlying purpose test

It is considerations of this nature that has led the courts to modify the test of simply asking whether there is an underlying purpose to the trust and then going on to consider whether it continues to subsist. While this will remain a most important factor for the court's consideration, modern case law has established that a general discretionary approach is to be taken. It

The general equitable approach

---

[7] (1976) 120 S.J. 100.
[8] *Ali* v. *Hussein* (1974) 231 E.G. 372; *Pariser* v. *Wilson* (1973) 229 E.G. 786 (parties agreed that the occupier should have a three month option to purchase).
[9] (1976) 238 E.G. 115.
[10] *Burke* v. *Burke* [1974] 1 W.L.R. 1063.
[11] [1964] P. 398 at 419.

was made clear in *Re Holliday (A Bankrupt)*,[12] when a trustee in bankruptcy of one co-owner sought a sale, that "the guiding principle in the exercise of the court's discretion is not whether the trustee or the wife is being reasonable but, in all the circumstances of the case, whose voice in equity ought to prevail . . . "

Relevant factors　In exercising this discretion, regard will be had to all the circumstances of the case. On the one hand is the desire for the non-occupying owner to realise the capital value of his share in the house. As against that is the accommodation needs of those in occupation. In particular, the "arrangements made by the court should take proper account of the need of the children for accommodation."[13] Where children are still living in the house, it is far less likely that a sale will be ordered than would otherwise be the case.

Occupation rent

If a petition for sale is refused, or the order for sale postponed, the effect of this is that one co-owner will derive no use from the property and be prevented from realising the capital value of his share. This consideration used to weigh very heavily with the courts, leading to a disposition towards ordering a sale. Partly as a response to this, the notion of ordering the occupying co-owner to pay an occupation rent to the other has emerged.

Ouster　The jurisdiction to order the payment of an occupation rent came to prominence in *Dennis* v. *McDonald*.[14] One tenant in common had effectively excluded the other from the house. Because children were living in the house with him, it was considered to be undesirable to order an immediate sale. It was further held that because one tenant in common had forcibly denied the other the right of occupation, he should pay her an occupation rent. This was assessed on the basis of one-half of what a registered fair rent, as assessed under section 70 of the Rent Act 1977, would be on this type of property. The figure of one-half reflected his own beneficial share in the house. Had it been only 30 per cent., he would have been ordered to pay 70 per cent. of what a fair rent would be.

Jurisdiction to order rent　Although the view has been expressed that an occupation rent can be ordered on the basis simply that this is fair,[15] the courts under the general law do not have this power. As was recognised in *Dennis* v. *McDonald*, there is an inherent jurisdiction to order the payment of rent only when one tenant in common has excluded the other. Ordinarily, both have the right to live in the house and if one simply chooses not to do so, no rent is payable.[16] Where there has been no exclusion by one co-owner

---

[12] [1981] Ch. 405 at 420, *per* Goff L.J. See also *Re Turner* [1974] 1 W.L.R. 1556 at 1558. For bankruptcy cases, see Chap. 6.
[13] *Chhokar* v. *Chhokar* [1984] F.L.R. 313 at 327, *per* Cumming-Bruce L.J.
[14] [1981] 1 W.L.R. 810 affirmed in principle [1982] 2 W.L.R. 275.
[15] *Chhokar* v. *Chhokar* [1984] F.L.R. 313 at 332, *per* Cumming-Bruce L.J. See also *Cousins* v. *Dzosens* (1984) 81 L.S.Gaz. 2855.
[16] See *McMahon* v. *Burchell* (1846) 5 Hare 322 and R. E. Annand (1982) 132 New L.J. 526.

of the other, the court cannot, in refusing a sale under section 30, directly order that a rent be paid.

Undertakings to pay rent

This problem is more apparent than real. If the court thinks that the appropriate disposition of the case is to postpone a sale of the property and, at the same time, ensure that an occupation rent is paid this can be done by undertakings. The person in occupation can be told that unless she undertakes to pay an occupation rent, a sale will be ordered under section 30. Conversely, the person not in occupation can be told that unless that offer is accepted, a sale will simply be refused.

Not a universal solution

It should not be thought that an indefinite postponement of sale coupled with an occupation rent is the panacea for all cases involving cohabiting co-owners of a house.[17] Indeed in many cases, particularly if the couple are young and childless, an immediate sale will be appropriate. The approach taken in *Dennis* v. *McDonald* and *Re Evers' Trust* does show, however, that once co-ownership has been established, the courts can treat questions relating to the disposition of the home with full regard to family law considerations, thereby achieving results similar to those achieved in matrimonial cases.

Orders under the Matrimonial Causes Act 1973[18]

Unlike the position when an unmarried couple is involved, when the court is resolving the problems concerning the matrimonial home in divorce proceedings, it need not pay "any too nice a regard to [the parties'] legal or equitable rights but simply [make an order] according to what is the fairest provision for the future—[for] mother and father and children."[19] Neither husband nor wife need establish a prior interest in the home; regard is simply had to the criteria listed in section 3 of the Matrimonial and Family Proceedings Act 1984 following which, the court makes such an order as is considered just under section 24 of the Matrimonial Causes Act 1973.

Co-ownership orders are common under the Act. When such an order is made, the court can also order the sale of the property under section 24(A) of the Matrimonial Causes Act 1973.[20] Where children are involved, the courts tend not to order an immediate sale of the property but are instead inclined to postpone a sale. This was done to provide a home for the children and led to the development of the Mesher Order,[21] whereby a sale would be postponed until the youngest child had reached a specified age, usually 16 or 17 years.

The Mesher Order

This type of order quickly became a popular one to make. It

---

[17] *Cousins* v. *Dzosens*, above n. 15 and *Stott* v. *Ratcliffe* (1982) 79 L.S.Gaz. 643.
[18] See generally M. Hayes and G. Battersby [1981] Conv. 404; (1985) 15 Fam.Law 213.
[19] *Hanlon* v. *The Law Society* [1981] A.C. 124 at 147, *per* Lord Denning M.R.
[20] Introduced by the Matrimonial Homes and Property Act 1981, s.7, to resolve the supposed difficulties caused by *Ward* v. *Ward and Greene* [1980] 1 W.L.R. 4n.
[21] *Mesher* v. *Mesher* [1980] 1 All E.R. 126n. (a case decided in 1973). See also *Browne* v. *Pritchard* [1975] 1 W.L.R. 1366.

Drawbacks of Mesher Order soon came to be realised, however, that it did not provide a satisfactory solution. This is because it has a tendency to store up trouble and hardship for a later date. The children may not stop needing a house at that time. The mother, who may have been out of the labour market for some time while looking after the children, may then be of advanced years and it could cause hardship to her to order a sale. Considerations such as these have led to the Mesher Order being currently out of favour.[22]

Flexible orders In steering away from the Mesher Order, the courts have adopted a more flexible approach. In *Harvey* v. *Harvey*[23] both parties after the divorce were in secure accommodation, the former wife living in the erstwhile matrimonial home with the children. Varying the original Mesher Order, the Court of Appeal ordered an indefinite postponement of sale coupled with an order that the mother pay to the father an occupation rent, that rent to become payable upon the youngest child attaining majority. The effect of this was to combine a Mesher Order with a right of indefinite occupation at a rent.

Cohabitation Whereas under section 24 of the Matrimonial Causes Act 1973, the courts can make this type of order directly, this cannot be done if the parties are unmarried. It may nevertheless be possible to achieve this result, again by obtaining undertakings. The court could indicate that an indefinite postponement of sale will be made, provided that an undertaking is given to pay an occupation rent from a specified date. As yet, there is no reported case where such an order has been made. There is no reason in principle why this course should not be adopted, however, if the circumstances of the case seem appropriate.

Subsequent sale orders If the original order refusing an immediate sale is made under section 30, there is no intrinsic difficulty in either side subsequently petitioning for a sale under the same section although, unless circumstances have changed, liability to pay costs will be an effective deterrent. If the original order is made under section 24 of the Matrimonial Causes Act 1973, however, the difficulty is that by section 31 of the same Act such orders are to be final. If the order made is a Mesher Order, the question arises whether there is jurisdiction to order a sale for reasons other than those specified in the original order: whether such an order would be a variation of the original order.

This issue was considered in *Thompson* v. *Thompson*.[24] The order made upon divorce was that the matrimonial home be held upon trust for sale and not to be sold "until the youngest child . . . reaches the age of seventeen years or finishes further education whichever is the later or further order." Two years later the wife, who occupied the house, wished to sell it and move to another area and sought an order compelling the husband to concur in the sale of the property.

On the issue of jurisdiction, it was held that regard must be

---

[22] See *Hanlon* v. *Hanlon* [1978] 1 W.L.R. 592; *Carson* v. *Carson* [1983] 1 W.L.R. 285; *Harman* v. *Glencross* [1986] Fam. 81; *Mortimer* v. *Mortimer-Griffin* [1986] 2 F.L.R. 315. See Bromley's *Family Law* (7th ed., 1987) pp. 707–709.
[23] [1982] Fam. 83; *Brown* v. *Brown* (1981) 3 F.L.R. 161. Jill Martin [1982] Conv. 305.
[24] [1986] Fam. 38.

Purpose of original order

had to the original purpose of the order. If, because of changed circumstances, that purpose was best furthered by an early sale, for example if the woman in the house remarried and transferred herself elsewhere with her minor children, then an early sale at the instance of the spouse out of possession would not amount to a variation of the order. In such an event, even if the current value of the house exceeded the jurisdictional value limit of the county court, the county court may still be petitioned for a sale under section 24A(1) of the Matrimonial Causes Act 1973, provided that, at the time when the original order was made, the value of the house did not exceed the limit of the county court. In the instant case, it was held that the county court did have jurisdiction to make an order under the 1973 Act as the reason why she wanted the sale was within the purpose of the original order.

County court jurisdiction

Premature sale

If a premature sale is sought for reasons which do not advance the original purpose of the order, perhaps if the spouse out of possession is currently in straitened circumstances and in urgent need to realise his beneficial share in the house, then any order of sale would amount to a variation of the original order. Accordingly the petition should be brought under section 30 of the L.P.A. 1925 and not under the 1973 Act. Which court the action should be brought in will then be determined by the current value of the house.

Legal aid

A common feature of disputes concerning the matrimonial or quasi-matrimonial home is that the litigation is financed by legal aid. When that is the case then, under section 9(6) of the Legal Aid Act 1974, the Law Society meets the deficiency between the contribution made by the assisted party and the costs actually incurred by taking a first charge, for the benefit of the legal aid fund, on any property which is recovered or preserved for him in the proceedings.

The existence of this charge has a significant impact on litigation concerning the family home. In assessing that impact, regard must first be had to the circumstances when it can be imposed. It was held in *Hanlon* v. *The Law Society*[25] that property is "recovered or preserved" whenever the ownership of the property is in issue between the parties. One does not first, in divorce proceedings, assess the beneficial interest before and after the court's judgment. If the wife is held to have a half share in the property then the Law Society charge will extend to that whole half share except for the first £2,500.[26] The property is also held to be in issue if the proceedings do not relate to the ownership of the house but as to whether it should be sold. Thus if a Mesher Order is made, although there was no dispute as to the quantum of the beneficial shares in the property, the assisted person will

Recovery or preservation of property

---

[25] [1981] A.C. 124.
[26] In so far as proceedings brought under s.24 of the Matrimonial Causes Act 1973 are concerned, the first £2,500 recovered or preserved is exempt from the charge: Legal Aid (General) Regulations 1980 (S.I. 1980 No. 1804), reg. 86.

Enforcement of the charge

still be regarded as having recovered or preserved her share in the house so that the Law Society is entitled to a charge on the property.[27]

When the property recovered or preserved is the house, then the charge is taken against it. If the house is sold, the Law Society is then entitled to have that charge satisfied from the proceeds of sale. This can have extremely unfortunate circumstances if the wife wishes to sell the matrimonial home and move to a smaller house, the upkeep of which is more within her means. In these circumstances, the Law Society has a discretion to transfer the charge from the previous house to the new one. In exercising that discretion, the Law Society should have regard not simply to the legal aid fund but to the scheme as a whole.[28] As a result a transfer of the charge is a likely outcome.

Lump sums

The statutory charge causes grave problems where one of the parties is given a cash award. A not unusual solution to the problems of reallocation of property on divorce is to allow one party to buy out the other's interest in the matrimonial home to enable the lump sum to be used to finance the purchase of a new property. The lump sum is itself subject to the Law Society charge. Unfortunately, regulations 88 to 91 of the Legal Aid (General) Regulations 1980 do not give the Law Society a discretion to impose the charge on the property bought by that lump sum. It has to be paid at once to the Law Society.[29]

The effect of these regulations would, of course, stultify completely the intent behind the order. To try to ensure that this does not occur, the courts have stressed the need to pay attention to the effect that the charge will have on any order that is made.[30] Accordingly, counsel should prepare an estimate as to costs so that it can be seen whether a lump sum would be swallowed up by the legal aid fund.[31]

Types of proceeding Clearly the costs involved in actual litigation will be recoverable by the Law Society by using the charge. Less obviously the costs incurred up until the time of a consent order or a compromise are treated in the same way.[32] Nevertheless, the costs will not be so great and the effect of the Law Society charge less damaging to the parties.

---

[27] *Curling* v. *Law Society* [1985] 1 W.L.R. 470.
[28] *Hanlon* v. *Law Society* [1981] A.C. 124.
[29] *Simmons* v. *Simmons* [1984] Fam. 17; *R.* v. *Law Society, ex p. Sexton* [1984] Q.B. 360; *Simpson* v. *Law Society* [1987] 2 W.L.R. 1390.
[30] *Singer* v. *Sharegin* [1984] F.L.R. 114.
[31] Practice Direction [1982] 2 All E.R. 800.
[32] *R.* v. *Law Society, ex p. Sexton*, above n. 29; *Van Hoorn* v. *Law Society* [1984] F.L.R. 203.

4 LEASEHOLD PROPERTY

It is, of course, true that it is not only freehold property that can be the subject of co-ownership. It is also possible for a lease to be owned by more than one tenant. In such cases, the tenants will, by virtue of section 36 of the L.P.A. 1925, hold the lease upon trust for sale.[1] Where a lease is jointly owned, however, particular problems can arise. These are caused in the main by the problems caused by accommodating joint tenancies within the provisions of the Rent Act 1977. Again, in the public sector, difficulties can be caused when the tenancy is jointly rather than solely owned. These problems will be addressed in turn later in this chapter. First the question of when a joint tenancy is created will be addressed.

Joint tenancies or licences?

The most straightforward case of a joint tenancy is, quite simply, when the landlord expressly grants a lease to several people as joint tenants. Such cases cause no difficulty at the outset. What is more problematic is where a freeholder enters into separate agreements with various people permitting them to occupy the house together. The question which then arises is whether the group as a whole become joint tenants of the property or whether they hold lesser individual interests.

    Before considering the judicial response to this problem, it is as well to state the context of it. For the purposes of section 1 of the Rent Act 1977, a tenancy under which a house or part of a house is let as a separate dwelling is a protected tenancy. The consequence of a tenancy being protected is that the tenant then enjoys the two principal benefits that the Act confers: rent restriction and security of tenure.

Rent Act 1977

Principal benefits

Rent Act avoidance: licences

    From the landlord's perspective, the Rent Act is undesirable and, therefore, many devices have been resorted to to avoid its provisions. Of these devices, a popular one is to seek to create a licence to occupy a house rather than a lease. If successful, the occupier is not a protected tenant within section 1 because the dwelling-house has not been "let." A popular licence agreement has involved admitting a number of occupiers into the house. They each sign a separate agreement with the freeholder which makes each one liable to pay a specified sum of money to him. Each person is also required to share the property with others. The object of such agreements is to establish that none of the occupiers has exclusive possession of the whole or any part: the right to exclude everyone else from the property. As a lease cannot exist unless exclusive possession has been granted, the effect of this device, if successful, is to cause the occupiers to be contractual licensees and therefore not entitled to the protection afforded to protected tenants.

No right to exclusive possession

[1] See above pp. 14–15.

Somma v. Hazlehurst

Rent

Per capita agreements: the judicial response A sharing arrangement such as the one outlined above was fully considered by the Court of Appeal in *Somma* v. *Hazlehurst*.[2] H and S, an unmarried couple, entered separate agreements for the use of a double bed-sitting room for a period of 12 weeks for the sum of £116.40 each, payable by three, four-weekly instalments. Each agreement reserved to the owner the right to use the room and to license one other occupier. On an application by the occupiers for registration of a fair rent, the issue arose as to whether they were tenants or licensees. The Court of Appeal held that they fell into the latter category.

In holding that there was not a joint tenancy, the crucial factor was that they were not jointly and severally liable to pay rent.[3] It was held that a joint interest coupled with a several liability for half the weekly payments was a logical inconsistency[4] and that consequently they could not be joint tenants. As they were not joint tenants, together thereby forming legally a single unit, they did not enjoy exclusive possession and were therefore merely licensees.

This decision occasioned much disquiet as it seemed to have opened the door to facile Rent Act avoidance schemes. In subsequent cases, similar schemes failed to prosper; in one case the whole payment had been extracted in advance, thereby causing the theoretical obligation of several liability to pay rent appear illusory[5] and, in another, the written document did not accord with what had been orally agreed.[6] The position with regard to these schemes was therefore unclear; a lack of clarity which, unfortunately, has not been dispelled by the House of Lords.

Street v. Mountford

Lease or licence?

Lease or lodgings?

A new approach? In *Street* v. *Mountford*,[7] the House of Lords reviewed the distinction between leases and licences. The House was seised of a single occupancy agreement which sought to avoid the Rent Act. Although the document signed by the occupier was called a licence, it was conceded that exclusive possession had been given.[8] In the light of this concession, unsurprisingly it was held that the transaction created a lease. Lord Templeman, who delivered the only speech, concluded that if exclusive possession for a fixed or periodic term at a rent was granted then, save for exceptional cases such as a service occupancy, a lease is created irrespective of what label has been attached to the document.

The thrust of Lord Templeman's speech was directed at the distinction between leases and lodgings: the latter category embracing transactions where the landlord provides attendance

---

[2] [1978] 1 W.L.R. 1014.
[3] See also *Aldrington Garages* v. *Fielder* (1978) 247 E.G. 557 and *Sturolson Co.* v. *Weniz* (1984) 17 H.L.R. 140. *Cf. Walsh* v. *Griffiths-Jones* [1978] 2 All E.R. 1002.
[4] [1978] 1 W.L.R. at 1926, *per* Cumming-Bruce L.J.
[5] *Demuren* v. *Seal Estates* (1978) 249 E.G. 440.
[6] *O'Malley* v. *Seymour* (1978) 250 E.G. 1083.
[7] [1985] A.C. 809. See Yates and Hawkins, *Landlord and Tenant Law* (2nd ed., 1986) pp. 23–24.
[8] Probably *de facto* exclusive occupation was meant rather than *de jure* exclusive possession. For a valuable discussion of the difference, see M. C. Cullity (1965) 28 Conv. (N.S.) 336.

or services which require him or his agents to exercise unrestricted access to and use of the premises.[9] In his speech, reference was also made to *Somma* v. *Hazlehurst*, which was disapproved. Lord Templeman expressed the view that the sham nature of the obligation in that case would have only been slightly more obvious if the couple had been married, or they had been furnished with a double bed instead of two single beds.[10] Accordingly in his view, the couple were joint tenants rather than licensees.

Shams

While the finding that the transaction in *Somma* v. *Hazlehurst* was a sham is to be welcomed, it remains unclear as to what the position would be if the documents do not misrepresent the transaction. A sham was defined by Diplock L.J. in *Snook* v. *London and West Riding Investment Co. Ltd.*[11] would be as involving "acts done or documents executed by the parties to the 'sham' which are intended by them to give to third parties or to the court the appearance of creating between the parties legal rights and obligations different from the actual legal rights and obligations (if any) which the parties intended to create." In *Somma*, it was clear that the separate transactions did not represent the reality of the matter; neither occupier would have left without the other, leaving the remaining occupier to be joined by another, as the agreements envisaged. Consequently the documents should have been disregarded. Had they been genuine, there is nothing in *Street* v. *Mountford* to suggest that the device would not work. Indeed, the very fact that it was disapproved solely on the ground that it was a sham suggests that it would have done.[12]

Per capita agreements after Street v. Mountford

If a freeholder wishes to admit a number of occupiers into his house, a key issue is whether or not agreements of the type used in *Somma* will operate to prevent the creation of a joint tenancy. If, for example, each occupier is charged a slightly different occupancy fee, and these agreements are adhered to, then it is difficult to construe the arrangement as a sham and the *ratio* of *Somma* would appear to apply to prevent them from being joint tenants. It is suggested that the courts would be reluctant to find this result had been achieved. Although it has been argued that there is nothing inimical to the notion of a joint tenancy that the joint tenants are only severally liable for the rent,[13] this, with respect, seems not to accord with the juristic nature of a joint tenancy and has been judicially regarded as a logical inconsistency.[14]

A method of avoiding this inconsistency would be to hold that the agreements entered into created a legal joint tenancy rendering the tenants jointly and severally liable to the landlord

---

[9] [1985] A.C. 809 at 818. For an example see *Marchant* v. *Charters* [1977] 1 W.L.R. 1181.

[10] *Ibid.* at 825.

[11] [1967] 2 Q.B. 786 at 802. See also *Miles* v. *Bull* [1969] 1 Q.B. 258 at 265, *per* Megarry J.

[12] *Cf. Crancour* v. *De Silvaesa* (1986) 18 H.L.R. 265 and see *Brooker Settled Estates Ltd.* v. *Ayres* (1987) 19 H.L.R. 246 and especially, *Hadjiloucas* v. *Crean* [1987] 3 All E.R. 1008. See also *Antoniades* v. *Villiers, The Independent*, March 23, 1988.

[13] Arden and Partington, *Housing Law* (1983) p. 131; citing in support *Demuren* v. *Seal Estates* (1978) 249 E.G. 440.

[14] *Somma* v. *Hazlehurst* [1978] 1 W.L.R. at 1026, *per* Cumming-Bruce L.J.

Tenancies in common at law for the rent. In equity, however, they would be tenants in common, so that a tenant who has paid more to the landlord than agreed in his document could claim the balance from the other tenants.[15] Despite the existence of separate agreements, if the negotiations have been conducted with the occupiers as a group, it is thought likely that the courts will construe the arrangements as creating a joint tenancy.[16]

Rather greater difficulty would be occasioned if the occupiers were not known to each other in advance and were admitted to the house at different times and required to pay different occupancy fees.[17] Such agreements, unless they misrepresent the reality of the position and are consequently vulnerable to attack as shams, appear to be completely **Joint tenancies** inconsistent with the notion of joint tenancy. Nevertheless, in *A. G. Securities* v. *Vaughan*,[17a] the Court of Appeal held, Sir George Waller dissenting, that a genuine series of agreements of this type did create a joint tenancy. This reasoning, with respect, minimises the difficulties in establishing that the necessary four unities are present and it is submitted that the dissenting judgment is to be preferred. Leave to appeal was granted, and it remains to be seen how the House of Lords will regard this issue.

If it transpires that there is no joint tenancy in these situations, then the only available method of finding that the occupiers were within the Rent Act would be to hold that, if each **Separate tenancies of rooms** occupier had a separate room, then section 22 of the Act applied to give then the status of protected tenants of such room, subject to their obligation to share the remaining living accommodation. If this course is adopted, or the decision in *A. G. Securities* v. *Vaughan* is upheld, then sharing arrangements of the type seen in *Somma* will fall into disuse. Pending a decision of the House of Lords, the current position is unclear.

Co-ownership and the exercise of landlord and tenant rights[18]

When either the freehold reversion or the tenancy itself is subject to co-ownership, difficult problems arise in determining whether the co-owners must act jointly or whether unilateral action by one of the co-owners will be effective. These difficulties are particularly acute when the issue concerns the construction of the statutory provisions regulating the rights of landlord and tenant, both in the private and public sectors. This is particularly so in the context of tenancies within the Rent Act 1977, because no thought was given in the drafting of these provisions, or their predecessors, to the problems that can be caused by co-ownership.[19]

---

[15] *Chalmers* v. *Guthrie* (1923) 156 L.T.J. 382.
[16] *Demuren* v. *Seal Estates Ltd.*, above n. 13; Arden and Partington, above n. 13, p. 59.
[17] See R. Street [1985] Conv. 325 at 332–333; N. Madge [1986] Legal Action 163 at 164.
[17a] [1988] 06 E.G. 112. See P. H. Kenny (1988) 85 L.S. Gaz. 17. But see also *Antoniades* v. *Villiers*, above n. 12.
[18] For a valuable discussion, see J. Martin [1978] Conv. 436.
[19] See *Lloyd* v. *Sadler* [1978] Q.B. 774 at 782, *per* Megaw L.J.

Co-owners comprise a single entity

The general law The basic position when leasehold property is subject to co-ownership is that any decisions made which affect the lease itself must be made by all the co-owners. This is in accordance with the theoretical basis of co-ownership. As the property must be held upon a legal joint tenancy, the co-owners together comprise a single legal entity and, as such, decisions made by that entity must be taken by all the constituent members.

Termination of the lease There are a number of illustrations of this principle. A fairly common provision in a lease is a break clause, whereby either or both parties can determine the lease at specified times. In *Re Viola's Indenture of Lease*,[20] joint tenants held under a lease which contained such a clause. One of the joint tenants purported to serve a notice to determine the lease but this was held to be invalid because there was no evidence that this action had been authorised by the other tenant. Similarly, in *Leek and Moreland Building Society v. Clark*[21] it was held that one of two joint tenants could not validly surrender the lease. It was further stated that if the lease contained an option to renew, the tenants must act together to exercise it.[22]

Relief against forfeiture

Similar reasoning is employed in the case of relief against forfeiture. In *T.M. Fairclough & Sons Ltd. v. Berliner*[23] the landlord sought to recover possession against its tenants for breach of repairing covenants. One of the tenants sought relief against forfeiture under section 146(2) of the L.P.A. 1925 but the other did not. Relief was refused as it was not sought by both of the tenants. To have granted relief to only one of them would have meant the continuation of the lease and the other would have remained liable for breaches of covenant in the future when he wished to end the tenancy.

Distress

In so far as the exercise of rights by one of two joint landlords is concerned, the position is less clear. In the old case of *Robinson v. Hofman*[24] it was held that one of the joint landlords could distrain for rent without the assent of the other. Whether or not this could have been done if the other co-owner had dissented was left open. In principle, it would seem that he could not. If rights incident to the relationship of landlord and tenant are to be exercised, it would seem to be necessary for all the co-owners to join in their exercise.

Notices to quit What at first sight might appear to be an exception to the above principle concerns the service of a notice to quit. In *Doe d. Aslin v. Summersett*,[25] one joint landlord served a notice to quit on a periodic tenant. This was held to be effective despite the other joint landlords not being party to the notice. The reason for this is that, where there is a periodic tenancy, each successive period operates as a renewal of the tenancy. For this to take place, each of the joint landlords must agree. The situation is

By landlord

---

[20] [1909] 1 Ch. 244.
[21] [1952] 2 Q.B. 788.
[22] *Ibid.* at 793, *per* Somervell L.J.
[23] [1931] 1 Ch. 60.
[24] (1828) 4 Bing. 562.
[25] (1830) 1 B. & Ad. 135; *Parsons* v. *Parsons* [1983] 1 W.L.R. 1390; *Leckhampton Dairies* v. *Actus Whitefield* (1986) 130 S.J. 225.

different from a surrender or the operation of a break clause in that both of these represent a decision to bring a premature end to the tenancy; here the decision is not to allow it to continue.

The principle which allows one joint landlord to serve a valid notice to quit applies *mutatis mutandis* to service of a notice by one of several joint tenants. The notice to quit will be valid to end the contractual tenancy regardless of the opposition of the others.[26] Where a notice to quit is served without consulting the other co-owners, however, the person who takes this action runs the risk of committing a breach of trust.[27] This is because the fact of co-ownership of either the lease or the reversion gives rise to a trust for sale. The legal owners are therefore trustees, frequently holding upon trust for themselves. Action by one, harmful to the beneficial interest of the other, is capable, therefore, of amounting to a breach of trust.

By tenant

Co-ownership and protective legislation

Much of the general law of landlord and tenant is now considerably affected by legislation. In so far as residential tenancies are concerned, the private sector is radically affected by the Rent Act 1977 and in the public sector the general law has to be read subject to the provisions of the Housing Act 1985. Again, commercial leases are governed by the Landlord and Tenant Act 1954 and agricultural tenancies fall within the ambit of the Agricultural Holdings Act 1986. Where either the lease or the reversion is jointly owned, problems of applying the statutory provisions can arise.

Rent control   If a tenancy is protected under section 1 of the Rent Act 1977, either the landlord or the tenant may apply to a rent officer for the determination and registration of a fair rent.[28] Similarly, if the occupancy is under a restricted contract, the occupier may apply to a rent assessment committee for the fixing of a reasonable rent.[29] It was held in *Turley* v. *Panton*[30] that, to be valid, all the occupiers must be party to an application to fix a reasonable rent. It should therefore follow that if a protected tenancy is held by joint tenants, they must all apply to the rent officer for the application to be valid. Similarly, if there are joint landlords, all would need to be party to an application for registration of a fair rent.

Parties to rent applications

Security of tenure   A feature of all the protective legislation in the field of landlord and tenant is that it confers security of tenure upon qualifying tenants. The means by which this goal is

---

[26] *Greenwich London Borough Council* v. *McGrady* (1983) 46 P. & C.R. 223. The doubt as to this expressed in *Howson* v. *Buxton* (1928) 97 L.J.K.B. 749 at 752, *per* Scrutton J. is unfounded although supported by F. Webb [1983] Conv. 194.

[27] *Parsons* v. *Parsons* above n. 25 at 1400, *per* Donald Rattee Q.C. See also *Harris* v. *Black* (1983) 46 P. & C.R. 366 at 374, *per* Slade L.J.

[28] Rent Act 1977, s.67.

[29] When performing this task, the rent assessment committee is known as a rent tribunal: Housing Act 1980, s.72.

[30] (1975) 119 S.J. 236.

implemented differs in the various statutory codes. These differences can be important in determining how the position of joint tenants is affected and must be considered in turn.

Rent Act 1977 **Private sector tenants** If a tenancy is protected under the Rent Act 1977, the Act confers upon the tenant security of tenure. This is done by section 2 which provides that after the termination of a protected tenancy, the person who immediately before the termination was the protected tenant of the dwelling-house shall, if and so long as he occupies the dwelling-house as a residence, be the statutory tenant of it. So long as the statutory tenancy continues, the landlord can only obtain possession by a court order obtained under section 98 or Schedule 15 to the Act.

Departure of one joint tenant The statutory tenancy continues so long as the tenant occupies the dwelling-house as a residence. If he departs with the intention not to return, then it terminates.[31] If there is a joint tenancy and one of the tenants leaves, in principle this should cause the statutory tenancy to terminate. This was recognised in **Lloyd v. Sadler** *Lloyd* v. *Sadler*[32] where it was held that to apply this principle would defeat the policy of the Act. Accordingly the Court of Appeal held that the ordinary law as to joint tenancies should not be applied strictly in this context. The remaining tenant was held to be the sole statutory tenant.

Remaining tenants This important decision makes this aspect of the security of tenure provisions clear. From it, it also follows that if one of the joint tenants leaves prior to the determination of the protected tenancy, the remaining occupier will be classed as the tenant when the statutory tenancy begins. Hence if a contractual periodic tenancy is terminated by a notice to quit served by only one of a number of joint tenants, this will end the contractual tenancy but the remainder will be entitled to remain as statutory tenants.

Public sector tenants Among the rights conferred upon council tenants by the Housing Act 1980, provisions now contained in **Housing Act 1985** the Housing Act 1985, was security of tenure. This is not done by the creation of a statutory tenancy. Instead, section 79 of the 1985 Act operates to make these tenancies secure. The effect of this is to preclude the landlord from terminating the lease except on the grounds specified in the Act.[33] Hence if the secure tenancy is a periodic tenancy, a notice to quit served by the landlord will be inoperative. If the original tenancy was for a fixed term, then on the term date, a periodic tenancy arises.[34]

For a secure tenancy to continue, the tenant condition must be satisfied. This is defined by section 81 as being that the tenant is an individual and occupies the dwelling-house as his only or

---

[31] *Brown* v. *Brash* [1948] 2 K.B. 247; *Colin Smith Music Ltd.* v. *Ridge* [1975] 1 W.L.R. 463; *Duke* v. *Porter* (1986) 280 E.G. 633.
[32] [1978] Q.B. 774.
[33] Housing Act 1985, ss.82–84; Sched. 2.
[34] *Ibid.* s.86. It has been argued that this tenancy is not itself secure; Yates and Hawkins, above n. 7 p. 550; [1982] Conv. 301. It is thought likely that the courts will accept the contrary view put by J. E. Alder [1982] Conv. 298, 304.

Provision for joint tenants

principal home. Specific provision is made for joint tenants in this section. The tenancy condition is satisfied if each of the joint tenants is an individual and at least one of them occupies the dwelling-house as his only or principal home. This reproduces, before any of the joint tenants serves a notice to quit, the effect of *Lloyd* v. *Sadler* in the public sector.

Notices to quit

An important consequence of not employing the concept of the statutory tenancy to confer security of tenure on tenants is that, except as modified by the Act, the common law continues to apply. Hence if the lease is terminated by the tenant, the occupation right ceases. In *Greenwich London Borough Council* v. *McGrady*[35] a husband and wife were secure weekly tenants of a council house. After divorce proceedings were instituted, the wife served a notice to quit upon the landlord. It was held that this terminated the tenancy and the landlord was entitled to possession against the husband.

Position of remaining joint tenant

The decision that the lease was ended by the notice to quit is clearly correct. It can cause hardship, however, if the other joint tenant would as a consequence be rendered homeless. Good administration should entail the remaining joint tenant being offered either a new lease of the house or a lease in alternative accommodation. Failure so to do has led to a finding against one council of maladministration.[36]

Landlord and Tenant Act 1954, Pt. II

Business tenancies Security of tenure in the case of business tenancies is conferred by Part II of the Landlord and Tenant Act 1954. Under section 24, the original tenancy can only be determined by the landlord in accordance with the statutory provisions. Upon receipt of a notice terminating the tenancy, section 26 entitles the tenant to apply for the grant of a new tenancy,[37] to which application the landlord can only object on the grounds stipulated in section 30 of the Act.

Applications for new tenancies

At common law, an application for a new tenancy, to be effective, had to be made by all the joint tenants.[38] This was reversed by section 9 of the Law of Property Act 1969[39] which enables a valid application for a new tenancy to be made by the joint tenants remaining in the property, regardless of the others having left and not wishing to take a new tenancy. The new tenancy is then granted to the remaining tenants who alone are liable for the payment of rent and the performance of the other obligations under the lease.

Qualification to apply

To qualify under this section, it is necessary that the business was at some time during the existence of the tenancy carried on in partnership by all the persons who were then the joint tenants, or by those and other persons, and the joint tenants' interest in the property was then partnership property. In addition, the business must be carried on by one or some of the joint tenants and no part of the property comprised in the

---

[35] (1983) 46 P. & C.R. 223.
[36] See D. Hughes, *Housing and Planning Review* (1984) Vol. 39, No. 6, pp. 10–11.
[37] Care must be taken to comply with the time limits of between two and four months.
[38] *Jacobs* v. *Chaudhuri* [1968] 2 Q.B. 470.
[39] This Act operated to insert s.41A into the 1954 Act.

tenancy is occupied in right of the tenancy for the purpose of a business carried on by the other or others.

Harris v. Black
In *Harris* v. *Black*[40] three people took a 14-year business tenancy to practise as solicitors. One died leaving the other two in possession. After a dispute, they dissolved their partnership and practised independently from the same building. On the expiry of the lease the plaintiff wished to apply for a new tenancy but the defendant did not. An application under the Landlord and Tenant Act 1954, s.26 would have failed as the second qualification introduced by the Law of Property Act 1969, s.9 was not satisfied.

Mandatory injunctions
In such a case, the only means by which one can apply for a new tenancy is to obtain a mandatory interlocutory injunction to compel the other joint tenant to join in the application. If the tenant who refuses is a beneficiary, this is most unlikely because such relief is not granted unless the court feels a high degree of assurance that at the trial such an order would be made.[41] Where business partners have fallen out, such a remedy is unlikely. The converse would be true if the refusing co-owner had no beneficial interest in the lease.

Agricultural tenancies In the case of tenancies that qualify for protection under section 1 of the Agricultural Holdings Act 1986, security of tenure is conferred by means of continuing the original tenancy. Under section 3(1) of the Act, a notice to quit an agricultural holding shall be invalid if it purports to terminate the tenancy before the expiration of 12 months from the end of the then current year of tenancy. If, within one month of receipt of such notice to quit, the tenant serves on the landlord a counter-notice in writing, then the notice to quit shall not have effect unless the Lands Tribunal consents to its operation.[42] Such consent can be refused on the grounds set out in Schedule 3, Part 1 to the 1986 Act.

Application of common law
No specific provision is made for joint tenants. Accordingly in that event, the common law rules apply and, therefore, a counter-notice, to be valid, must be signed by, or on behalf of, all the tenants.[43] this is so, unless one of the tenants is a company controlled by the landlord.[44] Where the tenancy does terminate, the tenant may be entitled to claim compensation from the landlord for "tenant-right" matters. The scope of what he can claim compensation for is outside the scope of this book.[45] Where there is a joint tenancy, it is not essential that all the joint tenants give notice of intent to claim. Each can claim separately with regard to his own loss.[46]

---

[40] (1983) 46 P. & C.R. 366. Such an order was made on unusual facts in the case of an agricultural tenancy: *Sykes* v. *Land* (1984) 271 E.G. 1264.
[41] *Locobail International Finance Ltd.* v. *Ayroexport* [1986] 1 W.L.R. 657.
[42] Agricultural Holdings Act 1986, s.26(1).
[43] *Newman* v. *Keedwell* (1978) 35 P. & C.R. 393; *Featherstone* v. *Staples* [1986] 1 W.L.R. 861. See C. P. Rodgers [1986] Conv. 429.
[44] *Featherstone* v. *Staples* [1986], above n. 43.
[45] Agricultural Holdings Act 1986, s.60. See Woodfall, *Landlord and Tenant* (28th ed. 1978) paras. 2 0142   2 0151.
[46] *Howson* v. *Buxton* (1928) 97 L.J.K.B. 749.

Grounds for possession

The security of tenure conferred by these Acts is not, of course, absolute. In the case of residential tenancies where security is conferred automatically, the landlord must establish one of the grounds for possession laid down in the Rent Act 1977 or the Housing Act 1985. In the case of tenancies within either the Landlord and Tenant Act 1954 or the Agricultural Holdings Act 1986, the landlord may object in the former case to the grant of a new tenancy, or in the latter to the continuation of the existing one. It is not intended to give a general exposition of the grounds for possession; rather, the cases where co-ownership gives rise to problems will be considered.

Residential tenancies A method of preventing a tenant from acquiring full security of tenure under the Rent Act 1977 is to take advantage of the resident landlord exception. Under section 12 of the Act,[47] a tenancy granted after August 14, 1974, shall not be a protected tenancy[48] if the dwelling-house forms part only of a building and the tenancy was granted by a person who occupied as his residence another dwelling-house which forms part of the same building.[49]

One resident landlord If there are joint landlords and only one of them resided in the tenanted property, then that landlord can rely on this provision.[50] It is not clear if the landlord who had not occupied could also rely on the residence of his co-owner to secure possession. It is thought that, as the tenancy is not protected, he should in principle be able to do so.

Possession actions Under the Rent Act 1977, the grounds for possession are divided into discretionary grounds and mandatory grounds. In the former category, the court must be satisfied that it is reasonable for possession to be granted[51] and either that the landlord has offered the tenant suitable alternative accommodation, or one of the Cases listed in Part 1 of Schedule 15 to the Act is made out.[52] Some of these Cases present difficulty when co-ownership occurs and those that do will be considered in turn, looking first at situations where there are joint landlords.

Discretionary grounds

Case 9 Under Case 9, a court may order possession where the dwelling-house is reasonably required by the landlord for occupation as a residence for:

(a) himself, or
(b) any son or daughter of his over 18 years of age, or
(c) his father or mother, or
(d) the father or mother of his wife or husband,

provided the landlord did not become a landlord by purchase.

---

[47] As amended by Housing Act 1980, s.65(1).
[48] It becomes instead a restricted contract: Rent Act 1977, s.20.
[49] For detailed consideration of this section which does not extend to a landlord who occupies a flat in a purpose-built block of flats, see Farrand and Arden, *Rent Acts and Regulations* (2nd ed., 1981) pp. 45–49.
[50] *Cooper* v. *Tait* (1984) 48 P. & C.R. 410.
[51] Rent Act 1977, s.98(1)(a).
[52] *Ibid.* s.98(1)(b).

Application of Case 9 to joint landlords

In *Baker* v. *Lewis*,[53] it was held that where there were joint landlords who both wished to take up residence in the tenanted property, they could rely on this case: the singular, "landlord" included the plural.[54] Divergent views were expressed as to whether if only one of the landlords reasonably required the dwelling-house as a residence, the Case applied. These doubts were resolved in *McIntyre* v. *Hardcastle*,[55] where it was held that reliance could not be placed on the Case in these circumstances.

It was held that the Case must be construed in the following way. In part (a) himself must be read as themselves; in part (b) any son or daughter of his means any son or daughter[56] of theirs and in (c) his father or mother is to be read as their father or mother.[57] Part (d) was added to this Case after *McIntyre* v. *Hardcastle* and must, for obvious reasons, be construed only in the singular.[58]

Trustees

If the landlords are trustees, problems also arise. In *Parker* v. *Rosenberg*[59] trustees for sale sought possession for a beneficiary under the trust. Despite the beneficiary being a co-plaintiff the action failed. The trustees did not want possession and the beneficiary was not a landlord. The solution is for the beneficiary to grant the lease. This will give rise to a tenancy by estoppel, to which the Rent Act applies. If he then requires the dwelling-house as a residence, he can rely on this case.[60]

Greater hardship provision

It should be noted that even if the landlords come within Case 9, the court may not make an order for possession if it is satisfied, having regard to all the circumstances of the case that greater hardship would be caused by making the order than by refusing it.[61]

Case 8: employees

Under Case 8, possession may be granted if the dwelling-house is reasonably required by the landlord for occupation as a residence for some person engaged in his whole-time employment. The issue of whether, if there are joint landlords, the employee has to be employed by both of them has yet to arise. It is submitted, by analogy with *McIntyre* v. *Hardcastle* that this will be necessary. There is no greater hardship provision with regard to this Case.

Case 11

Owner-occupiers Under Case 11 of Schedule 15 to the Rent Act 1977, the court must order possession where a person who, at any time before the letting, occupied the dwelling-house as his residence, let it on a regulated tenancy[62] and, the dwelling-house is required as a residence for the owner or any member of his

---

[53] [1947] K.B. 186.
[54] Interpretation Act 1889, s.1. See now Interpretation Act 1978, s.6(c).
[55] [1948] 2 K.B. 82. Applied in the context of what is now s.30(1)(g) of the Landlord and Tenant Act 1954 in *Wetherall & Co. Ltd.* v. *Stone* [1950] 2 All E.R. 1209.
[56] A daughter who is also an equitable co-owner of the freehold is nevertheless within this case: *Bostock* v. *Tacher De La Pagerie* (1987) 19 H.L.R. 358.
[57] [1948] 2 K.B. at 89, *per* Tucker L.J.
[58] Pettit, *Private Sector Tenancies* (2nd ed., 1981) p. 209.
[59] [1947] K.B. 371.
[60] *Stratford* v. *Syrrett* [1958] 1 Q.B. 507.
[61] Rent Act 1977, Sched. 15, Pt. III, para. 1. The onus of proving this is on the tenant: *Robinson* v. *Donovan* [1946] 2 All E.R. 731.
[62] Rent Act 1977, Sched. 15, Pt. V, para. 2.

family who resided with the owner when he last occupied the dwelling-house as a residence.[63] To take advantage of this Case, the landlord must give to the tenant, prior to the letting, written notice that possession may be recovered under this Case. This requirement can be waived by the court if it is just and equitable to do so.

Possession required by one landlord

It is important that this Case eschews the word "landlord." The difference in wording was regarded as a sufficient ground to distinguish *McIntyre* v. *Hardcastle* by the House of Lords in *Tilling* v. *Whiteman*,[64] where it was held by the majority that one of two joint landlords could recover possession under this Case. It would seem to be essential, however, that if one of the joint landlords seeks possession he must have been in occupation at some time prior to the letting. If A and B are joint landlords and only A was in occupation prior to the letting, it is submitted that A could recover possession under this Case but that B could not. However, if both A and B had been in occupation, though not together, for periods before the lease, the fact that B's occupation preceded A's would not, of itself, preclude B from recovering under this Case.

Importance of occupation

Expedited procedure

If possession is sought under this Case, the landlord can, instead of bringing an action for possession, apply by way of originating application. This must be accompanied by an affidavit to the effect that the tenant had been served with a written notice prior to the tenancy,[65] although this can be waived if just and equitable to do so, if the landlord honestly but wrongly states that the written notice had been served.[66] By using this procedure, possession can be obtained within seven days.

Case 12

Retirement A second mandatory ground for possession where the existence of joint landlords may cause difficulty is Case 12. Under this Case, possession must be granted if the landlord intends to occupy the dwelling-house at such time as he might retire from regular employment and has let it on a regulated tenancy prior to retirement. Possession can also be obtained under this Case, if the owner has died and the dwelling-house is required as a residence for a member of his family who was living with him at the time of his death or is required by a successor in title as his residence or for the purpose of disposing of it with vacant possession.[67]

Death of owner

Joint landlords

If there are joint landlords, then to come within the Case, it would seem to be necessary that both of them qualify. This is because the wording is similar to that used in Case 9 and so the reasoning in *McIntyre* v. *Hardcastle* should apply rather than that in *Tilling* v. *Whiteman*.

---

[63] Inserted by Rent (Amendment) Act 1985, s.1(1) to reverse *Pocock* v. *Steel* [1984] 1 W.L.R. 229.
[64] [1980] A.C. 1.
[65] Rent Act (County Court Proceedings for Possession) Rules 1981 (S.I. 1981 No. 139).
[66] *Minay* v. *Sentongo* (1982) 126 S.J. 674.
[67] Rent Act 1977, Sched. 15, Pt. V, para. 2(*b*)–(*d*). See also para. 2(*e*) and (*f*). As drafted, the case would not seem to apply to the self-employed: Farrand and Arden, above n. 49, p. 208.

Statutory grounds for possession

Conduct by the tenant Under both the Rent Act 1977 and the Housing Act 1985, the landlord may obtain possession as a result of certain conduct by the tenant. The provisions contained in Schedule 2 to the Housing Act 1985, which relate to the public sector, are closely modelled on the Cases for possession provided in Part 1 of Schedule 15 to the Rent Act 1977. For ease of exposition only the provisions of the 1977 Act will be referred to. The principles stated apply *mutatis mutandis* to the 1985 Act.

Part 1 of Schedule 15 lists a number of Cases whereby the court may order possession if it is reasonable to do so. Various types of conduct by the tenant are referred to in those Cases. The difficulty is that, ordinarily "tenant" is construed to mean all of the tenants if there is a joint tenancy. Consequently the view has been expressed that where there is a joint tenancy and there is a ground for possession against only one of them, it is not easy to read the Act as authorising any order for possession.[68] Despite this doubt, it is thought that the problems are more apparent than real.

Case 1 Under Case 1, possession may be ordered if the tenant is in arrears with the rent or in breach of other obligations under the lease. As the tenants are jointly and severally liable for obligations under the tenancy, the existence of a joint tenancy should not occasion any problems.

Case 2 Possession may be granted under Case 2 if the tenant has been guilty of conduct which is a nuisance or annoyance to adjoining occupiers[69] or has been convicted of using the dwelling-house or allowing it to be used for immoral[70] or illegal purposes. The Case extends to the acts of those residing with the tenant. This seems more apt to cover licensees of the tenant **Position of** rather than joint tenants.[71] Nevertheless, as the rationale of the **innocent joint** Case relates to conduct and the possible stigma attaching to the **tenants** property, it is submitted that if one joint tenant is guilty of misconduct within the Case, possession can be ordered despite the innocence of the other. That factor may be a consideration, however, in assessing whether it is reasonable to order possession.

Cases 3 and 4 Under Cases 3 and 4 a landlord is enabled to recover possession if the tenant or a person residing or lodging with him has caused the condition of the house,[72] or furniture provided for use under the tenancy, to deteriorate by waste, neglect or default. Possession can be ordered if the tenant has not taken such steps as he ought reasonably to have taken for the removal of the **Position of** lodger. The difficulty here is that one joint tenant cannot evict **innocent joint** the other, so that it is hard to see what reasonable steps an **tenants** innocent tenant can take to remove the other tenant, who is guilty of misconduct. It might appear, therefore, that the Court cannot order possession. The better view, however, is thought to be that the Court would, in an appropriate case, order possession,

---

[68] Megarry, *The Rent Acts* (10th ed., 1967) p. 262.
[69] The term "neighbours" is used in Housing Act 1985, Sched. 2. No difference in substance is caused by this.
[70] This does not include cohabitation: *Heglibiston Establishment* v. *Heyman* (1978) 36 P. & C.R. 351.
[71] *Green* v. *Lewis* [1947–51] 1 C.L.C. 8647.
[72] Case 4 in the Housing Act 1985 is wider, referring to deterioration in the condition of common parts.

focusing on the property damage rather than any attempt to oust a joint tenant. In the public sector, this problem could be overcome by the innocent joint tenant serving a notice to quit, having previously obtained the council's agreement to grant him a new tenancy.

Case 5

Service of notice to quit by one joint tenant

Case 5, which is not replicated in the Housing Act 1985, allows possession to be granted when a landlord has acted upon a notice to quit served by the tenant in such a way that it would be prejudicial to him not to get possession. Notice to quit served by one of a number of joint tenants is sufficient to terminate the protected tenancy and give rise to a statutory tenancy. If the landlord then contracts to sell the dwelling-house with vacant possession, it is thought that the Case will be satisfied. Nevertheless, if he takes this action without ascertaining the wishes of the remaining joint tenants who were not party to the notice to quit, it would, it is submitted, be unreasonable to make the order.

Succession

Under the general law, on the death of one joint tenant the title simply devolves on the remaining tenants by the operation of the right of survivorship. If there were only two joint tenants, on the death of one, the survivor is solely entitled to the lease and cannot look to the deceased's estate for any contribution to the rent.[73] If the deceased tenant was protected under the Rent Act 1977 or the Housing Act 1985, this principle may be modified.

Statutory succession

Under both the 1977 and 1985 Acts, provision is made for succession to a protected or statutory tenancy in the former and to a secure tenancy in the latter. Under section 2(1)(*b*) of the Rent Act 1977, Part 1 of Schedule 1 to the Act has effect to determine what person, if any, is the statutory tenant of a dwelling-house after the death of a person who, immediately prior to his death, was a protected or statutory tenant.

Rent Act 1977

Under paragraph 2 of Schedule 1, the surviving spouse of the original tenant shall become the statutory tenant provided that he or she occupied the dwelling-house immediately before the death of the original tenant. If there is no such person, then under paragraph 3 a person who was a member of the tenant's family who was residing with him at the time of and for a period of six months immediately prior to his death becomes the statutory tenant. Thereafter, upon the death of the successor, provided he was still a statutory tenant, the succession provisions operate again in the same way.[74]

Housing Act 1985

Similar provisions are included in section 87 of the Housing Act 1985, save that, unlike the position under the 1977 Act, there can only be one succession. In addition if the succession is by a member of the tenant's family, that person must have resided with the tenant at the time of death and for a period of 12 months immediately prior to the tenant's death.

Death of a joint tenant If a lease is held by joint tenants, it is important to know if the survivor was living in the

---

[73] *Cunningham-Reid* v. *Public Trustee* [1944] K.B. 602.
[74] Rent Act 1977, Sched. 1, paras. 5–7.

SUCCESSION 75

Succession in the public sector

dwelling-house at the time when the other one died. If that is the case, then the right of survivorship operates in the normal way: the survivor becomes the tenant. In the public sector, however, the survivor is deemed to have become a tenant by succession.[75] This means there can be no further succession. Thus if a husband and wife are secure joint tenants and the husband dies, his widow becomes the sole tenant. Upon her death, any children living with her at the time are not entitled to succeed to the tenancy.

Succession in the private sector

Under the Rent Act 1977, there is no similar provision and, accordingly, the survivor of two or more joint tenants should not be treated as a tenant by succession. Two further transmissions on death are therefore possible.

Non-occupying joint tenants

A conflict can arise between the general law and the statutory code of succession if the contractual tenancy is still in existence when the tenant dies. A member of his family may have been living with him for the requisite period prior to his death but, under his will, the tenancy is left to a third party. This occurred in *Moodie* v. *Hosegood*[76] where it was held that the contractual tenancy which passed under the will went into abeyance and that the person living with the deceased tenant became statutory tenant by succession.

A similar problem can arise if there is a joint tenancy. In *Halford's Executors* v. *Boden*[77] the daughter of one of a member of joint tenants lived with him in the dwelling-house. The other surviving joint tenant lived elsewhere. On the father's death, it was held that a statutory tenancy arose in the daughter's favour, which suspended the contractual tenancy which was vested by survivorship in the surviving joint tenant.[78] Although only county court authority, it is submitted that this result is correct in principle and will be followed.

Suspension of contractual tenancy

Who is a member of the family? Because the statutory transmission on death takes priority over testamentary provision or the normal right of survivorship, it is appropriate to consider who is entitled to succeed to the tenancy on death. If the original tenant's spouse was residing in the dwelling-house, then that person succeeds. If not, then it is necessary to determine whether people who shared residence with him were members of his family.

Public sector

The Housing Act 1985, s.113 defines people who are members of the tenant's family and therefore entitled to succeed to the secure tenancy. This includes the spouse of that person or a person who lived with the tenant as husband or wife. This latter definition does not include the survivor of a homosexual union.[79] Also included as members of the family are parents, grandparents, legitimate and illegitimate children, brothers, sisters, uncles, aunts, nephews and nieces. Further, a relationship by marriage is treated as a relationship of blood, as is a relationship of half-blood. Finally, a step-child of the tenant is treated as his child.

---

[75] Housing Act 1985, s.88(1)(*b*).
[76] [1952] A.C. 61.
[77] [1953] 103 L.J. 78.
[78] This was unaffected by the daughter being a minor.
[79] *Harrogate Borough Council* v. *Simpson* (1985) 17 H.L.R. 205. See generally H. W. Wilkinson (1987) 137 New L.J. 586.

Private sector

Unlike the Housing Act 1985, the Rent Act 1977 contains no definition or list of who is to be regarded as a member of the tenant's family. This is left to common law. In substance, however, the position in the private sector is the same as that which pertains under the 1985 Act.

Cohabitees

Originally, the position was that a person who cohabited with the tenant was not regarded as being a member of his family.[80] The position now is that if a couple were cohabiting in a stable relationship, equivalent to that of a married couple,[81] then the survivor will be regarded as a member of the deceased tenant's family.[82] This is true even if the tenant has a spouse but lived in a stable union with another partner.[83]

Platonic relationships

Although the 1977 Act contains no reference to a couple living together as husband and wife, it seems clear that it is only this relationship which will constitute the surviving partner as being a member of the tenant's family. Thus it has been held that a platonic relationship akin to that of aunt and nephew did not constitute the male survivor a member of the tenant's family in the absence of a blood relationship.[84] It is also thought probable that a surviving homosexual partner will not be considered a member of the tenant's family.

Qualifying members

It may transpire that more than one member of the tenant's family had resided with him for the requisite period prior to his death. In this event, it has been held that there can be no joint succession; one person alone can succeed.[85] The notion of joint succession was regarded as giving rise to fearful confusion and absurd consequences,[86] although it is difficult to see the force of this.

Resolution of disputes between qualifying members

If there is more than one person qualified to succeed, any dispute should be resolved by agreement amongst them.[87] In the absence of such agreement, the county court decides between them. In so doing, attention is paid to any wishes of the deceased, although this is not a decisive factor.[88] It is not necessary for the landlord to be party to the resolution of the dispute.[89] This is so, except in the case of succession to a secure periodic tenancy where, in default of agreement, the landlord is given the right, under section 89(1)(b) of the Housing Act 1985, to choose the tenant.

The right to buy

When the legislative framework of council housing was reshaped by the Housing Act 1980, and now consolidated in the 1985 Act, the most significant right conferred upon tenants was the right to buy. Unusually, the position when there is a joint tenancy was provided for and the law can therefore be stated fairly briefly.

[80] *Gammans* v. *Elkins* [1950] 2 K.B. 328.
[81] *Helby* v. *Rafferty* [1979] 1 W.L.R. 13. Cf. *Chios Property Investment Co.* v. *Lopez* (1987) 138 New L.J. 20.
[82] *Dyson Holdings Ltd.* v. *Fox* [1976] Q.B. 503.
[83] *Watson* v. *Lucas* [1980] 1 W.L.R. 1493.
[84] *Carega Properties S.A.* v. *Sharratt* [1979] 1 W.L.R. 928. See also *Sefton Holdings Ltd.* v. *Cairns* (1987) 138 New L.J. 19.
[85] *Dealex Properties Ltd.* v. *Brooks* [1966] 1 Q.B. 542.
[86] *Ibid.* at 550–551, *per* Harman L.J.; at 554, *per* Diplock and Russell L.JJ.
[87] Rent Act 1977, Sched. 1, paras. 3 and 7.
[88] *Williams* v. *Williams* [1970] 1 W.L.R. 1530.
[89] *General Management Ltd.* v. *Locke* (1980) 255 E.G. 155.

Joint tenancies	If the dwelling-house is a house and the landlord owns the freehold, a secure tenant has the right to buy the freehold.[90] If the secure tenancy is a joint tenancy then, whether or not each of the joint tenants occupies the dwelling-house as his only or principal home, the right to buy belongs jointly to all of them or to such one or more of them as may be agreed between them. Such an agreement is not valid unless the person or at least one of the persons to whom the right to buy is to belong occupies the dwelling-house as his only or principal residence.[91]
Occupation by one joint tenant	The only potential source of difficulty here is where there is a joint tenancy but only one of the joint tenants occupies the house. If it cannot be agreed that the occupier has the right to buy the house, then it would appear that it cannot be exercised by him alone as the right to buy, in the absence of agreement, belongs to the joint tenants jointly. In such circumstances, the occupying tenant should ask the council to grant him a new tenancy and, if they are willing, terminate the existing one by service of a notice to quit. He would then have the sole right to buy.
Joint tenancy after purchase	In addition to dealing with the situation where the lease is jointly owned, the 1985 Act makes provision for joint purchase when the lease is vested in only one person but occupation is shared. Under section 123(1) a secure tenant may, when serving notice of the exercise of his right to buy, pursuant to section 122, require that not more than three members of his family, who are not joint tenants but occupy the dwelling-house as their only or principal home, shall share the right to buy with him. He may only do so if the member of his family is his spouse or has been residing with him for 12 months prior to serving the notice or the landlord consents. The right to buy then belongs to them all jointly and they are treated as joint tenants.[92]
Registration	It should be observed that, on the completion of the sale under the right to buy provisions, title should be registered irrespective of whether the house is in an area of compulsory registration.[93]
Length of residence and calculation of discount	**Discount** In addition to conferring upon tenants the right to buy, the Act also gives a discount from the price payable. This is based upon the length of residence. When the right to buy is exercised by joint tenants, then the Housing Act 1985, s.129(3) provides that regard is had to the occupation of the joint tenant whose length of residence will produce the largest discount. The discount to which the tenant is entitled is calculated under section 129. For up to three years residence, the discount is 32 per cent.[94] Thereafter the discount is increased in the case of a

---

[90] Housing Act 1985, s.118(1); Sched. 4, para. 9.
[91] *Ibid.* s.118(2).
[92] *Ibid.* s.123(2)(3).
[93] *Ibid.* s.154.
[94] To be eligible to exercise the right to buy, the tenant must have resided in the house for at least two years: Housing Act 1985, s.119(1). In the case of a joint tenancy, this is satisfied by the residence of one of them: *ibid.* s.119(2). A higher rate of discount is available in the case of flats: Housing and Planning Act 1986, s.2(2). The maximum discount for a dwelling-house is £35,000: Housing (Right to Buy) (Maximum Discount) Order 1986 (S.I. 1986 No. 2193).

house by 1 per cent. for every year's extra residence up to a maximum discount of 60 per cent. In the case of a flat, the discount under the Housing and Planning Act 1986, s.2(2)(*b*) is 44 per cent. plus 2 per cent. per annum for each complete year by which the qualifying period exceeds two years, up to a maximum of 70 per cent.

Covenant to repay on resale   If a discount is given on the purchase of a house then, the conveyance must contain a covenant by the tenant to repay the discount if the house is resold within a period of three years from the original sale.[95] When this occurs, should the tenant exercise the right to buy on a subsequent occasion, the discount he is entitled to on that transaction will be reduced by the amount of discount previously received, disregarding any of the original discount that has been repaid.[96] Where a discount has been received by joint tenants, then each for this purpose is to be treated as having received an equal share.[97]

Right to a mortgage   Together with the right to buy conferred on the secure tenant, he is also given the right to leave an amount of the purchase price outstanding on the security of a first mortgage.[98] Where there is a joint right to buy, then the right to a mortgage is also joint.[99]

Amounts that can be borrowed   The amount which it is possible to leave outstanding on the mortgage is calculated in accordance with the Housing Act 1985, s.133 in conjunction with the Housing (Right to Buy) Mortgage Limit Regulations 1980.[1] Where the right to a mortgage belongs to more than one person, then the amount that can be left outstanding is an aggregate amount of the available incomes after each has been multiplied by the appropriate multipliers under the regulations.[2]

Multipliers   Under the regulations, the principal income must first be ascertained. This is then multiplied by the appropriate factor as determined by age. This is determined as follows.

Age of Tenant	Multiplier
Under 60	2.5
Over 60 but under 65	2.0
65 and over	1.0

The multiplier for the non-principal income is one.

Example   A husband and wife, both aged 45, exercise their right to buy. His available income is £6,000 and hers is £4,000. The total that can be left outstanding on the mortgage is £6,000 × 2·5 + £4,000 × 1. The sum is £19,000.

---

[95] Housing and Planning Act 1986, s.2(3). The amount repayable is reduced by one-third for each complete year that elapses after the original sale.
[96] Housing Act 1985, s.130(1)(4).
[97] *Ibid.* s.130(3).
[98] *Ibid.* s.132(1)(*a*).
[99] *Ibid.* s.132(3).
[1] (S.I. 1980 No. 1423), retained in force by the Housing (Consequential Provisions) Act 1985, s.2.
[2] Housing Act 1985, s.133(2)(*b*).

5 THE PROTECTION AND REGULATION OF OCCUPATION

In modern society, enforceable rights to remain in occupation of a home can be as important as a claim to a share in the proceeds of sale of it. This is particularly marked in the context of leasehold property where, under the Rent Act 1977, on the termination of the contractual tenancy, enforceable rights of occupation remain under the ensuing statutory tenancy despite the tenant having no beneficial ownership of the house. An account of co-ownership must, therefore, concern itself with shared rights of occupation, not necessarily derived from shared ownership of the property, and how the law protects and regulates rights of occupation.

Spouse's right of occupation

At common law, a wife who did not have a beneficial interest in the matrimonial home had only limited rights of occupation in it. By virtue of the marriage, she acquired the right of cohabitation with her husband and the right to support from him.[1] This was only enforceable indirectly by an order for the restoration of conjugal rights buttressed by sanctions against the husband for non-compliance with any such order.[2] Additionally, it seemed that she had a right to restrain by injunction any dealing with the matrimonial home by her husband in a manner which infringed those rights.[3]

Deserted wife's equity Despite the somewhat limited nature of the rights of a wife without a beneficial interest in the home, a series of cases in the 1950s nevertheless held that she had a right of occupation enforceable, not only against her husband, but also against third parties.[4] This right, which was termed "the deserted wife's equity" was regarded as a form of licence, protected in equity, and binding upon all but the bona fide purchaser for value without notice. Its status was always regarded as highly controversial until, in *National Provincial Bank* v. *Ainsworth*,[5] the House of Lords held there to be no such thing and that a wife, with no beneficial interest in the matrimonial home, had merely personal rights against her husband which could not survive a disposition of the property by him.

Statutory right of occupation The position of a wife with no beneficial interest in the matrimonial home was considered to be unacceptably vulnerable. In response, the Matrimonial Homes

---

[1] *National Provincial Bank* v. *Ainsworth* [1965] A.C. 1175 at 1243–1248, *per* Lord Wilberforce.
[2] *Weldon* v. *Weldon* (1883) 9 P.D. 52. Such an action has now been abolished: Matrimonial Proceedings and Property Act 1970, s.20.
[3] *Lee* v. *Lee* [1952] 2 Q.B. 489.
[4] *Bendall* v. *McWhirter* [1952] 2 Q.B. 466; *Street* v. *Denham* [1954] 1 W.L.R. 624; *Westminster Bank Ltd.* v. *Lee* [1956] Ch. 7.
[5] [1965] A.C. 1175.

Matrimonial Homes Act 1983

Act 1967 was enacted, the amended provisions of which are now to be found in the Matrimonial Homes Act 1983. The Act deals even-handedly with both spouses but, for ease of exposition, it will be assumed that the legal owner of the matrimonial home is the husband.

Section 1 of the Act provides that where one spouse is entitled to occupy a dwelling-house by virtue of a beneficial estate or interest or contract or by virtue of any enactment giving him the right to remain in occupation then the spouse not so entitled has the right, if in occupation, not to be evicted or excluded from the house or any part thereof by the other spouse except with the leave of the court given by an order under this section. If she is not in occupation, she has the right, with the leave of the court, to enter into and occupy the dwelling-house.

Entitlement under the Act

The first limitation on those entitled to the statutory right of occupation is that it is only conferred on spouses. This includes parties to polygamous marriages[6] but excludes unmarried cohabiting couples. In addition, the statutory right of occupation applies only in respect of a house that has at one time been a matrimonial home.[7] If the husband is the tenant of a house and it has never been used as a matrimonial home, his wife has no rights under the Act with regard to that property.[8]

Co-owners

The 1967 Act did not confer a statutory right of occupation on a wife who had an equitable interest in the matrimonial home. It was later thought that this might put an equitable co-owner in a worse position with regard to a purchaser than a wife with no proprietary interest at all.[9] Under section 1(11) of the 1983 Act a spouse who has an equitable interest in a dwelling-house or in the proceeds of sale thereof, not being a spouse in whom is vested the legal estate in the dwelling-house, is to be treated for the purpose only of determining whether she has rights of occupation under this section as not being entitled to occupy the dwelling-house by virtue of that equitable interest. This means, quite simply, that in addition to her rights as a beneficial co-owner, she also enjoys the occupation rights conferred by the Act.[10]

Registration Before the enactment of the original Matrimonial Homes Act 1967, perhaps the greatest weakness in the wife's position was that if the husband mortgaged the property or sold it, she, in the absence of a proprietary claim, had no enforceable rights against the mortgagee or purchaser. The Act overcomes this problem by providing that the statutory right of occupation can be enforced against a third party. Section 2(1) of the 1983 Act

Right of occupation enforceable against third parties

provides that during the subsistence of the marriage,[11] where one spouse is entitled to occupy a dwelling-house by virtue of a beneficial estate or interest in it, the other spouse's right of occupation be a charge on that estate or interest created at whichever of the following is the latest:

---

[6] Matrimonial Homes Act 1983, s.10(2).
[7] *Ibid.* s.1(10).
[8] *Hall* v. *King* (1987) 19 H.L.R. 440.
[9] For the enforcement of beneficial interests against purchasers, see Chap. 7.
[10] For a similar provision with regard to legal joint tenants, see Matrimonial Homes Act 1983, s.9.
[11] The statutory right of occupation does not generally survive the ending of the marriage: *ibid.* s.2(4); see p. 84 below.

(a) the date when the spouse so entitled acquires the estate or interest;
(b) the date of the marriage; and
(c) January 1, 1968.

Section 2(5) then further provides that if a wife registers her statutory charge then the statutory rights have like effect against a person deriving title from the other husband as they would have done against her husband. In other words, a purchaser is bound by the statutory right of occupation. This is also the case if the husband becomes bankrupt, as the trustee in bankruptcy is now bound by the wife's right, if registered.[12]

Trustee in bankruptcy

Methods of registration

In the case of land where title is registered, the appropriate method of protecting the statutory right of occupation after February 14, 1983, is by registering a notice under the Land Registration Act 1925. The right is not capable of being an overriding interest.[13] This right used to be protected by the lodging of a caution. Cautions lodged prior to February 13, 1983, remain effective by virtue of section 11 of the Act.

Unregistered land

In the case of unregistered land, the wife should protect her interest by registering a Class F land charge against her husband.[14] This, unfortunately, may not be an easy task as, to be effective, registration must be against the name of her husband.[15] This means the version of his name as it appears on the title deeds and not as it appears on his birth or marriage certificate.[16] Registration against an incomplete version of the husband's name will be ineffective, provided that a search is requisitioned against the full names.[17] If registration is effected against what may be fairly described as a version of the full name, it will be effective against a purchaser who either searches against the wrong name or does not search at all.[18] There may well be problems for the wife in ascertaining the name which is on the conveyance, this difficulty being a direct consequence of the defective system of registration against estate owners introduced in 1925 by the Land Charges Act.

Who can register?

The Act makes clear that only spouses are given a statutory right of occupation. It is only proper to register this right, however, in order to protect occupation rights. If registration is effected simply to cause difficulty in disposing of the house and not to secure occupation rights, this is an abuse of the Act and the registration will be cancelled.[19] It is not essential for the wife to be in occupation, however, in order to register her statutory right. Under section 1(1)(b) of the 1983 Act, if a wife is not in occupation, she has a right, with the leave of the court, to enter and occupy. It was originally held that until leave had been given, she had no right to occupy and so nothing to register.[20] This

---

[12] Insolvency Act 1986, s.336(2). For insolvency, see Chap. 6.
[13] Matrimonial Homes Act 1983, s. 2(8)(b).
[14] Land Charges Act 1972, s.2(7).
[15] *Ibid.* s.3(1).
[16] *Standard Property Investment plc* v. *British Plastics Federation* (1987) 53 P. & C.R. 25.
[17] *Diligent Finance Co. Ltd.* v. *Alleyne* (1972) P. & C.R. 346.
[18] *Oak Co-operative Building Society* v. *Blackburn* [1968] Ch. 370.
[19] *Barnett* v. *Hassett* [1981] 1 W.L.R. 1385.
[20] *Protheroe* v. *Protheroe* [1970] 1 W.L.R. 1480.

decision was overruled in *Watts* v. *Waller*[21] and the position now is that a wife seeking to go into occupation may validly register her statutory right.

One house Finally, it should be noticed that only one charge should be registered at any one given time. Section 3 of the Act provides that where one spouse is entitled to a registered charge in respect of each of two or more dwelling-houses only one of the charges shall be registered at any one time and, if more than one is registered, the Chief Land Registrar shall cancel the registration of the charge first registered.

Effect of registration The principal effect of registration of a charge is to enable the wife's statutory rights to subsist against a purchaser. This may cause serious conveyancing difficulty as is shown by *Wroth* v. *Tyler*.[22] Mr. Tyler, the sole registered proprietor of a house, wished to move into a smaller house on his retirement. He exchanged contracts to sell it for £6,000 but a day later his wife lodged a caution to protect her statutory charge. This was not known to Mr. Tyler until the purchasers discovered it upon making their search prior to completion. Mrs. Tyler, who was in no danger of being made homeless, but was unwilling to move, adamantly refused to release her rights.[23] This caused her husband to be in breach of contract in that he was unable to give vacant possession. These events occurred at a time of spiralling house prices. At the time of the breach of contract the property was worth £7,500 and at the date of the hearing, £11,500. Megarry J. assessed the damages at £5,500, being the difference between the contract price and the current value of the property.[24]

Precautions The result of this case was financially catastrophic for Mr. Tyler. To avoid the risk of this recurring, a husband should, prior to entering a contract of sale, ensure that his wife is willing to move. In that event, as a counsel of extreme prudence, he should secure from her a written release of her rights under the Act. This will avoid a post-exchange registration causing havoc to the conveyancing transaction. If the charge has already been registered, he will not be informed of this at the time by the Land Registry[25] and, again, should not enter into any contracts affecting the property unless he can secure her consent to the transaction.

Mortgages A second important consequence of a wife registering her statutory charge is that it helps to safeguard her position against a mortgagee of the property. Normally, the purchase of a matrimonial home will be financed by a mortgage. If her husband leaves her, having defaulted on the mortgage, she **Right to take over** is entitled under section 1(5) of the 1983 Act to take over **the mortgage** mortgage payments which are then as good as if they were made **payments** by her husband, the mortgagor. If she has registered her statutory charge, she is entitled under section 8(3) to be given

---

[21] [1973] Q.B. 153.
[22] [1974] Ch. 30. See D. G. Barnsley [1974] C.L.P. 76.
[23] Matrimonial Homes Act 1983, s.6. The court may, however, in the exercise of its discretion under s.1(2)(3) terminate the wife's right of occupation as against a purchaser: *Kaur* v. *Gill*, *The Independent*, March 16, 1988.
[24] See now *Johnson* v. *Agnew* [1980] A.C. 387 at 400, *per* Lord Wilberforce.
[25] Ruoff and Roper, *Registered Conveyancing* (5th ed., 1986) p. 841. For criticism, see *Wroth* v. *Tyler* [1979] Ch. 20 at 29.

notice of any action for the enforcement of the mortgagee's security and to be made a party to the action.[26] Her chances of retaining possession of the home will correspondingly be increased.[27]

Non-registration One of the practical problems caused by the deserted wife's equity as developed at common law was the difficulty caused to purchasers and mortgagees. Its existence necessitated embarrassing enquiries prior to entry into the contract. To obviate this, the enforceability of the wife's right of occupation was made dependent on registration. The consequence of this is that the wife may lose her right of occupation by a transaction effected by her husband without her knowledge.

Void against purchasers If title to the land is unregistered, her statutory right is void against a purchaser of the land or any interest in the land unless it is registered.[28] This is so, irrespective of whether the purchaser knew of her existence and even if the purpose of the transaction was to defeat her rights.[29] If she has not registered her charge, her only chance to assert her statutory rights is to establish that the transaction effected by her husband was a sham.[30] If title is registered, a transferee takes subject to entries appearing on the register and to overriding interests.[31] The statutory charge cannot be an overriding interest and, therefore, if it has not been registered, a transferee will take free from her statutory rights.

If a wife has not registered her statutory charge, to assert any rights against a purchaser, she must establish a beneficial interest in the land.[32] She cannot rely on her status as a spouse.

Leasehold property[33] A spouse's statutory right of occupation applies to leasehold as well as freehold property. Because of the statutory regimes in existence, which confer security of tenure on tenants, special provisions are necessary to accommodate the right conferred by the 1983 Act.

Termination of the tenancy If the husband is the sole tenant of the property, he can terminate it by surrendering the lease. If he does this, the wife can nevertheless continue in occupation, provided that she has registered her statutory charge. In this event, the surrender shall have effect subject to the charge and the persons thereafter entitled to the other estate or interest shall, for so long as the estate or interest surrendered would have endured if not so surrendered, be treated for all purposes of this Act as deriving title to the other estate or interest under the other spouse by virtue of the surrender.[34]

Security of tenure If a tenancy is protected under section 1 of the Rent Act 1977, then on the termination of the tenancy, the person who was

---

[26] Matrimonial Homes Act 1983, s.8(2).
[27] The effect of insolvency will be considered in full in Chap. 6.
[28] Land Charges Act 1972, s.4(8).
[29] *Midland Bank Trust Co. Ltd.* v. *Green* [1981] A.C. 513.
[30] *Ferris* v. *Weaven* [1952] 2 All E.R. 233; *National Provincial Bank* v. *Ainsworth* [1965] A.C. 1175 at 1223 and 1257. See M. P. Thompson [1985] C.L.J. 280 at 286–289.
[31] Land Registration Act 1925, s.20.
[32] See Chap. 7.
[33] For the position with regard to cohabitees, see p. 94 below.
[34] Matrimonial Homes Act 1983, s.2(6).

the tenant immediately before the end of that tenancy will become the statutory tenant of the dwelling-house if and so long as he occupies the dwelling-house as his residence.[35] Under section 1(6) of the Matrimonial Homes Act 1983, a spouse's occupation by virtue of this section shall be treated for the purposes of the Rent Act 1977 as possession by the other spouse. The effect of this is that if the tenant leaves the property and his wife remains in possession then, even if he has no intention to return, the statutory tenancy will continue in her favour while she continues to occupy the dwelling-house. Her position is equated with that of a joint tenant.[36]

Council housing Security of tenure is conferred on council tenants by section 82 of the Housing Act 1985. This prevents the landlord from terminating a secure tenancy. For a tenancy to be secure, the tenant condition must be satisfied.[37] This is defined by section 81 to mean that the tenant is an individual and occupies the dwelling-house as his only or principal home. As with the private sector, section 2(6) of the 1983 Act provides that a spouse's occupation by virtue of this section shall be treated for the purposes of the Housing Act as occupation by the other spouse. If the tenant simply leaves the council house, his wife remains as a secure tenant. If, however, he ends the lease there is no statutory tenancy in the public sector. For the deserted wife to remain, she will have to rely on the council granting her a new tenancy.

Transfer of tenancies A wife's statutory right of occupation does not survive the termination of the marriage. Power is given to the court by Schedule 1 to the 1983 Act to transfer protected, statutory and secure tenancies from one spouse to the other on the making of an order to terminate the marriage or for judicial separation. This can also be done under the Matrimonial Causes Act 1973, however, and there seems little advantage in proceeding under this Schedule.[38] Once the marriage has been terminated, however, there is no power to order such a transfer.[39] If no application for a transfer is made before the decree absolute then the former wife will lose all her occupation rights if her former husband ends the tenancy.[40]

Regulation of occupation—ouster orders

As has been seen, a spouse has been given by statute considerable protection in so far as occupation of the matrimonial home is concerned. These rights derive from the status of spouse and is not dependent on the possession of a beneficial interest in the home. At least as important as these rights to stay in the home is

---

[35] Rent Act 1977, s.2(1)(*a*).
[36] See p. 67 above.
[37] Housing Act 1985, s.79.
[38] See annotations to Matrimonial Homes Act 1983 by C. Hand.
[39] Except after an application for financial relief after an overseas divorce: Matrimonial and Family Proceedings Act 1984, s.22; Sched. 1.
[40] *Metropolitan Properties Co. Ltd.* v. *Cronan* (1982) 44 P. & C.R. 1.

Power to exclude a spouse from occupation

the power given to the courts to exclude either a spouse or a cohabitee from shared accommodation. As will be seen, the courts are now armed with considerable powers to make orders regulating the occupation of the home. Unfortunately, the statutory jurisdiction can, with justice, be described as "a hotchpotch of enactments,"[41] with the result that the law is more complex than it need be.

Jurisdiction to make ouster orders There are three statutes under which courts are expressly empowered to exclude a person from the home. These are the Matrimonial Homes Act 1983, the Domestic Violence and Matrimonial Proceedings Act 1976 and the Domestic Proceedings and Magistrates Courts Act 1978. It will first be convenient to consider the orders that can be made under each Act and then consider the principles that the courts adopt and the procedure to be followed.

Married couples

The provisions of the Matrimonial Homes Act 1983 and the Domestic Proceedings and Magistrates Courts Act 1978 can only be used by parties to a marriage. As has been seen, the 1983 Act confers on a spouse with no beneficial interest in the matrimonial home a statutory right to occupy it. As well as this, the Act also empowers the court to vary the occupation rights. Section 1(2) of the Act provides:

> "So long as one spouse has rights of occupation, either of the spouses may apply to the court for an order—
> (a) declaring, enforcing, restricting or terminating those rights, or
> (b) prohibiting, suspending or restricting the exercise by either spouse of the right to occupy the dwelling-house,[42] or
> (c) requiring either spouse to permit the exercise by the other of that right."[43]

Jurisdiction

The jurisdiction to make orders under this section is conferred, by section 1(a) of the Act on both the High Court and the county court, the jurisdiction of the county court being exercisable, notwithstanding that the net annual value for rating of the dwelling-house exceeds that for which the county court would ordinarily have jurisdiction.

The principles on which a court will exclude a spouse from the matrimonial home under this Act, whether permanently or temporarily, will be considered shortly. First, it is apposite to

Orders that can be made

point out the limits of the court's jurisdiction. The Act deals solely with occupation of the home. It does not confer any jurisdiction to make direct orders for the protection of the spouse or children personally. Neither does it empower a court to make orders prohibiting a spouse from the vicinity of the matrimonial home. Should these types of order be appropriate, an application should be made under one of the other statutes. It should be noted, however, that if the court makes an exclusion order under

---

[41] *Richards* v. *Richards* [1984] A.C. 174 at 206, *per* Lord Scarman.
[42] This includes part of a house. Matrimonial Homes Act 1983, s.3(a).
[43] Where the legal estate is vested in both spouses jointly, similar orders can be made under *ibid.* s.9.

Occupying spouse to make payments section 1(2), it may order the occupying spouse to make periodical payments to the other in respect of the occupation and also impose on either spouse obligations as to the repair and maintenance of the dwelling-house or the discharge of any liabilities in respect of it.[44] In appropriate cases, therefore, a spouse who has been ordered to leave the house may nevertheless be required to pay the mortgage instalments or the rent.

Magistrates court jurisdiction Under the 1983 Act, a spouse may apply to the High Court or county court for an order excluding the other from the matrimonial home. A similar order may also be obtained in the magistrates court, although the criteria for making such an award are rather different. Under section 16(3) of the Domestic Proceedings and Magistrates Courts Act 1978, either party to a marriage may apply to the court for an order requiring the respondent to leave the matrimonial home and/or an order prohibiting him from entering it. An order may also be made under section 16(4) in addition to an order under section 16(3) requiring the respondent to permit the applicant to enter and remain in the matrimonial home.

Violence The power given to the magistrates court to make an exclusion order is part of the legislative response to violence in the home. To obtain such an order, the applicant must show either that:

> "(a) the respondent has used violence against the person of the applicant or a child of the family, or
> (b) that the respondent has threatened to use violence against the person of the applicant or a child of the family and has used violence against some other person,[45] or
> (c) that the respondent has in contravention of an order made under subsection (2) [above] threatened to use violence against the person of the applicant or the child of the family,
>
> and that the applicant or a child of the family is in danger of being physically injured by the respondent (or would be in such danger if the applicant or child were to enter the matrimonial home)."[46]

Personal protection The order referred to in paragraph (c) is what is known as a personal protection order. Such an order can be obtained under section 16(2) prohibiting the respondent from using or threatening to use violence against the applicant or child of the family. Such an order may be granted if the court is satisfied that the respondent has used or threatened to use violence in the past and that it is necessary for the protection of the applicant or child of the family. No such order is available under the 1983 Act.

Power of arrest The court can, when making one of the orders under section 16 attach to it a power of arrest, whereby a constable may arrest without warrant a person whom he reasonably suspects to be in breach of a personal protection or an exclusion order.[47] The

---

[44] Matrimonial Homes Act 1983, s.1(3)(*b*)(*c*).
[45] An exclusion order can therefore be made against a person with a conviction for violence not directed towards a member of the family, *e.g.* a football hooligan.
[46] Domestic Proceedings and Magistrates Court Act 1978, s.16(3).
[47] *Ibid.* s.18(1)(2).

attachment of a power of arrest will be considered together with the similar jurisdiction under the Domestic Violence and Matrimonial Proceedings Act 1976.

Domestic Violence and Matrimonial Proceedings Act 1976 The third statute which empowers a court to exclude a person from a home is the Domestic Violence and Matrimonial Proceedings Act 1976. This Act resulted from a private member's Bill and was a direct response to the mounting evidence of violence occurring both between husband and wife and also cohabiting couples.[48] The central thrust of the Act is found in section 1, which provides:

> "Without prejudice to the jurisdiction of the High Court, on an application by a party to a marriage a county court shall have jurisdiction to grant an injunction containing one or more of the following provisions, namely—
> (a) a provision restraining the other party to the marriage from molesting the applicant;
> (b) a provision restraining the other party from molesting a child living with the applicant;
> (c) a provision excluding the other party from the matrimonial home or from a specified area in which the matrimonial home is included;
> (d) a provision requiring the other party to permit the applicant to enter and remain in the matrimonial home or a part of the matrimonial home;
> whether or not any other relief is sought in the proceedings."

Section 1(2) provides that subsection (1) above shall apply to a man and a woman who are living with each other in the same household as man and wife as it applies to the parties to a marriage and any reference to the matrimonial home shall be construed accordingly.

Section 2 of the Act enables the court to attach a power of arrest and this also applies to a man and woman living with each other in the same household as man and wife.

Jurisdiction One of the main features of the Act is that it enables an injunction to be granted whether or not other relief is sought in the proceedings. Before the Act, a court would only grant an injunction in support of an independent cause of action.[49] In the case of a married couple, this meant proceedings for divorce or judicial separation would have to be lodged in order to obtain injunctive relief. This is no longer necessary. The Act expressly confers jurisdiction on the county court to grant an injunction despite there being no claim to other relief. Although this was expressed to be without prejudice to the jurisdiction of the High Court, extended jurisdiction was not actually conferred on that court. It has since been held that the High Court does not

---

[48] For a particularly horrific example see First Special Report from the Select Committee on Violence in Marriage (1974–1975), para. 10. See also E. Pizzey, *Scream Quietly or the Neighbours Will Hear* (1974) and S. Maidment (1977) 26 I.C.L.Q. 403.
[49] *The Siskina* [1979] A.C. 210. See Cretney, *Principles of Family Law* (4th ed.) pp. 263–264.

have jurisdiction to grant injunctions under the Act unless other relief is sought.[50] The county court will, therefore, be the main forum for applications under the 1976 Act.

Cohabitees Perhaps the most important aspect of the Act was that it extended to a man and a woman living with each other in the same household as man and wife although not actually married. This reflects both the increased incidence of non-marital cohabitation and the fact that violence is a problem in this context as well as between married couples. The Domestic Violence and Matrimonial Proceedings Act 1976 is the only one of the three statutes dealing expressly with ouster orders which applies to unmarried couples so that, if the parties are unmarried, applications for non-molestation or exclusion orders must be made under it.

Shortly after the Act was passed, a series of cases came before the courts where the issue was whether the courts had jurisdiction under this Act to order the owner of property to leave the home. At first, the view was taken that the courts could not interfere with property rights. The Act was construed to mean that a sole owner of the property could use the procedure to secure the removal of a non-owning cohabitee but that there was no jurisdiction to order the exclusion of either the sole owner or a co-owner of the home.[51] These cases were, however, overruled in the leading case of *Davis* v. *Johnson*.[52]

In *Davis* v. *Johnson*, an unmarried couple were joint tenants of a council flat, where they lived with their three year old daughter. He committed various acts of extreme violence towards her as a result of which she fled with her child to a women's refuge, which was grossly overcrowded. She then sought an order under the Act excluding him from the flat to enable her to return there and this was granted by the House of Lords.

The jurisdiction under this Act empowers the court to regulate the enjoyment of the property. It does not enable the courts to adjust the beneficial interests in the home.[53] Thus if the sole owner is excluded on the application of the person with whom he shares the house, he retains his beneficial interest in it. He is simply prohibited from living in the property for a given period of time.[54]

Living together as man and wife In the case of unmarried couples, the jurisdiction of the court to make non-molestation or exclusion orders depends upon them living with each other in the same household as man and wife. This raises two problems. First the question can arise as to whether a couple who are estranged, but are still in the same house, are living together as man and wife and secondly, whether a woman who has been forced to leave as a result of violence can nevertheless apply for an order.

The courts have approached both questions in a liberal manner. If the couple are in the same household, sharing

---

[50] *Crutcher* v. *Crutcher* (1978) 128 New L.J. 981.
[51] *B.* v. *B. (Domestic Violence: Jurisdiction)* [1978] Fam. 26; *Cantliff* v. *Jenkins* [1978] Fam. 47.
[52] [1979] A.C. 264. See H. A. Finlay (1978) 52 A.L.J. 613.
[53] *Ibid.* at 335, *per* Viscount Dilhorne.
[54] The period of exclusion orders is considered, see p. 93–94 below.

amenities, they will be considered as being within the Act. There is no point in reviving cases of desertion when the couple are in the same house.[55] With regard to the second point it was made clear in *Davis* v. *Johnson* itself, that the fact that the woman has left the property is no bar to her applying for an order. To hold otherwise would be to defeat the purpose of the Act.[56] Instead, the court will be prepared to make an order if the couple were living together when the acts complained of occurred; but the longer the interval between the cohabitation and the application, the less likely it is that the court will make any order.[57] A couple may be regarded as living together as man and wife if cohabitation resumes after a divorce, but, unless it does, there is no longer jurisdiction to make an order under the Act.[58]

Leaving property is no bar to applying for an order

Criteria for making an order

Having sketched the types of order that can be made under the various Acts, one must now turn to the question of what must be established before an order can be made. This in turn will lead to consideration of which Act applications should be made under and the procedure to be adopted. Finally one must examine the extent of the protection available and the sanctions that may be imposed in the case of any orders being breached.

Under which Act should an application be made

In so far as unmarried couples are concerned, the only available jurisdiction by which an exclusion order can be made, at least where disputes concerning children are not at issue, is under the Domestic Violence and Matrimonial Proceedings Act 1976. Where married couples are involved there would seem to be a choice between three statutes. Until recently, however, little attention seemed to be paid to the courts' jurisdiction to make exclusion orders, a situation which has now changed radically.

Exclusion orders: position before Richards

Before the decision in *Richards* v. *Richards*,[59] the most common way for a non-molestation or exclusion order to be sought was by seeking an injunction ancillary to another form of matrimonial relief, normally a divorce.[60] As other relief was being sought, an injunction excluding the husband from the matrimonial home could be granted in the county court. A petition was filed for an injunction by notice of application in the suit and an affidavit lodged in support of that petition. The 1976 Act was used if no matrimonial relief apart from a non-molestation or ouster order was sought, or if an application was made to attach a power of arrest to the injunction. The 1983 Act was scarcely used at all.

Conflicting authorities

The courts regularly awarded injunctions in respect of these proceedings but a conflict of authority arose as to what criteria the court should adopt in making these orders. Under one line of

---

[55] *Adeoso* v. *Adeoso* [1980] 1 W.L.R. 1535.
[56] See *White* v. *White* [1983] Fam. 54 at 63, *per* Cumming-Bruce L.J.; *McLean* v. *Nugent* [1979] F.L.R. 26.
[57] *O'Neill* v. *Williams* [1984] F.L.P. 1.
[58] *Ainsbury* v. *Millington* [1986] 1 All E.R. 73. Where children are also involved, an ouster order can be made: *Wilde* v. *Wilde*, *The Independent*, December 2, 1987.
[59] [1984] A.C. 174.
[60] For a valuable discussion, see G. Gypps [1983] Lit. 53.

authority, it was held that an order excluding the husband from the house should not be made unless the wife had reasonable grounds for refusing to continue to live with him[61]; in the other, this was not considered to be important if there were children. In that event, their welfare became the dominant criterion.[62]

Richards v. Richards

In *Richards* v. *Richards* a married couple lived in a council house with their two children. In January 1982, she filed a divorce petition which was defended. The grounds for this petition were variously described as "flimsy" and "rubbishy."[63] She left the matrimonial house with the children in June 1982, to stay with a friend. When she was asked to leave, she was offered a caravan by the local authority. She then sought an injunction excluding her husband from the matrimonial home. This was reluctantly granted by the county court judge, who felt bound to make the order in the interest of the children, although he felt such an order to be unjust to him. This was confirmed in the Court of Appeal but reversed in the House of Lords.

The House of Lords were highly critical of the way in which the courts had approached these matters in the past. In particular, the failure to advert to the statutory basis for the making of exclusion orders was condemned. The previous practice was to make such orders in matrimonial proceedings as part of the court's inherent jurisdiction. It was held that this jurisdiction had been superseded by the Matrimonial Homes Act 1967, which empowered the courts to exclude a spouse from the home, and laid down the matters to which the courts were to have regard in making such orders.

Grounds for making orders

Statutory criteria

On an application for an order under section 1(2) of the Matrimonial Homes Act 1983, the court is directed by section 1(3) to make such order as it thinks just and reasonable having regard to the conduct of the spouses in relation to each other and otherwise, to their respective needs and financial resources, to the needs of any children and to all the circumstances of the case. As the previous cases had not considered all the listed criteria, they were based on incorrect reasoning although not necessarily wrongly decided on the facts.[64]

Welfare of the children paramount?

Because the House took the view that the jurisdiction to make ouster injunctions now derived from the Matrimonial Homes Act, it followed that it was wrong to treat the welfare of any children as paramount. This test derives from section 1 of the Guardianship of Minors Act 1971 and when the custody of upbringing of a minor is in question is to be applied in deciding that question. It was held, Lord Scarman dissenting, that deciding whether to make an ouster order did not decide the issue of custody and so this test was not to be applied. The needs of the children was simply one factor amongst others to be taken into account.[65]

---

[61] *Myers* v. *Myers* [1982] 1 W.L.R. 247.
[62] *Samson* v. *Samson* [1982] 1 W.L.R. 252.
[63] [1984] A.C. 174 at 198.
[64] *Ibid.* at 204, *per* Lord Hailsham L.C.
[65] The court can, however, make an ouster order ancillary to an application under Guardianship of Minors Act 1971, and the Guardianship Act 1973 in which case the needs of the children will be regarded as paramount: *T.* v. *T.* (1986) 136 New L.J. 391. See also *Wilde* v. *Wilde*, *The Independent*, December 2, 1987.

Importance of the needs of children   This does not mean to say, however, that the needs of children will not be considered as important, Lord Hailsham recognised that in a given case the needs of the children may be so clamant that, in the proper exercise of its discretion, the court should give them paramountcy.[66] Equally, where the other factors are evenly balanced, the needs of children, including those as yet unborn, may tip the balance in favour of making an order.[67] It is a matter of discretion.

Exercise of discretion   It was made clear by the House of Lords that the discretion to make ouster orders was to be exercised in accordance with the criteria laid down in the Matrimonial Homes Act. This is true also of orders made under the Domestic Violence and Matrimonial Proceedings Act 1976 by which county courts were given an additional power to make ouster orders. Lord Brandon thought it was a necessary inference that the legislature intended such additional power to be exercised in accordance with the principles laid down in the Matrimonial Homes Act.[68]

In exercising this discretion, it is clear that cases have limited utility as precedents in that the factual scenarios are likely to differ. Nevertheless, the courts must decide whether to make an ouster order having regard only to the statutory criteria. It is not open to a judge to have regard to other factors, such as a desire to give the spouses a breathing space from each other.[69]

Draconian remedy   It was stressed in *Richards* that ouster orders should not be made lightly. The consequence of such an order is likely to be serious, in that the person ordered to leave will have to go at short notice,[70] and will often experience difficulty in finding alternative accommodation.[71] Before making such an order, a judge should be satisfied that no lesser order would give the wife adequate protection[72] and that the respondent is given the opportunity to test the applicant's affidavit evidence by cross-examination.[73]

It is wrong to see the ouster jurisdiction as being essentially a housing matter.[74] Nevertheless housing aspects can be a legitimate consideration in the exercise of discretion. If a wife has left the matrimonial home with the children, and is refused an order ousting her husband so that she can return, she will have a priority need within section 59 of the Housing Act 1985 and will **Homelessness** not be regarded as intentionally homeless. She will therefore be provided with accommodation by the local authority under the Act. If the ouster order is made, the husband, as a single person,

---

[66] [1984] A.C. 174 at 204.
[67] *Anderson* v. *Anderson* (1984) 14 H.L.R. 241. See also *Summers* v. *Summers* [1986] F.L.R. 343.
[68] [1984] A.C. 174 at 222 applied in *Lee* v. *Lee* (1983) 12 H.L.R. 116.
[69] *Summers* v. *Summers*, above n. 67.
[70] They should take effect within a week or two; not as some sort of "ouster nisi": *Burke* v. *Burke* (1987) 137 N.L.J. 11; *Chadda* v. *Chadda* (1981) 11 Fam. Law 142.
[71] [1984] A.C. at 215, *per* Lord Brandon.
[72] *Reid* v. *Reid*, The Times, 30 July, 1984. See also *Wiseman* v. *Simpson* [1988] 1 W.L.R. 35.
[73] *Harris* v. *Harris* [1986] F.L.R. 12. See also *Wiseman* v. *Simpson*, above n.72, at 40 *per* Ralph Gibson L.J.
[74] This approach in *Spindlow* v. *Spindlow* [1979] Fam. 52 at 59, *per* Ormrod L.J. was rejected in *Richards* v. *Richards* [1984] A.C. at 208, *per* Lord Scarman.

will not have corresponding rights. This is a matter to which the court can properly have regard, but it is not a decisive consideration. A court may nevertheless make the order even if it would leave him homeless.[75]

Procedure *Richards* v. *Richards* established that the discretion to make an ouster order must be exercised in accordance with the criteria contained in the Matrimonial Homes Act. The substantive law decided in this case has been said to pale into significance compared with the procedural implications.[76] The particular difficulties caused related to the method of applying for orders and the manner in which the various statutes interrelate.

Procedural implications of Richards v. Richards

Prior to *Richards* v. *Richards* the practice in matrimonial cases when seeking an ouster order was to apply for it ancillary to the matrimonial proceedings. Lord Brandon, however, emphasised that as ouster orders should be sought under the Matrimonial Homes Act, the procedures under that Act should be followed. This entailed issuing an originating summons under rule 107(1) of the Matrimonial Causes Rules.[77] Separate proceedings became necessary, thereby adding cost and complexity to such applications.[78] These difficulties have now largely been eradicated by changes to the rules of the court.

High Court

If matrimonial proceedings have been instituted in the High Court and an application is made under the Matrimonial Homes Act 1983, the procedure is governed by the new rule 107 of the Matrimonial Causes Rules.[79] This provides that when a cause is pending in the High Court an application under section 1 or section 9 of the Matrimonial Homes Act 1983 shall be made as an application in that cause.

County court

A similar amendment to the county court rules was made in response to *Richards* v. *Richards*. The new County Court Rules, Order 47, r. 4(9) introduced by the County Court (Amendment) Rules 1984[80] provides that where matrimonial proceedings are pending between the parties in the county court, an application under sections 1 or 9 of the Matrimonial Homes Act 1983 shall be made in those proceedings in accordance with Order 13, r. 1. This means that the application is made by notice filed with the court together with an affidavit and the draft order. These must be served on the respondent two clear days before the hearing, unless the application is *ex parte*.[81] If an ouster order is sought under the 1983 Act, when matrimonial proceedings are pending, the procedure introduced by these rules is mandatory.

Interrelation of the statutes

The existence of three statutes under which ouster orders can be made serves only to complicate unnecessarily the law relating to

---

[75] *Wooton* v. *Wooton* [1984] F.L.R. 871; *Thurley* v. *Smith* [1984] F.L.R. 875.
[76] Gypps [1983] Lit. 53 at 57.
[77] (S.I. 1977 No. 344).
[78] M. Rae and J. Levin [1983] L.A.G. Bull. 145.
[79] (S.I. 1984 No. 1511).
[80] (S.I. 1984 No. 576) amended by County Court Amendment Rules 1986 (S.I. 1986 No. 636).
[81] Passingham and Harmer, *Law and Practice in Matrimonial Causes* (4th ed., 1985) p. 340.

Choice of statutes

this area. In the absence of consolidating legislation, the problem for a married person seeking an ouster order will be to decide which of the statutes to apply under. For unmarried persons living together as man and wife, there is no such difficulty; the application must be under the Domestic Violence and Matrimonial Proceedings Act 1976.

There are passages in *Richards* v. *Richards* which seem to suggest that during the subsistence of the marriage an application to the High Court or county court must be made under the Matrimonial Homes Act 1983.[82] The problem with this is that the orders that can be made under the 1983 Act are limited to those regulating occupation of the matrimonial home. In addition to such an order, a wife may seek to exclude the husband from the vicinity of the home and to obtain a non-molestation order. Additionally, it might be sought to attach a power of arrest and it is doubtful if this can be obtained under the 1983 Act, as jurisdiction exists to make orders rather than injunctions and the jurisdiction to attach such a power is based on the award of an injunction.[83] As these wider orders can be obtained under the Domestic Violence and Matrimonial Proceedings Act 1976, a wife may wish to apply under that Act rather than the 1983 Act. It seems that the stress on the jurisdiction under the 1983 Act was to emphasise that the courts should not decide ouster injunctions as a matter of inherent jurisdiction. Notwithstanding the emphasis on applying under the 1983 Act, it seems that a wife can simply apply for the wider orders under the 1976 Act without also applying under the 1983 Act.[84] Should a wife instead seek an order in the magistrates court, this is unaffected by *Richards*.

Limitations of the 1983 Act

Exclusion and non-molestation orders

Power of arrest

Applications under the Domestic Violence and Matrimonial Proceedings Act   Applications under section 1 of the 1976 Act should be made by originating application to the court for the district in which either the applicant or respondent resides or the matrimonial home is situated. The return day is four days after service and the application is dealt with in chambers unless the court otherwise directs.[85] In determining whether to issue an injunction excluding the respondent from the home, the criteria applied in applications under sections 1 or 9 of the Matrimonial Homes Act 1983 are also applied.

Period of exclusion   One of the innovations of the 1976 Act was that it enabled the owner of a house to be ordered from it on the application of a person living there with him, or one joint owner to be excluded on the application of the other. This clearly marks a considerable interference with the normal incidents of beneficial ownership. As a consequence, when a person is excluded the period of that exclusion tends to be relatively

---

[82] [1984] A.C. 174 at 202, *per* Lord Hailsham; at 222, *per* Lord Brandon.
[83] Gypps [1983] Lit. 53 at 59; Passingham and Harmer, *Law and Practice in Matrimonial Causes* (4th ed.) p. 340.
[84] Passingham and Harmer, above n.81, p. 338. *Cf.* Cretney, above n.49, p.252. There were vastly more applications in 1986 under the Domestic Violence and Matrimonial Proceedings Act 1976 than the Matrimonial Homes Act 1983. See Judicial Statistics, Tables 4.12 and 4.14.
[85] C.C.R. 1981, Ord. 47, r. 8.

Time limit usually imposed

brief.[86] This was stressed in *Davis* v. *Johnson*,[87] the Act being seen as primarily a first aid provision for battered wives.[88] In line with this, the terms of a Practice Direction require that consideration should be given to imposing a time limit on the operation of the injunction. In most cases a period of up to six months is likely to suffice.[89]

Extended exclusion

There are, of course, exceptional cases where a more extended period of exclusion will be necessary.[90] This is most likely to occur if acts of violence are repeated. In *Spencer* v. *Camacho*[91] one joint tenant of a council flat obtained an injunction excluding the other from it, originally for a period of three months. Because of further acts of violence, she obtained an extension of the period but had to return to court again after a further incident. On this occasion, the Court of Appeal held that an indefinite exclusion was justified.

Leasehold property The purpose of an ouster injunction may be defeated in the case of leasehold property, in so far as cohabitees are concerned, by the conduct of the excluded tenant.

Private sector In the private sector,[92] security of tenure is conferred by the continuation of a statutory tenancy after the termination of the protected tenancy. If the couple are joint tenants and one is excluded, the continued occupation of the other will keep the statutory tenancy in being.[93] If the sole tenant is excluded, however, and he forms the intention not to return, then the statutory tenancy will terminate and the woman will have no further right to occupy the dwelling-house.[94]

Council housing In the case of council housing,[95] both spouses and cohabitees are potentially vulnerable if the excluded tenant serves a notice to quit. This is arguably in breach of an order under section 1(1)(d) of the Domestic Violence and Matrimonial Proceedings Act requiring the other party to enter and remain in the house but it would nevertheless end the tenancy, whether the excluded party is the sole tenant or a joint tenant. The local authority may in those circumstances by sympathetic to an application for a new tenancy.

Emergency procedure In some cases it may be necessary to seek an order as a matter of extreme urgency. The methods available to do this are by making an *ex parte* application and by the use of the expedited procedures available. In both cases, a

---

[86] *Cf.* Matrimonial Homes Act 1983, s.1(2)(*a*) where the court is empowered to terminate a right of occupation.
[87] [1979] A.C. 264 at 343, *per* Lord Salmon.
[88] Despite its title, the Act is not applicable only in cases of violence: *ibid.* at 334, *per* Viscount Dilhorne, at 341, *per* Lord Salmon.
[89] *Hopper* v. *Hopper* [1979] 1 W.L.R. 1342; *Freeman* v. *Collins* (1983) 13 Fam. Law 113.
[90] See *Fairweather* v. *Kolosine* (1984) 11 H.L.R. 61; *Galan* v. *Galan* [1985] F.L.R. 905.
[91] (1983) 13 Fam. Law 114.
[92] See J. Martin (1978) 128 New L.J. 154.
[93] *Lloyd* v. *Sadler* [1978] Q.B. 774.
[94] *Colin Smith Music Ltd.* v. *Ridge* [1975] 1 W.L.R. 463. A wife can, of course, rely on her statutory right of occupation. Matrimonial Homes Act 1983, s.1(6).
[95] See A. Arden (1981) 131 New L.J. 165; S. Blandy (1981) 131 New L.J. 520; J. Luba [1981] L.A.G. Bull. 82.

Ex parte applications

remedy can be obtained very rapidly; an essential requirement in cases of extreme violence.

An *ex parte* application for an injunction to exclude a person from the home should only be done in cases of extreme urgency, where there are exceptional circumstances, it always being desirable in such applications that both sides are heard. A failure to do this can lead to injustice being caused. In consequence, solicitors who make unnecessary *ex parte* applications can be made personally liable in costs.[96] Where such an order is necessary, it should be limited to the shortest possible period and should not be expressed to last until further order.[97]

Practice Direction

As a consequence of too many *ex parte* applications being made, a Practice Direction was issued in 1978 expressing concern both at the increasing number and the fact that nearly half of them were unjustified.[98] It was stated that an application should not be made *ex parte* unless there is a real and immediate danger of serious injury or irreparable damage. Attention was also drawn to the special arrangements which exist at the Royal Courts of Justice whereby the applicant's solicitor is able to select for the hearing any day on which the court is sitting.[99]

Applications under the Domestic Proceedings and Magistrates Court Act As an alternative to bringing proceedings in the county court, an application may be made by one spouse to exclude the other from the matrimonial home to the magistrates court under section 16(3) of the Domestic Proceedings and Magistrates Court Act 1978. If the court considers it essential to hear the application without delay, an expedited order can be made.[1] Such an order continues for 28 days and does not take effect until the order is served on the respondent or until such later date as is specified in the order.[2] Under section 16(6) of the Act, service on the respondent may be dispensed with in the case of personal protection orders but not for exclusion orders.

Expedited order

Powers of arrest

One of the problems for the victims of domestic violence was the unwillingness of the police to become involved with family disputes. As a consequence the criminal law provided little protection in this type of case. To combat this problem, the courts were given the power to attach a power of arrest to injunctions.

Under section 2(1) of the Domestic Violence and Matrimonial Proceedings Act 1976, a judge is empowered, on the grant of an injunction excluding a person from the home or from a specified area in which the house is included, to attach a power of arrest to that injunction. He can attach such a power if he is

---

[96] *Masich* v. *Masich* (1977) 121 S.J. 645; *Ansah* v. *Ansah* [1977] Fam. 138.
[97] *Morgan* v. *Morgan* (1978) 9 Fam. Law 87.
[98] Practice Note (Matrimonial Cause: Injunction) [1978] 1 W.L.R. 925.
[99] Practice Direction (Divorce Registry: Injunction) [1972] 1 W.L.R. 1047. See also C.C.R. Ord. 13, r. 4(4).
[1] Domestic Proceedings and Magistrates Court Act 1978, s.16(5).
[2] *Ibid.* s.16(8).

satisfied that the other party has caused actual bodily harm to the applicant, or as the case may be, to the child concerned and considers that he is likely to do so again.[3] The need for actual bodily harm to have occurred already is unfortunate, in that a judge who suspects strongly that the respondent will cause bodily harm in the future cannot attach a power of arrest if the respondent has not already caused bodily harm.[4]

Not a routine remedy It has been stressed in the Court of Appeal that a power of arrest should not routinely be attached to an injunction granted under the 1976 or 1978 Acts, but should be seen as an exceptional remedy.[5] To counter any suggestion that it has simply been attached as a matter of course, it is good practice for reasons to be given for its attachment. If a power of arrest is attached, it should not ordinarily last for a period of longer than three months. This period can be extended should the need arise.[6]

Procedure on arrest If the county court judge attaches a power of arrest to an exclusion order under the Act, a copy of that injunction should be delivered to the officer in charge of any police station for the applicant's address.[7] A constable can arrest without warrant a person whom he has reasonable cause for suspecting is in breach of that injunction.[8] After the arrest, the police should forthwith seek directions from the court as to when he should be brought before a judge, but he must in any event be brought before the judge within 24 hours of the arrest and should not be released before then.[9] The judge may then punish for contempt, notwithstanding non-compliance with the procedure requirements of Order 29 of the County Court Rules 1981.[10]

Committal The ultimate sanction which the court can impose for breach of an injunction is to commit the respondent to prison for a period not exceeding two years.[11] To apply for a committal order, care must be taken to ensure that the procedural rules are complied with. These requirements are laid down in Order 29 of the County Court Rules 1981 and these requirements will, in general, be strictly applied by the courts.

C.C.R. 1981, Order 29

Procedure Order 29, r. 1(3) requires a penal notice to be indorsed on an injunction or like order. This puts the respondent on warning that he may be committed to prison for breach of it. If the order is breached, then, at the request of the complainant, the proper officer should serve notice on the party, two clear days before the hearing, requiring him to show cause why a committal order

---

[3] A similar jurisdiction exists under Domestic Proceedings and Magistrates Court Act 1978, s.18 save that it can be attached to an injunction preventing him from returning to the matrimonial home but not to one ordering him to leave it.
[4] *McLaren* v. *McLaren* (1978) 9 Fam. Law 153; Parker, *Cohabitees* (1981) p. 96.
[5] *Lewis* v. *Lewis* [1978] Fam. 60 at 63, *per* Ormrod L.J. Nevertheless, in 1986 over 4,000 such orders were made: Judicial Statistics 1986, Table 4.14.
[6] *Widdowson* v. *Widdowson* [1983] F.L.R. 121 at 125, *per* Sir John Arnold P.
[7] Practice Note [1981] 1 W.L.R. 27.
[8] C.C.R. 1981, Ord. 47, r. 8(5).
[9] Domestic Violence and Matrimonial Proceedings Act 1976, s.2(4)(5). No account is taken of Christmas Day, Good Friday or any Sunday. Domestic Proceedings and Magistrates Court Act 1978, Sched. 2, para. 53.
[10] C.C.R. 1981, Ord. 47, r. 8(7).
[11] Contempt of Court Act 1981, s.14 as amended by the County Courts (Penalties for Contempt) Act 1983, s.1.

should not be made against him. This should set out in detail the acts alleged to be in breach of the injunction or undertaking, as someone is not to be deprived of his liberty unless he knows in advance what he is alleged to have done.[12]

Dispensing with service
The judge has power under Order 29, r. 1(7) to dispense with service on the alleged contemnor. This should only be done in exceptional circumstances, such as where the contemnor has persistently breached the injunction and cannot be found so as to serve notice upon him.[13] Neither is a court precluded from taking account of alleged breaches which occur after the notice has been served; there is no need to serve a fresh notice. Notice that this course has been taken should be recorded in the committal order but a failure to do so will not in itself be a ground for interfering with the order.[14]

The court will not lightly commit a contemnor to prison, although it may do so, notwithstanding that criminal charges are pending arising out of the same incidents.[15] A person should not be committed for a technical breach of the order.[16] It is a remedy of the very last resort which should be resorted to only when other attempts to secure compliance with the order have failed.[17]

Remedy of last resort

Conclusion

The statutory jurisdiction both to allow a non-owning spouse to remain in the matrimonial home and to exclude owners of property from it is a significant alteration of the normal incidents of beneficial ownership. Although the beneficial rights in the property itself are not changed, the right to enjoy occupation of it are. Because these rights can be protected in the courts, it is now possible to see cohabitees and spouses having a form of quasi co-ownership, in that they have shared rights of occupancy, which can become exclusive, despite not having necessarily a right to share in the proceeds of sale of the house.

---

[12] *Dorrell* v. *Dorrell* (1986) 16 Fam. Law 15; *Williams* v. *Fawcett* [1986] Q.B. 604.
[13] *Wright* v. *Jess* [1987] 1 W.L.R. 1077. *Ex parte* committals can also be ordered. *Newman* v. *Benesch* [1987] F.L.R. 262.
[14] *Ibid.*; *Linnett* v. *Coles* [1987] Q.B. 555. But *cf. Linklater* v. *Linklater* (1987) 137 New L.J. 67 for a more stringent approach to procedure.
[15] *Szczpanski* v. *Szczpanski* [1985] F.L.R. 468.
[16] *Boylan* v. *Boylan* (1981) 11 Fam. Law 76; *Smith* v. *Smith* (1987) 137 New L.J. 767.
[17] *Ansah* v. *Ansah* [1977] Fam. 138.

6 INSOLVENCY

Personal insolvency is, regrettably, by no means an uncommon event. If a person becomes insolvent, often his only major asset will be the house in which he lives. In this event, the creditors or, in the case of bankruptcy, the trustee in bankruptcy, will want the house to be sold in order to meet the existing debts. This will create problems if the property is jointly owned, the co-owner wishing to remain in the house and continue to use it as a home. This chapter examines the impact of insolvency when the house is subject to co-ownership.

Charging orders

Charging Orders Act 1979 Under the Charging Orders Act 1979, provision is made for a judgment creditor to obtain a charge against the debtor's property. This procedure can be used when a person has by order of either the High Court or a county court been required to pay a sum of money to another person. Then, for the purpose of enforcing that order, the appropriate court may make an order imposing a charge on the debtor's property. The effect of this charge is that the person in whose favour it is imposed becomes a secured creditor.[1]

Jurisdiction When a creditor seeks to impose a charge, he should apply to the High Court in respect of judgment debts in excess of £5,000. For lesser sums, he should apply to the county court.[2]

Property Under section 2 of the Act, the property against which a charge may be imposed by a charging order includes any beneficial interest which the debtor holds in land. Prior to this Act, a charging order could not, owing the drafting of section 35(3) of the Administration of Justice Act 1956, be made against a beneficial interest in land when the land was jointly owned. This was a consequence of the doctrine of conversion, whereby the debtor's interest was regarded as being in the proceeds of sale of the land, rather than the land itself.[3] One of the purposes of the Act was to remove this unfortunate gap and it is now clear that a charging order can be made against a beneficial interest existing behind a trust for sale.[4]

Enforcement against purchasers Although a charging order can be imposed against a beneficial share existing behind a trust for sale, such a charge can only be equitable and would not appear to be registrable, and will be overreached on a sale of the legal estate. It can be protected against a purchaser of the debtor's equitable interest by notifying the trustees for a sale.[5] Such a sale is most likely to occur when the debtor purports to mortgage the property forging the other co-owner's signature. This fraudulent practice will be insufficient to create a legal mortgage but will, by virtue of section 63 of the

---

[1] Charging Orders Act 1979, s.1.
[2] County Court Jurisdiction Order 1981.
[3] *Irani Finance Ltd. v. Singh* [1971] Ch. 59.
[4] *National Westminster Bank Ltd. v. Stockman* [1981] 1 W.L.R. 67.
[5] L.P.A. 1925, s.137.

section 63 of the L.P.A. 1925, operate on his own beneficial interest in the property.[6]

Procedure An application for a charging order can be made *ex parte* and should be supported by an affidavit identifying the judgment to be enforced and the amount owed, the name of the debtor and of any creditor the applicant can identify, full particulars of the subject matter of the intended charge and verifying that the interest to be charged is owned beneficially by the debtor. The court will then make an order nisi. This will then be followed by an order to show cause why the order should not be made absolute which will be served on the judgment debtor.[7] The court may also direct that copies of the order should be served on any other creditor or any other interested party.[8] On further consideration of the matter, the court should then either make the charge absolute, with or without modifications, or discharge it.[9]

Making the order absolute Obtaining an order nisi is a fairly simple process. The issues involved in the dispute will be resolved at the later hearing when the court determines whether or not the charging order should be made absolute. That the court has a discretion in this matter is clear from section 1(5) of the Act which directs the court, in deciding whether to make a charging order, to consider all the circumstances of the case and, in particular, any evidence before it as to the personal circumstances of the debtor and whether any other creditors of the debtor would be likely to be unduly prejudiced by the making of the order.

Principles to be applied The general principles that the court will adopt were laid down in the Court of Appeal by Lord Brandon, in *Roberts Petroleum Ltd. v. Bernard Kenny Ltd.*[10] Although the question of whether to make the order absolute is one for the court, the burden of showing cause why it should not be made absolute is on the debtor. The court in considering all the circumstances of the case, should have regard to other creditors. As the effect of a charging order is to make the judgment creditor a secured creditor, this can operate unfairly on other creditors in the event of a bankruptcy. If the debtor appears to be insolvent, this may cause the court to refuse to make the order. In the absence of this consideration, the court is likely to make the order absolute.

The family home Of the various assets against which a charging order can be made, it is the home which can cause the greatest difficulty. This is because it may be jointly owned and

---

[6] *First National Securities Ltd. v. Hegerty* [1985] Q.B. 850. *Cf. Thames Guaranty Ltd. v. Campbell* [1985] Q.B. 210. *Cedar Holdings Ltd. v. Green* [1981] Ch. 129 to the contrary was overruled in *Williams & Glyn's Bank v. Boland* [1981] A.C. 487. The strange county court decision in *Ainscough v. Ainscough (Cedar Holdings Ltd. intervening)* (1987) 17 Fam. Law 347 is submitted to be wrong. See further, p. 134 below.
[7] R.S.C., Ord. 50, r.1(2). A similar procedure obtains in the county court. See C.C.R. 1981, Ord. 31, r. 1(2).
[8] R.S.C., Ord. 50, r. 2(1); C.C.R. 1981, Ord. 31, r. 2(2). Below p. 102.
[9] R.S.C., Ord. 50, r. 3; C.C.R. 1981, Ord. 31, r. 3.
[10] [1982] 1 W.L.R. 301, reversed on the facts [1983] 2 A.C. 192.

one co-owner may be anxious that it should not be sold to enable the charge to be realised. An additional complication that can arise is if the debtor is married and, at the time when it is sought to impose the charge, the debtor's spouse is seeking a property adjustment order under the Matrimonial Causes Act 1973.

First National Securities Ltd. v. Hegarty

These issues have been considered twice by the Court of Appeal. In *First National Securities Ltd.* v. *Hegarty*[11] a married couple bought a house as beneficial joint tenants. The husband, ironically a retired policeman, obtained a loan from the plaintiffs, forging his wife's signature on the mortgage. The plaintiffs obtained judgment in default against him and obtained a charging order nisi. She then filed a divorce petition and sought ancillary relief seeking, *inter alia*, a transfer of his share in the house to her. She then argued that the charging order should not be made absolute.

Presumption in favour of order

The starting position was held to be that the judgment creditor was justified in expecting that the order should be made absolute unless the debtor could persuade the court that in all the circumstances such an order should not be made.[12] Stressing that the order nisi had been made prior to the wife lodging her divorce petition, the Court of Appeal held that there was no basis for interfering with the judge's decision to make the order absolute. The argument that the matter should be transferred to the Family Division was similarly rejected, it being emphasised that the court should not use its powers under Part II of the Matrimonial Causes Act 1973 to override the claims of a creditor seeking security for a debt.[13] Ultimately, the issue would be the enforcement of the charge which would be considered on an application by the creditor for a sale of the house under section 30 of the L.P.A. 1925.[14]

Family considerations Harman v. Glencross

The Court of Appeal in *Hegarty* displayed considerable sympathy for the position of creditors and little for the wife. In contrast, in *Harman* v. *Glencross*[15] a somewhat different approach was taken. In 1981, the debtor's wife filed a divorce petition and sought an order transferring his interest in the house to her. Afterwards the debtor's partner obtained a judgment of £9,250 against him and obtained a charging order nisi which was subsequently made absolute. The wife, who had had no notice of the charging order proceedings, applied under section 3(5) of the Charging Orders Act 1979 to have the order varied. Both this application and the divorce petition were then heard in the Family Division where the registrar varied the charging order and ordered that the debtor's share in the house be transferred to her. This was upheld by Ewbank J.[16] and by the Court of Appeal.

The order made in this case effectively terminated the debt owed to the judgment creditor, because the debtor's only

---

[11] [1985] Q.B. 850; P. F. Smith [1983] Conv. 129.
[12] *Ibid.* at 866, *per* Sir Denys Buckley.
[13] *Ibid.* at 868, *per* Stephenson L.J.
[14] A secured judgment creditor is a person interested in the property within L.P.A. 1925, s.30: *Stevens* v. *Hutchinson* [1953] Ch. 299.
[15] [1986] Fam. 81. See N. P. Gravells (1985) 5 O.J.L.S. 132; J. Warburton [1986] Conv. 218.
[16] [1985] Fam. 49. This decision had been doubted in *First National Securities Ltd.* v. *Hegarty* [1985] Q.B. 850 at 868, *per* Stephenson L.J.

substantial asset was his beneficial share in the house.[17] Because this is likely to be the result if the court refuses to make the order absolute, and transfers the debtor's beneficial interest in the house to his wife, such an order should not be seen as the norm. In *Harman* v. *Glencross*, the Court of Appeal stressed various unusual features present, the most important being that the creditor had declined to give evidence as to his financial position. In addition, the creditor knew that the wife had a half interest in the house before seeking to enforce his judgment debt.

Principles to be applied

Chronology of actions

The opportunity was taken in *Harman* v. *Glencross* to lay down the principles to be applied in cases where the debtor's wife has filed a divorce petition and has sought ancillary relief. The first factor was the chronology of the two actions. If the judgment creditor has obtained a charging order nisi, and his application to have it made absolute is heard before the wife starts divorce proceedings, then it is difficult to see why the court should refuse to make the charging order absolute and the wife's right of occupation should be adequately protected under section 30 of the L.P.A. 1925.[18] Alternatively, if the charging order nisi is made after the wife's petition, the court should consider whether it is appropriate to make the order absolute even before the application for ancillary relief has been heard by the Family Division. Such a course would be appropriate when after a sale of the house there would be sufficient funds available to make adequate provision for the wife. If the facts are not so clear, the normal practice should be to transfer the case to the Family Division so that both claims can be heard together.

Balancing of interests

When the case has been transferred to the Family Division, the starting point is to recognise that the judgment creditor is justified in expecting that a charging order will be made against the debtor's beneficial interest in the matrimonial home.[19] The court should then consider whether the charge should be made absolute and enforced at once, even if the result would be that the wife and any children would as a result have a lower standard of housing than would have been the case had only the husband's interest been taken into account. Failing that, the court should only make such order as might be necessary to protect the wife's right to occupy the matrimonial home with the children. This would entail a *Mesher* type order being made, postponing a sale of the house until the children had attained a specified age, thereby holding a balance between the wife and the judgment creditor.[20] One of the personal circumstances of the debtor which the court is obliged to have regard to, by section 1(5)(*a*) of the Act, was held to be the fact that the debtor is obliged to make provision for his wife and young children and that he has no other property with which to do so.[21]

Outright transfer unusual

Although the order transferring the husband's beneficial interest in the house was upheld in *Harman* v. *Glencross*, the Court of Appeal stressed that this course of action would be

---

[17] *Harman* v. *Glencross* [1986] Fam. 81 at 104, *per* Fox L.J.
[18] *Ibid.* at 99, *per* Balcombe L.J.
[19] *Ibid.* approving the statement in *First National Securities Ltd.* v. *Hegarty* [1985] Q.B. 850 at 866, *per* Sir Denys Buckley.
[20] *Harman* v. *Glencross* [1986] Fam. 81 at 100, *per* Balcombe L.J.; at 104–105, *per* Fox L.J.
[21] *Ibid.* at 103, *per* Fox L.J.

exceptional. This course would leave the judgment creditor with nothing on which the charging order could bite in the future. To frustrate a pending application for a charging order by directing an immediate transfer of the house was not thought to be of proper exercise of the jurisdiction under section 24 of the Matrimonial Causes Act 1973.[22]

Factors in favour of a sale While seeking to effect a compromise between the creditor on the one hand and the wife and children on the other, the Court of Appeal recognised that there may be cases where it would not be appropriate for the enforcement of the charging order to be delayed. Regard must be had to any hardship that the creditor may suffer if his right to recover the debt is postponed. Not all judgment creditors are faceless corporations and there is no reason why evidence should not be admitted as to any hardship that would be caused by delayed enforcement.[23] Secondly, the court should also consider whether there is any point in delaying the enforcement of the order, if the wife's right of occupation could be defeated by making the husband bankrupt.[24]

Timing of the writs It is evident that the approach taken in *Harman* v. *Glencross* is quite different from that taken in *Hegerty*, in that considerably more sympathy was shown for the wife's position and the claim of the creditor was not accorded absolute priority. *Hegerty* was distinguished on the basis that in that case, the application for a charging order preceded her claim to ancillary relief. Balcombe L.J. in *Harman* v. *Glencross* indicated that in such circumstances the charging order should normally be made absolute, whereas if the divorce petition is entered first, both claims should be heard together in the Family Division. It has been pointed out that this acts as an inducement for both a judgment creditor and a spouse to bring an action sooner rather than later, which may not facilitate out of court settlements.[25]

Enforcing the charge The fact that a charging order has been made absolute does not mean that the house will necessarily be sold at once. If there is legal co-ownership, then after an order **Notice** nisi has been made, notice to show cause should be served on that co-owner as well as on the debtor thereby allowing representations to be made by her.[26] If no notice is served then this will be one of the exceptional cases when the court will entertain an action to vary or discharge the order.[27]

Postponing the sale A co-owner of the property, whether married or simply cohabiting with the debtor, should be able, in cases where the debtor is not made bankrupt, to cause the sale to be postponed, if this is desirable to protect her and their children's occupation needs. It is clear from *Harman* v. *Glencross* that the courts are quite willing to balance the creditor's desire to realise his debt, on the one hand, with the housing needs of his partner and their children on the other. This compromise is to make a *Mesher* type

---

[22] *Harman* v. *Glencross* [1986] Fam. 81 at 100, *per* Balcombe L.J.; at 103, *per* Fox L.J.
[23] *Ibid.* at 93, *per* Balcombe L.J.
[24] *Ibid.* at 100, *per* Balcombe L.J. See below, pp. 108–112.
[25] J. Warburton [1986] Conv. 218 at 220.
[26] *Harman* v. *Glencross* [1986] Fam. 81 at 89, *per* Balcombe L.J. Notice should also be served on a spouse who has registered her statutory right of occupation, *ibid.*
[27] *Ibid.*

order. The original charge can itself be made conditional, the condition being that it is not enforced until the youngest child reaches a specified age. Alternatively, on an application by the judgment creditor under section 30 of the L.P.A. 1925, a postponement of the sale could be ordered for a similar period.

Continuation of relationship   The above discussion has tended to assume that the relationship between the debtor and his spouse or partner has broken down, with the wife or cohabitee remaining in the house with the children and anxious to resist the sale sought by the judgment creditor. The wife is in a stronger position as she can register her statutory right of occupation and seek a property variation order but either can, if they are a co-owner of the property, assert that interest against the creditor. In such an event, the courts seek to balance, where possible, the conflicting interests. As yet, no case has emerged where the relationship between the debtor and his partner has not broken down but a realisation of the creditor's charging order by sale is nevertheless resisted by a co-owner. It is thought to be likely that the courts will be less sympathetic of the housing needs of the co-owner and children in these circumstances and more amenable to the claim of the judgment creditor.

Bankruptcy[28]

When a person becomes bankrupt, his property vests in the trustee in bankruptcy as soon as that person is appointed; such vesting taking effect without any conveyance, assignment or transfer.[29] The trustee's duty is then to get in, realise and distribute the bankrupt's estate in accordance with Chapter IV of the Insolvency Act 1986.[30] In the exercise of these duties the following matters may be in issue: first, whether the trustee in bankruptcy will be able to set aside the transaction by which the co-owner acquired her beneficial interest in the property and, secondly, the ability of the trustee to obtain a sale of a jointly owned home.

Setting transactions aside   The jurisdiction to set aside transactions effected by the bankrupt prior to his bankruptcy was originally contained in two statutory provisions, section 42 of the Bankruptcy Act 1914 and section 172 of the L.P.A. 1925. Neither provision was regarded by the Cork Committee on Insolvency Law and Practice as being entirely satisfactory.[31] Pursuant to recommendations made by that Committee, new provisions dealing with this matter were enacted in the **Insolvency Act 1986**   Insolvency Act 1986. These new provisions, to be considered shortly, apply only to acts occurring after December 29, 1986. For acts occurring before that date, the matter will be governed by the two earlier statutory provisions.[32] Even though a bankruptcy takes place under the Insolvency Act 1986, the

---

[28] See N. Furey (1987) 17 Fam. Law 316.
[29] Insolvency Act 1986, s.306(1), (2).
[30] *Ibid.* s.305(2).
[31] Cmnd. 8558 (June 1982) paras. 1210–1215, 1221–1227.
[32] Insolvency Act 1986, Sched. 11, paras. 17 and 20.

earlier sections will therefore continue to have effect for a period of years.

Defrauding creditors Under section 172 of the L.P.A. 1925 every conveyance of property with intent to defraud creditors shall be voidable at the instance of any person thereby prejudiced. This section does not extend to any conveyance for valuable consideration in good faith or for good consideration in good faith to any person not having, at the time of the conveyance, notice of the intent to defraud creditors. This provision has been replaced by section 423 of the Insolvency Act 1986 and operates to enable various transactions **Transactions at an** at an undervalue to be set aside at the instance of a victim of the **undervalue** transaction.[33] In actions to set aside a transaction under section 423, the intent that must be proved on the part of the transferor is that the purpose of the transaction was to put assets beyond the reach of a person who is making or may, at some time in the future, make a claim against him or of otherwise prejudicing the interests of such a person in relation to the claim he is making or may make.[34]

These provisions can be invoked by any creditor and it is not necessary that the debtor be adjudicated bankrupt. These provisions are unlikely to be of much utility where property has **Joint property** been put into joint names. This is because it will be extremely difficult to prove the requisite intent, especially if the property is a house. If a man puts a house into the joint names of himself and his wife, or the person with whom he lives, it is most unlikely that a creditor could prove the intent specified in either section 172 or section 423. A more obvious explanation is a desire to share property together. It is therefore possible, but unlikely, that these provisions will be relevant when property is owned jointly.

Setting transactions aside in bankruptcy Under section 42(1) **Bankruptcy Act** of the Bankruptcy Act 1914, any settlement of property, not **1914** being a settlement made before and in consideration of marriage, or made in favour of a purchaser or incumbrancer in good faith and for valuable consideration shall, if the settlor becomes bankrupt within two years after the date of the settlement, be void against the trustee in bankruptcy. It will also be void against the trustee in bankruptcy if the settlor becomes bankrupt within 10 years of the settlement unless the parties claiming under the settlement can prove that the settlor was, at the time of making the settlement, able to pay all his debts without the aid of the property comprised in the settlement.

Although this section has been replaced by sections 339–342 **Continuing** of the Insolvency Act 1986, acts committed before the Act came **relevance of Act** into force, December 29, 1986, are subject to the Bankruptcy Act. The first limb of section 42(1), which avoids settlements against the trustee in bankruptcy if the settlor becomes bankrupt within two years of making the settlement, can only apply until December 28, 1988, and is consequently of little importance. The second limb, which permits a settlement to be set aside up to 10 years after it was made, will continue to have the potential to affect settlements until 1996, provided that the actual settlement occurred before the Insolvency Act 1986 came into force. It is necessary therefore to consider its scope.

[33] Insolvency Act 1986, s.424.
[34] *Ibid.*, s.423(3).

Bankruptcy

Voidable not void
Although the section states that a settlement is void against the trustee in bankruptcy, it is valid unless he seeks to set it aside. Void is regarded as meaning voidable.[35]

Settlement
Section 42(4) of the Bankruptcy Act 1914 defines settlement to include any conveyance or transfer of property.[36] The nature of a settlement is that there is an element of bounty in the transfer of property from one to another. It must be contemplated that the transferee will retain the property in its original or in a traceable form[37] and it is immaterial whether the transfer is formal or informal.[38]

Operation of the Bankruptcy Act 1914, s.42 In *Re Densham (A Bankrupt)*[39] a matrimonial home was bought and conveyed into the husband's name. It was found as a fact that the husband and wife had agreed that it should be owned equally. In terms of **Financial contribution** financial contribution to its purchase, however, the wife had made only a limited contribution, amounting to one-ninth of the value of the property. Goff J. held that because there was an **Agreement as to beneficial ownership** agreement as to the beneficial ownership of the property, and the wife had contributed to the purchase of the house, it would be fraudulent for the husband to rely on the lack of writing as required by section 53(1)(b) of the L.P.A. 1925 to deny her a beneficial interest in the property. Accordingly a constructive trust was imposed to give effect to the oral agreement, giving her a half share in the property. Had there been no such oral agreement, however, she would have been entitled on resulting trust principles to a one-ninth beneficial share in the property, based on her financial contribution to the purchase of the house.[40] It was held that the difference between a half and **Settlement?** one-ninth, seven-eighteenths, amounted to a settlement. As the husband had been adjudicated bankrupt within 10 years, this was liable to be set aside at the behest of the trustee in bankruptcy as the debtor could not have met his debts without recourse to the property comprised in the settlement.

Although a settlement had been found to exist, the wife nevertheless sought to resist the claim of the trustee to set it **Exceptions to the statute** aside. The two exceptions to section 42 that the wife sought to rely on were that, if the settlement was made before and in consideration of marriage or in favour of a purchaser in good faith and for valuable consideration, the trustee cannot have it set aside. In *Re Densham (A Bankrupt)*, although the settlement was made on the occasion of the marriage, it was not conditional on the marriage taking place and done with a view to encouraging or facilitating the marriage.[41] It was therefore held that the settlement was not in consideration of marriage.

Valuable consideration
The wife's claim to be a purchaser for valuable consideration rested on her financial contribution to the acquisition of the

---

[35] *Re Carter and Kenderdine's Contract* [1897] 1 Ch. 776. Snell's *Principles of Equity* (28th ed. 1982) p. 135.
[36] See Hanbury and Maudsley, *Modern Equity* (12th ed. 1985) pp. 355–356.
[37] *Re Plummer* [1900] 2 Q.B. 790.
[38] *Re Densham (A Bankrupt)* [1975] 1 W.L.R. 1519.
[39] [1975] 1 W.L.R. 1519.
[40] See above, pp. 38–40.
[41] [1975] 1 W.L.R. 1519 at 1526–1527, applying *Rennell* v. *I.R.C.* [1964] A.C. 173.

house. This too failed. Goff J. held that valuable consideration did not mean that her contribution had to be equal in value to what he had given her. It must, however, be looked at in a commercial sense with the result that a contribution which would in any event entitle her to an aliquot share, could not be valuable consideration for the transfer of a larger interest than that aliquot share.[42]

Matrimonial orders

In *Re Abbott (A Bankrupt)*[43] a wife petitioned for divorce and sought an order transferring the jointly owned matrimonial home to her. The couple arrived at a compromise, which was incorporated into a consent order, whereby the house was sold and from the proceeds of sale he paid her a lump sum. On his bankruptcy, the trustee sought to recover £9,000 from the wife, that sum being the amount in excess of the value of her half share in the house. The Divisional Court held, however, that she was a purchaser for valuable consideration, her consideration being the withdrawal of a bona fide claim to a property adjustment order.

This seems a generous interpretation of valuable consideration. It is the case that a court may set aside an order made under section 24 of the Matrimonial Causes Act 1973 under section 42 of the Bankruptcy Act,[44] and arguably, as was recognised in *Re Abbott (A Bankrupt)*, an order made in the absence of a compromise would be a voluntary settlement.[45] If that is the case, it would be strange and anomalous if a wife was better off by compromising her claim to matrimonial relief.[46]

Adjustment of transactions under the Insolvency Act 1986   Section 42 of the Bankruptcy Act 1914 applies only to transactions which took place before the Insolvency Act 1986 came into force. Under section 339 of the Insolvency Act 1986, the trustee in bankruptcy may apply for an order where the bankrupt has entered into a transaction at a relevant time with any person at an undervalue. On such an application, the court may make such order as it sees fit for restoring the position to what it would have been if that individual had not entered into that transaction.

Section 339

Transactions at undervalue

Under section 339(3), an individual enters into a transaction with a person at an undervalue if—

"(a) he makes a gift to that person or he otherwise enters into a transaction with that person on terms that provide for him to receive no consideration,
(b) he enters into a transaction with that person in consideration of marriage, or
(c) he enters into a transaction with that person for a consideration the value of which, in money or money's worth, is significantly less than the value, in money or money's worth, of the consideration provided by the individual."

Relevant time

The time in which the trustee can apply to have a transaction at an undervalue set aside is laid down by section 341 of the Act.

---

[42] [1975] 1 W.L.R. 1519 at 1529. See also *Re Windle* [1975] 1 W.L.R. 1628.
[43] [1983] Ch. 45; *Re Pope* [1908] 2 K.B. 169.
[44] Matrimonial Causes Act 1973, s.39.
[45] [1983] Ch. 45 at 57, *per* Peter Gibson J. See also *Harman* v. *Glencross* [1986] Fam. 81 at 97, *per* Balcombe L.J.
[46] See R. Griffith [1983] Conv. 249.

The initial period that is stipulated is that a transaction at an undervalue can be set aside if it took place within five years of the presentation of the bankruptcy petition. This initial five-year period is then extended by a further two years, if when the transaction was entered into, the individual was either insolvent at the time, or became insolvent in consequence of the transaction.[47]

Insolvency For the purposes of this subsection, insolvency is defined by section 341(3) of the Act to mean that the individual is either unable to pay his debts as they fall due, or that the value of his assets is less than the amount of his liabilities, taking into account his contingent and prospective liabilities.

Onus of proof Under section 346(2) there is a presumption that a person was insolvent, unless the contrary is proved, in relation to any transaction at an undervalue which is entered into by an individual with a person who is an associate of his, otherwise than by reason only of his being an employee. Associate is defined by section 435 of the Act to include the individual's husband or wife. This expression includes a former husband and wife and a reputed husband or wife.[48] Also included are relatives of the individual. In many cases where property is jointly owned, therefore, the onus will be on the co-owner to prove the individual's solvency at the time of the settlement.

Effect of the Insolvency Act The provisions of the 1986 Act are potentially more wide-ranging than those in the Bankruptcy Act 1914 which they have replaced. If a husband and wife have **Co-owners** the house conveyed to them jointly and they become equal owners of it, but the husband is the only person who contributes to the purchase of it, then his giving her a half share in the property would amount to a transaction at an undervalue within **Petition lodged** section 339(3)(a) of the Act. Accordingly if he is made bankrupt **within five years** and the petition was lodged within five years of the acquisition of the house, the trustee will be able to claim the wife's beneficial share, regardless of whether he was solvent at the time of the **Between five and** transaction. If the petition is lodged between five and seven years **seven years** of the acquisition of the house, then the transaction can only be set aside if he was insolvent when the house was acquired. As the wife is an associate, the onus will be upon her to prove that this was not the case. A similar result would occur in a case such as *Re Densham (A Bankrupt)* in that the half share had been acquired at an undervalue. To the extent that it had been so acquired, it would be liable to be set aside on an application by the trustee in bankruptcy.

In *Re Abbott (A Bankrupt)* the Divisional Court held that a wife had given valuable consideration by withdrawing her **Divorce** property adjustment application and accepting a compromise **settlements** with the result that the trustee could not set the transaction aside under the Bankruptcy Act 1914. Accepting this, it would nevertheless appear to be the case that the transaction would be at an undervalue in that the value in money or money's worth would seem to be significantly less than the consideration provided by

---

[47] Insolvency Act 1986, s.341(2).
[48] Query whether a cohabiting couple who make no secret of the fact that they are not married would be a reputed husband and wife.

the individual. It is submitted that compromise orders are liable to be set aside under section 339 of the Insolvency Act 1986.

Petitions for sale by the trustee in bankruptcy[49]

The normal position when a person is declared bankrupt is that his property automatically vests in the trustee in bankruptcy.[50] In the case of land which is in the joint names of a bankrupt and another, the legal title will not vest in the trustee. This is because the legal title is held by joint tenants and it is not possible for a legal joint tenancy to be severed.[51] There is no such impediment regarding his beneficial interest in the property and the bankrupt's share will vest in the trustee. In the exercise of his statutory duty to realise the bankrupt's estate, the trustee will apply under section 30 of the L.P.A. 1925 for a sale of the house. This petition will then frequently be opposed by the other co-owner of the house who wishes to continue to use it as a home.

Vesting of legal title

Vesting of beneficial interest

Applications after bankruptcy

Prior to the enactment of the Insolvency Act 1986, the trustee in bankruptcy would petition for a sale in the normal way. In addition, he would not be bound by any rights that the bankrupt's spouse had under the Matrimonial Homes Act 1983. This has now been changed. Section 336(2) provides that where a spouse's rights of occupation under the Matrimonial Homes Act 1983 are a charge on the bankrupt's estate, the charge continues to subsist notwithstanding the bankruptcy. Any applications made under section 1 of the 1983 Act should then be made to the court having jurisdiction in the bankruptcy. Similarly, when the bankrupt and his spouse or former spouse are the trustees for sale, in any application by the trustee in bankruptcy for a sale of the property under section 30 of the L.P.A. 1925, section 336(3) of the 1986 Act requires that application to be made to the court having jurisdiction in the bankruptcy.

Discretion to order a sale Prior to the enactment of the Insolvency Act 1986, the decision as to whether or not to order a sale was solely a matter for the courts. In virtually all the reported decisions, however, where the contest was between the trustee and the bankrupt's co-owner, a sale was ordered. Following recommendations of the Cork Committee,[52] which were not fully implemented, some legislative guidance is now given as to how the courts should approach such matters.

Statutory criteria

Under the Insolvency Act 1986, if an application is made to the court under either section 1 of the Matrimonial Homes Act 1983 or section 30 of the L.P.A. 1925 then the court shall make such an order as it thinks just and reasonable having regard to—

"(a) the interests of the bankrupt's creditors,
(b) the conduct of the spouse or former spouse, so far as contributing to the bankruptcy,

---

[49] See J. G. Miller [1986] Conv. 393.
[50] Insolvency Act 1986, s.306.
[51] L.P.A. 1925, s.36(2).
[52] Cmnd. 8558 (June 1982), paras. 1120 et seq.

(c) the needs and financial resources of the spouse or former spouse,
(d) the needs of any children, and
(e) all the circumstances of the case other than the needs of the bankrupt."[53]

Presumption after one year

The Act having laid down the criteria to which the court is to have regard to, section 336(5) goes on to provide that:

"Where such an application is made after the end of the period of one year beginning with the first vesting of . . . the bankrupt's estate in a trustee, the court shall assume, unless the circumstances of the case are exceptional, that the interests of the bankrupt's creditors outweigh all other considerations."

Applications within the first year

Although the Act makes it clear that, except in exceptional circumstances, the creditor's interests are to prevail over those of the bankrupt's spouse in the case of an application for a sale made a year after the bankruptcy, it is silent on what the position is to be in the case of applications made prior to that date. Equally the Act makes no reference to the needs of a co-owner of the property who is not married to the bankrupt. One is, therefore, left to speculate as to what the position would be in such circumstances.

No presumptions

The fact that there is a presumption in favour of the creditors when an application is made a year after the bankrupt's property has vested in the the trustee implies that there is no such presumption if the application is made within the year. It does not follow from this, however, that there is any presumption to the contrary: that the interests of the bankrupt's spouse or of any children are to prevail. Rather, it is submitted that the role of the court during that initial period is simply to balance the competing interests without any predisposition in favour of one side. It is feasible, therefore, that a sale within a year of the bankruptcy could be ordered, although it is more likely that the courts will grant a postponement of the sale until a year has elapsed.

Cohabitees

A co-owner of the property who cohabits with the bankrupt is not mentioned in section 336 of the Insolvency Act 1986. If she was one of the trustees for sale and will not co-operate in a sale of the property, the trustee must petition for a sale under section 30. In this case, there is no requirement that the petition be made to the court having jurisdiction in the bankruptcy. As the criteria listed in section 336(4) and (5) of the Insolvency Act 1986 apply only to cases involving spouses or former spouses, it would appear that the matter is one for the common law, in which case it is likely that a sale will be ordered.

Children

One of the factors which may weigh with the court in refusing an immediate sale of the property is the existence of young children living in the home. If the bankrupt is living in the house with children below 18 years of age, he is given rights of occupation against the trustee in bankruptcy.[54] These rights are conferred by giving the bankrupt rights of occupation under the Matrimonial Homes Act 1983.[55] Section 337(5) of the 1986 Act directs the court, on an application made under section 1 of the

---

[53] Insolvency Act 1986, s.336(4).
[54] *Ibid.* s.337(2).
[55] *Ibid.* s.337(3).

Matrimonial Homes Act 1983, to make such an order as it thinks just and reasonable having regard to the interests of the creditors, to the bankrupt's financial resources, to the needs of the children and to all the circumstances of the case other than the needs of the bankrupt. Again, however, where the application is made more than a year after the vesting of the property in the trustee, the court is required by section 337(6) of the 1986 Act to assume, unless the circumstances of the case are exceptional, that the interests of the bankrupt's creditors outweigh all other considerations.

Cohabitees with children The Act makes no mention of the position if an unmarried co-owner of the bankrupt remains in the house with young children, the bankrupt having left, and the trustee in bankruptcy applies for the house to be sold. This is a matter for the common law. It is thought likely that the court will grant her a postponement of sale for a year, by analogy with the protection afforded to the bankrupt himself in similar circumstances.

Exceptional circumstances The Insolvency Act 1986 adopts the approach that, in cases of bankruptcy, the enforcement of the creditors' rights can be delayed but not suspended indefinitely. Except in exceptional circumstances, the court is required to assume after one year that the creditors' interests outweigh all other considerations. The question which arises is to ascertain what are likely to be regarded as exceptional circumstances. Light is shed on this area by considering the pre-Act cases[56] as, in those decisions, the courts have consistently held that, unless there are exceptional circumstances, when the trustee in bankruptcy petitions for a sale his voice should prevail in equity.

Re Solomon (A Bankrupt) The judicial tone to applications for a sale of a house, made by a trustee in bankruptcy under section 30 of the L.P.A. 1925, was set in *Re Solomon (A Bankrupt)*.[57] The case concerned a matrimonial home which had been conveyed to the couple as joint tenants. In matrimonial proceedings, she had obtained an undertaking from him not to dispose of the property. After he had been adjudicated bankrupt, the trustee petitioned for a sale of the house under section 30 of the L.P.A. 1925. Goff J. held that the issue was not one simply between husband and wife but between the wife and the husband's creditors. In the case of such **Presumption in favour of trustee** a contest, the trustee's voice should prevail. The house was ordered to be sold, the wife being given a short time in which to order her affairs.

The courts have consistently stated that whether or not a sale should be ordered is a matter for the exercise of discretion. Nevertheless, that discretion has almost always been exercised in favour of the trustee in bankruptcy. A not untypical example of the judicial attitude is that of Walton J. who said in *Re Bailey (A Bankrupt)*[58] "One's debts must be paid, and paid promptly, and if they cannot be paid promptly, then the trustee in bankruptcy must take over." Similarly, in *Re Densham (A Bankrupt)*[59] Goff J. said that "where, as here, there are no other assets and the

---

[56] See generally, C. Hand [1983] Conv. 219.
[57] [1967] Ch. 573. For criticism, see C. Palley (1969) 20 N.I.L.Q. 132.
[58] [1977] 1 W.L.R. 278 at 283.
[59] [1975] 1 W.L.R. 1519 at 1531; see also *Re Turner* [1974] 1 W.L.R. 1556.

co-owner is not in a position to make any proposition to the trustee, the voice of the trustee should normally prevail in equity, because of his statutory duty."

Homelessness It is clear that at common law, exceptional circumstances would be necessary before there was any significant postponement of sale. It has been argued that the fact that the co-owner of property and the children would be made homeless by such an order should cause a sale to be refused. This, however, is seen by the courts to be a normal consequence of a bankruptcy and not one which should prevent a sale order being made.[60] It is simply "yet another case where the sins of the father have to be visited upon the children, but that is the way in which the world is constructed, and one must be just before one is generous."[61]

Education A consideration which has been pressed upon the courts in these cases is that a sale of the property could cause disruption to the children's education. An argument that there should be no sale because it might mean that the children would have to move schools is unlikely to persuade a court that there were exceptional circumstances.[62] If, however, important examinations are to be taken in the near future, the courts may be more sympathetic. Thus in *Re Lowrie*,[63] the Divisional Court postponed the sale of the house for 12 months to avoid disrupting a child's education. Given that the Insolvency Act envisages postponements of this order, however, it is perhaps unlikely that the courts will be willing to grant further postponements beyond a year from the bankruptcy.

Illness If the co-owner of the bankrupt or another member of the household suffers from an illness or disability, that factor is not in itself likely to persuade a court that the circumstances are exceptional. Where such matters might be relevant, however, is if the house has features which make it especially suitable for that person's needs. In *Re Bailey (A Bankrupt)*[64] Walton J. thought that if a house had been specially adapted to suit the needs of a handicapped child, the court would hesitate long before ordering an immediate sale. In such a case, a court may be disposed to allow a postponement of sale beyond a year.

Re Holliday (A Bankrupt) In only one reported decision has the court sanctioned a lengthy postponement of sale, when the trustee in bankruptcy has petitioned under section 30. In *Re Holliday (A Bankrupt)*[65] a matrimonial home had been bought in joint names. The wife obtained a decree nisi and was seeking ancillary relief, whereupon the husband lodged his own petition for bankruptcy. After he was adjudicated bankrupt, the trustee petitioned for a sale of the house. Owing to the needs of the wife and their three children, the Court of Appeal postponed the sale for five years.

The case was most unusual, in that the creditors, who were essentially his solicitors and the bank, were not pressing for payment and his bankruptcy petition was in reality a device to avoid a property adjustment order being made against him. As

---

[60] *Re Lowrie* [1981] 3 All E.R. 353.
[61] *Re Bailey, (A Bankrupt)* [1977] 1 W.L.R. 278 at 284, *per* Walton J.
[62] *Ibid.*
[63] [1981] 3 All E.R. 353.
[64] [1977] 1 W.L.R. 278 at 284.
[65] [1981] Ch. 405.

such the facts were clearly extremely unusual[66] and shows that something quite out of the ordinary was necessary at common law for a court to accede to a co-owner's request for a lengthy postponement of sale. A similar approach can be expected to applications for a postponement of sale beyond one year in cases under the Insolvency Act 1986.

Consequences of postponement Should the sale of the dwelling-house which is occupied by the bankrupt or his spouse or former spouse be postponed, or for any reason the trustee is unable to realise it, he may apply to the court under section 313 of the Insolvency Act 1986 for an order imposing a charge on the property for the benefit of the bankrupt's estate. If such an order has been applied for, then the trustee can call a final meeting of creditors under section 332 of the Act. Ordinarily, such a meeting can only be called when it appears to the trustee that the administration of the bankrupt's estate is substantially complete.[67]

Conditional postponement The court can permit the bankrupt to continue to live in the property he owns notwithstanding the bankruptcy. This may be made conditional on him making payments under a mortgage or other outgoings of the property. If this is the case, then section 338 of the Act provides that the bankrupt does not, by virtue of those payments, acquire any interest in the premises.

Mortgage possession actions

As more people have become owner-occupiers of houses, the number of possession actions by mortgagees has also risen. Various problems can arise when the property is jointly owned. First, to obtain possession, the mortgagee must have priority over the holders of beneficial interests in the house. This issue is considered in detail in Chapter 7. Even when priority has been established, the court can postpone a possession order. This can occur at the instance of a spouse of the mortgagor who has shared occupation rights, without necessarily having a beneficial share in the house. This jurisdiction will now be considered.

Sole legal owner Where a married couple are joint legal owners of the house, they will be joint mortgagors and no particular difficulty is caused by co-ownership. The situation where one spouse, normally the husband, is the sole legal owner can, however, give rise to problems for the mortgagee in securing possession of the property. The difficulty arises when the husband stops paying the mortgage instalments and then, usually, leaves the property altogether. In this situation, the wife may wish to take over the mortgage payments.

Rights under the Matrimonial Homes Act Under section 1(5) of the Matrimonial Homes Act 1983,

"Where a spouse is entitled . . . to occupy a dwelling house or any part thereof, any payment or tender made or other thing done by that spouse in or towards satisfaction of any

---

[66] See *Re Lowrie* [1981] 3 All E.R. 353 at 356, *per* Walton J; *Harman* v. *Glencross* [1986] Fam. 81 at 95, *per* Balcombe L.J. *Cf. Thames Guaranty Ltd.* v. *Campbell* [1985] Q.B. 210 at 239, *per* Slade L.J.
[67] Insolvency Act 1986, s.331.

liability of the other spouse in respect of rent, rates, mortgage payments or other outgoing affecting the dwelling house shall, whether or not it is made or done in pursuance of an order under this section, be as good as if made or done by the other spouse."

Acquisition of interest

A wife, therefore, has the right to take over the mortgage payments and if able to do so will be able to continue in occupation of the house. It is further provided by section 1(7) of the Act that although the mortgagee is required to regard the payments made by the wife as having been made by the husband, the mortgagor, that will not affect any claim by the wife to have acquired an interest in the property.

Arrears A possession action will, in practice, only be brought by a mortgagee if the mortgage repayments are in arrears. Possession is then sought as a prelude to the exercise of the power of sale. The mortgagor's spouse will only be able to resist this action if she is able both to meet the continuing liability and also to discharge the accrued arrears. To do this, she may need to avail herself of the statutory jurisdiction to defer the mortgagee's action for possession.

Administration of Justice Acts 1970 and 1973[68] Under section 36 of the Administration of Justice Act 1970, the court is given the power, when a mortgagee brings a possession action with regard to land which consists of or includes a dwelling-house, to adjourn the proceedings. Alternatively, on giving judgment or making an order for the delivery of possession, the court may stay or suspend execution of the judgment or order, or postpone the date for the delivery of possession. These powers can only be exercised, however, if it appears that the mortgagor is likely to be able, within a reasonable period, to pay any sum due under the mortgage or to remedy a default consisting of a breach of any other obligation contained in the mortgage.

Default clauses

The problem with the Act of 1970 as drafted was that it ignored the effect of default clauses commonly contained in mortgages. If default is made in a number of instalments, the effect of a default clause is that the whole capital sum borrowed becomes payable. This occurred in *Halifax Building Society* v. *Clark*,[69] where it was held that for the court to exercise its jurisdiction under the Act of 1970, the mortgagor, or in this case his wife, must be able to repay the whole capital sum borrowed within a reasonable time, rather than simply the arrears that had accrued. This unfortunate decision undermined considerably the purpose of the Act and, as a result, section 8 of the Administration of Justice Act 1973 was passed to repair the damage.

Instalments and deferred payments

Section 8(1) of the Administration of Justice Act 1973 provides that when the mortgagor is entitled or is to be permitted to pay the principal sum secured by instalments or otherwise to defer payments of it in whole or in part, but provision is also

---

[68] See generally R. J. Smith [1979] Conv. 266; A. Clarke [1983] Conv. 293; S. Tromans [1984] Conv. 91.

[69] [1973] Ch. 307. For a more reasonable approach to default clauses, see *First Middlesbrough Trading Mortgage Co. Ltd.* v. *Cunningham* (1974) 28 P. & C.R. 69.

made for earlier payment in the event of any default by the mortgagor or of a demand by the mortgagee then, for the purposes of section 36 of the Administration of Justice Act 1970, a court may treat as due under the mortgage only such amounts as the mortgagor would have expected to pay if there had been no such provision for earlier payment. Section 8(2) further directs the court not to exercise its discretion under section 36 of the 1970 Act unless it is satisfied that not only can the arrears be paid within a reasonable time but also that the normal repayments expected during that period can be paid as well.

Notice of action It is fairly evident that a spouse's ability to take advantage of these provisions is going to be affected by how much notice she had of the fact that her husband has stopped paying the mortgage. If she is not told until late in the day, perhaps when a possession order has been obtained, the arrears may have accumulated to such an extent that she cannot repay them within a reasonable period. Had she known of the situation earlier, this problem may not have arisen. At common law, the mortgagee was under no obligation to inform the wife of her husband's arrears, to give her notice of the possession proceedings or make her a party to the action.[70] This issue is now regulated by statute.

Registration Under section 8(3) of the Matrimonial Homes Act 1983, if a mortgagee of land which consists or substantially consists of a dwelling-house brings an action for the enforcement of his security, and at the relevant time the spouse's statutory right of occupation is registered in the appropriate manner,[71] then notice of the action shall be served by the mortgagee on that spouse if she is not a party to the action. The spouse, who is entitled to meet the mortgage payments, can then apply to the court under section 8(2) of the Act to be made a party to the action. The spouse is entitled to be made a party to the action, if the court does not see any special reason against it, and is satisfied that the applicant may be expected to make such payments as might affect the outcome of the proceedings or that the expectation of it should be considered under section 36 of the Administration of Justice Act 1970.

Discretion to postpone possession Although both of the relevant provisions refer to default on the part of the mortgagor, it has been held that the court is empowered to postpone a possession action in any case where the mortgagee is seeking to enforce his security, regardless of whether the mortgagor is actually in default on the mortgage.[72] This result was achieved by adopting a purposive approach to the interpretation of the legislation. A similar approach has had to be adopted in other cases in order for the rationale of the sections to be furthered.

Instalment mortgages The type of mortgage most clearly envisaged by section 8 of the Administration of Justice Act 1973 is one where capital and interest is paid in instalments and the whole sum becomes

---

[70] *Hastings & Thanet Building Society* v. *Goddard* [1970] 1 W.L.R. 1544.
[71] In the case of unregistered land by a Class F land charge; in the case of registered land by a notice, or a caution if registered under s.2(7) of the Matrimonial Homes Act 1967: Matrimonial Homes Act 1983, s.2(8).
[72] *Western Bank Ltd.* v. *Shindler* [1977] Ch. 1.

payable in the event of default in payments. Other types of mortgage present some difficulty. In *Centrax Trustees Ltd.* v. *Ross*[73] the mortgage deed stipulated that the loan be repaid in six months. The mortgage also envisaged instalments being paid over a prolonged period with the whole sum becoming due on default. The problem was whether section 8 applied. This was, because the provision for the whole sum becoming payable did not require earlier payment, the whole sum was due six months from the date of the mortgage. Goulding J. held that on a liberal construction of the section he did have jurisdiction to postpone possession. He considered the obligation in equity as well as at law and concluded that the mortgagor had been permitted to defer payment and that the default clause operated as a provision for earlier payment than the mortgage envisaged.

Endowment mortgages

Under an endowment mortgage, the mortgagor pays interest on the sum borrowed for the period of the loan. He also pays the premiums on an assurance policy which matures at the end of the loan period, thereby redeeming the mortgage. The difficulty was whether section 8 of the 1973 Act applies to this type of mortgage, in that it is not clear that the mortgagor is entitled or permitted to defer payment of the principal sum.

Deferred payment

Habib Bank Ltd. v. Tailor

The potential problem emerged as a result of *Habib Bank Ltd.* v. *Tailor*.[74] The defendant executed a mortgage over his house to secure an overdraft with the plaintiff. He exceeded his overdraft limit and the plaintiff sought possession under the mortgage. In granting possession, the Court of Appeal held that there was no jurisdiction to postpone the order under section 8. This was because the mortgagor had not been permitted to defer payment of the principal sum; there was no legal obligation to repay it until that sum was demanded by the bank. This reasoning created a potential problem for endowment mortgages, as there is no legal liability to pay the principal sum until the end of the loan or an earlier demand. It seemed, therefore, that there was no provision for deferral of payment.[75]

Bank of Scotland v. Grimes

Endowment mortgage default

This difficulty has now been resolved in *Bank of Scotland* v. *Grimes*[76] where £15,015 had been borrowed to finance the purchase of a home, the mortgage to be repaid after 25 years when an endowment policy matured. The mortgagor defaulted on the interest and policy payments and the mortgagee sought possession, and an application was made for that order to be postponed under the Administration of Justice Acts. The Court of Appeal found section 8 of the Act extremely difficult to construe and so felt able to interpret it in order to give effect to its underlying policy. Distinguishing *Tailor* on the basis of the type of loan involved, it was held that a loan which was not to be repaid for 25 years was within section 8. On the facts, a reasonable time to pay the arrears was granted and possession refused.

Acquisition mortgages

It now seems clear that the courts, by a process of liberal interpretation, are prepared to bring within the section all types of mortgage commonly employed to finance the purchase of a house. Mortgages which will not be within the section are

---

[73] [1979] 2 All E.R. 952.
[74] [1982] 1 W.L.R. 1218.
[75] See S. Tromans [1984] Conv. 91 at 96–102.
[76] [1985] Q.B. 1179.

short-term mortgages to secure loans. As such, a wife will be able in most situations to qualify as a person able to take over the mortgage payments and pay the arrears, thereby continuing to enjoy her shared occupation rights after her husband has left.

Finance The court will only postpone a possession order, if there is a realistic prospect of the arrears being paid off within a reasonable time. The court will not postpone possession if the wife's prospect of making the repayment is dependent on some hypothetical windfall such as winning the pools.[77] If the wife is not in employment, however, she is entitled, as a deserted spouse, to apply for housing benefit to meet the interest payments on the mortgage.[78] Capital repayments will have to be met from other resources.

Length of postponement If the court is willing to grant a postponement of a possession order under the Administration of Justice Acts, it should not do so for an unlimited time. The court should assess what is a reasonable time in which the arrears should be paid and stipulate that in the postponement order.[79]

Equity of exoneration

When one of the two co-owners becomes insolvent, the other may be able to take advantage of the equity of exoneration. This doctrine is based upon the principle that when two co-owners are jointly liable to a secured creditor, but the money that is borrowed is for the exclusive benefit of one of them, then, as between the two co-owners, it is the one who has had the benefit of the loan whose beneficial share in the property is primarily liable to make good the sum borrowed. The doctrine is best explained by an example.

Co-owner as surety In *Re A Debtor (No. 24 of 1971)*[80] a father wished to help his son in business. He conveyed his freehold house into the joint names of his son and himself as tenants in common in equal shares. They then charged the house to a bank, the father acting as surety, to secure a loan for the son. The business failed and the son was adjudicated bankrupt. The house was valued at £10,300 and the son owed £4,739. The bank did not seek to enforce its security but the trustee in bankruptcy sought a sale of the house.

Implied intention as to burden The Divisional Court held that an intention should be implied as between the father and the son that the son's beneficial interest should bear the burden of the loan. On that basis, when the son's beneficial interest vested in the trustee in bankruptcy, it was subject to an inchoate right of indemnity if the father as surety was called upon to pay, or the debt fell to be discharged. The debt being primarily payable out of the son's half-share in the house, the trustee in bankruptcy was only entitled to the small sum that was the remainder of the son's half share in the house.

---

[77] *Hastings & Thanet Building Society* v. *Goddard* [1970] 1 W.L.R. 1544, 1548, *per* Russell L.J.
[78] Supplementary Benefit (Housing Requirements and Resources) Amendment Regulations 1987, reg. 2(3) (S.I. 1987 No. 17) amending Supplementary Benefit (Requirements) Regulations 1983, reg. 15(1)(ii) (S.I. 1983 No. 1399).
[79] *Royal Trust Co. of Canada* v. *Markham* [1975] 1 W.L.R. 1416.
[80] [1976] 1 W.L.R. 952. See also *Gee* v. *Liddell* [1913] 2 Ch. 62 at 72, *per* Warrington J.

As the value of the trustee in bankruptcy's share in the property was only £150, no sale was ordered.

Operation of the doctrine   For the equity of exoneration to arise, there must be a charge on jointly owned property to secure the debts of only one of the co-owners. The other co-owner is then entitled, as against the other, to have the secured indebtedness discharged so far as is possible out of the equitable interest of the debtor.[81] For the equity to arise, the money must be for the sole benefit of one of the parties. If the secured loan is used in part for general household expenditure and in part for the individual business purposes of one of the co-owners, the equity only applies with regard to the proportion of the loan used for the latter purpose. Where both benefit from the loan then, as between themselves, their beneficial interests bear the burden of the loan *pari passu*.

When the equity of exoneration arises, its effect is not simply to entitle one co-owner to be indemnified by the other. The indebtedness is thrown primarily on the share of the person who has benefited from the loan, thereby enhancing the beneficial share of the other.[82] The holder of the equity is entitled to prove in the bankruptcy of the other co-owner.[83] The existence of the equity may, therefore, cause the trustee in bankruptcy to acquire little of value when the bankrupt's beneficial interest vests in him. The secured creditor, however, will be able to obtain a sale to enforce his security.

---

[81] *Re Pittortou (A Bankrupt)* [1985] 1 W.L.R. 58 at 61, *per* Scott J.
[82] *Ibid.*
[83] *Re Cronmire* [1901] 1 K.B. 480.

7 PRIORITIES

The mortgagees' problem

In the previous Chapter, possession actions by mortgagees were considered. If the beneficial co-owner and the mortgagor are married, then, as has been seen, the co-owner may be able to retain possession by exercising the right to take over the mortgage repayments and pay off any arrears that have accrued. In such a situation, it is irrelevant that the co-owner has a beneficial interest in the house; the protection derives from that co-owner's status as the mortgagor's spouse. Acute problems for mortgagees, and indeed purchasers, can occur, however, if beneficial co-ownership of the home occurs. The difficulty then is that the mortgagee can find itself bound by that beneficial interest and consequently unable to obtain possession of the property as against that co-owner. Similar problems can arise if an interest is acquired through the medium of estoppel.

Decision in *Williams & Glyn's Bank* v. *Boland*

Overriding interest

The starting point in a consideration of these issues must be the landmark decision of the House of Lords in *Williams & Glyn's Bank* v. *Boland*.[1] Mr. Boland was the sole registered proprietor of a house but his wife had contributed substantially to its purchase. This, it was conceded, meant that there was beneficial co-ownership with the result that he held the house on an implield trust for sale for himself and his wife as beneficial tenants in common.[2] For purposes of his own, he then borrowed money from the bank and a legal charge was executed. On making the loan, the bank made no enquiries of Mrs. Boland, who was living in the house, as to what rights, if any, she had in the property. When Mr. Boland defaulted on the mortgage, the bank began possession proceedings which were resisted by Mrs. Boland on the basis that her beneficial interest in the house, coupled with her actual occupation of it, meant that she had an overriding interest in the property, under section 70(1)(g) of the Land Registration Act 1925, which bound the bank. This defence was upheld in the House of Lords and the bank was refused possession of the house.

The response to Boland

The decision in *Boland* aroused considerable interest and generated a substantial literature.[3] Much of this centred on the conveyancing implications of the case and so much concern was felt that the matter was referred to the Law Commission, who recommended statutory reversal of the decision.[4] The response to this was the introduction of the Land Registration and Law of

---

[1] [1981] A.C. 487. The case was heard together with the substantially identical case of *Williams & Glyn's Bank* v. *Brown*.
[2] See above pp. 15–16.
[3] See M. D. A. Freeman (1981) 11 Fam. Law 37; S. Freeman (1980) 43 M.L.R. 692; W. T. Murphy (1979) 42 M.L.R. 467; J. Martin [1980] Conv. 361; [1981] Conv. 219; C. Sydenham [1980] Conv. 427.
[4] Law Commission (1982) No. 115. But for a reversal of opinion, see now Law Commission (1987) No. 155, para. 2.64.

Property Bill 1985 which, if enacted, would have retained the decision in so far as spouses were concerned, but required all other co-owners to protect their beneficial interests by registration, if those rights were to be asserted against purchasers of the legal estate. Such discrimination between spouses and other co-owners was considered to be unacceptable and the Bill was withdrawn. The issue, therefore, remains for the common law and close attention must be paid to the basis of the decision itself and its wider conveyancing implications.

Legal title The view has been expressed that a conveyance or mortgage by a single trustee for sale should not operate to pass the legal estate.[5] The basis of this argument was that a trustee for sale derives his powers principally from section 28(1) of the L.P.A. 1925 which gives the trustees for sale all the powers possessed by the tenant for life and the trustees of the settlement in the case of settled land. In the case of settled land, while there exists a power to mortgage the property, this power does not extend to mortgages used either to finance the acquisition of the land, nor to later mortgages, except for the purpose of authorised improvements.[6] The answer to this is that the fact that a transaction is unauthorised does not make it void, so that the unauthorised transaction should still pass a legal interest to the mortgagee.[7] The courts have consistently adopted this latter view, admittedly without considering the alternative argument, and treated the matter as being whether the beneficial interest can be enforced in equity, either through the doctrine of notice or as an overriding interest.[8]

Co-owner's rights in equity In resisting the bank's claim for possession, Mrs. Boland had to establish both that she had a right to possess the land and also that that right was capable of enduring through successive ownerships of that land.[9] In establishing this, the argument had to be countered that, as a tenant in common behind a trust for sale, she had only an interest in the proceeds of sale of the land, rather than in the land itself.

Bull v. Bull In analysing the rights of a tenant in common behind a trust for sale, Lord Wilberforce in *Boland* drew heavily on the Court of Appeal decision in *Bull* v. *Bull*.[10] In that case, the plaintiff and his mother together bought a house for their use as a joint home but it was conveyed into his name alone. After four years of living together, he brought an action for possession but this was dismissed by the Court of Appeal.

The right of occupation Delivering the only judgment, Denning L.J. held first that the existence of a beneficial tenancy in common caused the land to be held upon an implied trust for sale.[11] It was then held that a beneficial tenant in common, in this case the mother, had a right

---

[5] S. M. Clayton [1981] Conv. 19.
[6] Settled Land Act 1925, s.71(1); Clayton [1981] Conv. 19 at 20–21.
[7] See R. J. Smith (1986) 49 M.L.R. 519 at 523 n. 16. See also Trustee Act 1925, s. 17.
[8] *Caunce* v. *Caunce* [1969] 1 W.L.R. 286; *Williams & Glyn's Bank* v. *Boland* [1981] A.C. 487.
[9] *National Provincial Bank Ltd.* v. *Ainsworth* [1965] A.C. 1175 at 1237, *per* Lord Upjohn; at 1261, *per* Lord Wilberforce.
[10] [1955] 1 Q.B. 234.
[11] See above pp. 15–16.

to remain in the house as against the other tenant in common.[12] This conclusion was arrived at by equating the rights of equitable tenants in common with the rights of legal tenants in common prior to 1926. When a tenancy in common was possible at law, each was, as against the other, entitled to possession. Section 34 of the L.P.A. 1925 prevents the creation of a legal tenancy in common. This section is, however, in Part I of the L.P.A. 1925 and section 14 provides that nothing in that Part of the Act shall prejudicially affect the rights of people in actual occupation. As the mother was in actual occupation, it was held that the abolition of legal tenancies in common by section 34 should not prejudicially affect her rights. She had the same rights as a legal tenant in common enjoyed prior to 1926, which included a right not to be ousted by a co-owner.

By holding that the mother could not be ousted from the house by the sole legal owner, who was also a beneficial co-owner, the Court of Appeal effectively gave her a power of veto over any sale of the property. This was recognised in terms by Denning L.J., who held that, unless the other beneficial tenant in common consented, there could be no sale with vacant possession by the sole legal owner, unless the sale was ordered under section 30 of the L.P.A. 1925.[13] Because section 14 of the L.P.A. 1925 was an integral factor in this reasoning, the fact of occupation is significant. The right that the beneficial tenant in common has is to remain in occupation, rather than to insist upon acquiring it.[14] The significance of this is that the equitable co-owner must be in occupation of the land to assert a right of possession against a mortgagee. If she is not, it is possible that a prior claim to a share of the proceeds of sale may be sustained but, in principle, the mortgagee would have a better right to possession.

Limits of Bull v. Bull

Purpose of the trust

A further limitation on the right of a beneficial tenant in common to occupy the property is that it must be an underlying purpose of the trust that the house is to be used for joint occupation. In *Barclay* v. *Barclay*[15] a testator devised a bungalow with a direction that it be sold and the proceeds of sale divided equally between five people. One of the five had lived in the bungalow with the testator prior to his death and continued to live there afterwards. The plaintiff acquired the legal title and sought possession as against the defendant prior to selling the bungalow. In ordering possession, the Court of Appeal distinguished *Bull* v. *Bull* as being a case where the principal purpose of the trust was to provide a home. Here it was not. The purpose of the trust was to sell the bungalow and divide the proceeds of sale. Accordingly the defendant, although having the right to a share in the proceeds of sale, had no right of occupation as against the legal owner. On a sale of the property, therefore, there would have been no right of possession against the purchaser.

---

[12] See also *Re Warren* [1932] 1 Ch. 42; *Cook* v. *Cook* [1962] P. 235; *Jones* v. *Jones* [1977] 1 W.L.R. 438. *Cf. Re Landi* [1939] Ch. 828. For critical comment, see H. Gray (1955) 18 M.L.R. 408; V. Latham (1955) 18 M.L.R. 303; F. R. Crane (1955) 19 Conv. (N.S.) 146.

[13] [1955] 1 Q.B. 234 at 239. For strong criticism, see H. W. R. Wade (1955) 14 C.L.J. 155.

[14] *Re Bagot's Settlement* [1894] 1 Ch. 177; G. A. Forrest (1956) 19 M.L.R. 312.

[15] [1970] 2 Q.B. 677.

The distinction made in *Barclay* v. *Barclay* has been criticised as coming perilously close to drawing a line between express and implied trusts for sale.[16] This is, however, a little misleading. Where there is an express trust for sale there will usually be two trustees for sale. The courts still have regard to the underlying purpose of the trust, but to consider whether or not to order a sale of the property. After a sale takes place, the beneficial interests behind the trust will be overreached.[17] Nevertheless, until the sale occurs a beneficiary may still have the right to remain in possession, even if she is not a trustee. If, as is likely, she is a trustee, then she will have the right, in her capacity as a legal joint tenant, not to be excluded from the property.

Co-owner's rights as an overriding interest Denning L.J.'s analysis in *Bull* v. *Bull* was expressly approved in *Williams & Glyn's Bank* v. *Boland*, where it was described as "illuminating."[18] As there was only one trustee for sale, she had the right as against him to remain in possession and to be consulted prior to any transaction affecting the house. Given the existence of those rights, to describe her interest as existing merely in the proceeds of sale seemed to Lord Wilberforce to be "just a little unreal."[19] Without actually holding her interest to be in the land itself, Mrs. Boland was held to be within the ambit of section 70 of the Land Registration Act 1925 as having rights subsisting in reference to the land,[20] which was sufficient for her beneficial interest to qualify as at least a potential overriding interest.

Interest in land?

A further argument put by the mortgagee was that, because an interest behind a trust for sale is included within the definition of minor interests,[21] it could not be an overriding interest. It was argued that these categories were mutually exclusive. Although finding the argument "formidable,"[22] Lord Wilberforce held that the effect of actual occupation was to upgrade a minor interest into an overriding interest; a finding of considerable significance to the general law of registered conveyancing and not merely to co-ownership.[23]

Conversion of minor interests

Actual occupation It was also argued in *Boland* that the wife was not in actual occupation of the house for the purposes of section 70(1)(g) of the Act. The basis of this argument was that this expression should be construed to reach the same result as the application of the principles of constructive notice would in unregistered land and that, if the vendor shared occupation of the house with another, there would be no constructive notice of that

---

[16] M. J. Prichard (1971) 29 C.L.J. 44 at 46. *Cf.* S. M. Cretney (1971) 44 M.L.R. 441 at 443 and A. E. Boyle [1981] Conv. 108.
[17] *City of London Building Society* v. *Flegg* [1988] A.C. 54. See below pp. 129–133.
[18] [1981] A.C. 487 at 507, *per* Lord Wilberforce. See also p. 510, *per* Lord Scarman.
[19] *Ibid.* at 507. *Cf. City of London Building Society* v. *Flegg* [1988] A.C. 54 at 78 and at 82–83, *per* Lord Oliver of Aylmerton.
[20] *Ibid.* at 507.
[21] Land Registration Act 1925, s.3(xv)(*a*).
[22] *Williams & Glyn's Bank* v. *Boland* [1981] A.C. 487 at 506.
[23] See *e.g. Webb* v. *Pollmount* [1966] Ch. 584; *Kling* v. *Keston Properties Ltd.* (1985) 49 P. & C.R. 412.

Question of fact

other's rights. It was argued that a wife's occupation was merely a shadow of her husband's.[24] This argument was totally rejected. The basic premise that the meaning of actual occupation was to be equated with constructive notice was not accepted. Section 70(1)(g) was interpreted literally, so that the question of whether a person is in actual occupation is one of fact[25]; "the law as to notice as it may affect purchasers of unregistered land . . . has no application even by analogy to registered land."[26]

It is now entirely clear that a person who shares a house with the vendor may assert any proprietary rights that he or she possesses as overriding interests against a purchaser of the land. *Boland* applies not only to spouses, but to all occupiers. Rather

Absences more difficult issues are raised if the occupier is absent from the property at the time of the transaction. In *Chhokar* v. *Chhokar*[27] a wife was in hospital having a child when her husband transferred the house to a purchaser and registration took place. It was nevertheless held that she was in actual occupation although, in reaching that conclusion, some reliance was placed on her furniture remaining there.[28]

There is at least a suggestion from *Chhokar* v. *Chhokar*, that

Visible signs it made a difference whether the wife had left furniture in the house. It is thought that this should not be significant. A person may be held to be in actual occupation of land, despite that occupation being virtually undiscoverable.[29] It is suggested that the court will be more concerned with the regularity of occupation and the length of any absences from the house,[30] rather than looking for outward manifestations of that occupation,[31] which in any event could be removed by an unscrupulous legal owner of the house. The courts are likely to regard such cases as matters of fact and degree. So, for example, it is thought that a student who has an interest in the family home will not be held to be in actual occupation in the term time periods when he is away studying. Where there is a prolonged absence, it is suggested that actual occupation would not continue, during that period.

Time of occupation In registered conveyancing, the crucial time for assessing priorities is generally thought to be the time of registration, rather than the time when the conveyance or transfer takes place.[32] This is because it is registration that effects

---

[24] *Williams & Glyn's Bank* v. *Boland* [1981] A.C. 487 at 490–492, *per* Mr. D. J. Nicholls Q.C.
[25] *Ibid.* at 506, *per* Lord Wilberforce; at 511, *per* Lord Scarman.
[26] *Ibid.* at 504, *per* Lord Wilberforce.
[27] [1984] F.L.R. 313.
[28] *Ibid.* at 317, *per* Ewbank J. This was not considered in the Court of Appeal.
[29] *Kling* v. *Keston Properties Ltd.* (1985) 49 P. & C.R. 212 at 222, *per* Vinelott J. See also *Hodgson* v. *Marks* [1971] Ch. 892 at 932, *per* Russell L.J.
[30] *Cf. Kingsnorth Finance Co. Ltd.* v. *Tizard* [1986] 1 W.L.R. 783. See also *Epps* v. *Esso Petroleum Ltd.* [1973] 1 W.L.R. 1071. (Sporadic parking of a car on a strip of land did not amount to actual occupation of it.)
[31] *Cf.* in the context of the Rent Act 1977, s.2, *Brown* v. *Brash* [1948] 2 K.B. 247.
[32] *Re Boyle's Claim* [1961] 1 W.L.R. 339; *E.S. Schwab & Co. Ltd.* v. *McCarthy* (1975) 31 P. & C.R. 196 at 204. *Cf. Epps* v. *Esso Petroleum Ltd.* [1973] 1 W.L.R. 1071 at 1078 *Paddington Building Society* v. *Mendelsohn* (1985) 50 P. & C.R. 244 at 247. See Barnsley, *Conveyancing Law and Practice* (2nd ed., 1982) p. 52; Law Commission (1982) No. 115, paras. 16 and 34. For the opposite view, see P. Sparkes [1986] Conv. 309.

the transfer or completion of the legal interest in the property[33] and so, on principle, that is the date for ascertaining what overriding interests the land was subject to. This was thought to create a potential trap, because there is often a gap between the transfer of the property and the creation of the mortgage and the application for registration. In that time, a person who has a beneficial interest in the land could go into occupation and therefore have an overriding interest in the property when the mortgage came to be registered.[34] It now seems, however, that this trap has been largely removed.

Potential problem

First mortgages

In *Paddington Building Society* v. *Mendelsohn*[35] a mother and son agreed to buy a flat together. She provided £15,000 and the balance was advanced by the plaintiffs by way of mortgage. The son was responsible for the mortgage payments and the flat was transferred into his name. The transfer was effected in July 1979, but the mortgage was not registered until October. In the interim period, the mother had moved into occupation of the flat. After the son defaulted on the mortgage and left the flat, the plaintiffs sought possession and the mother argued that she had an overriding interest binding upon them.

Bristol and West Building Society v. Henning

The Court of Appeal held, following its decision of the same day in *Bristol and West Building Society* v. *Henning*,[36] and distinguishing *Boland*, that the building society was entitled to possession. It was held that in the absence of an express trust, a right to a beneficial interest in land can only be established by proving an express or implied intention that the person who is not a legal owner should acquire an interest in the property. As the mother knew that the finance for the house was to be derived by means of a mortgage then, although no thought at all had actually been given to the matter, the intention would be imputed to her that the mortgagee was to have priority over her interest.

Imputed intention

Practical implications

The significance of these decisions for building societies is considerable. It was widely thought that the decision in *Boland* had put in jeopardy the security of many existing building society mortgages and also made it much more difficult to ensure that future mortgages of this type would have priority over competing interests. The danger was thought to be that if there was only one legal owner, a beneficial co-owner may exist whose interest may have priority over that of the mortgagee's even when the loan was for the purpose of financing the purchase. Simply asking the mortgagor if anyone was living with him who might have an interest in the property is not a sufficient safeguard. The mortgagor may reply untruthfully, and "Reliance upon the untrue ipse dixit of the vendor will not suffice"[37] to protect the mortgagee. The decisions in *Henning* and in *Mendelsohn* assuage all these fears, in that they held that the co-owners do not possess rights which are capable of binding this type of mortgage.

Extent of co-owners' rights

---

[33] Land Registration Act 1925, ss.19(1), 20(1), 26(1). Registration is effective from the date of the application for registration: Land Registration Rules, r. 83(2) as substituted by Land Registration Rules 1978, r. 8(2).
[34] See Law Commission (1982) No. 115, para. 34; J. Martin [1980] Conv. 361 at 369 and correspondence at [1981] Conv. 84. Murphy and Clarke, *The Family Home* (1983) pp. 161–162.
[35] (1985) 50 P. & C.R. 244. For criticism, see M. P. Thompson [1986] Conv. 57.
[36] [1985] 1 W.L.R. 778. Astonishingly, *Williams & Glyn's Bank* v. *Boland*, above n. 1 was not cited in this case.
[37] *Hodgson* v. *Marks* [1971] Ch. 892 at 932, *per* Russell L.J.

In the light of these cases, lending institutions will not be bound by beneficial interests behind a trust for sale if the loan is used to acquire the house itself. The only potential worry remaining is if further advances are made which cannot be tacked on to the original mortgage.

Critique   Both *Henning* and *Mendelsohn* have done much to reduce the impact of *Boland*, in that they have effectively confined that decision to second mortgages. The basis of the two decisions has been criticised.[38] In *Gissing* v. *Gissing*,[39] which the Court of Appeal purported to apply, Lord Diplock stated quite clearly that if the parties had not applied their minds at all to the question of how a beneficial interest in a family asset was to be

Intention   held at the time when it was acquired, then a court cannot give effect to a common intention on this matter which it was satisfied that they would have formed as reasonable persons if they actually had thought about it.[40] Yet in *Henning*, Browne-Wilkinson L.J. expressly found that the parties had not addressed their minds to the position of the mortgagee but nevertheless felt able to impute to them the intention that the building society were to have priority over Mrs. Henning's beneficial interest.[41] It is difficult to reconcile this with the reasoning employed in *Gissing*.

     The decisions in *Henning* and *Mendelsohn*, while not
Estoppel   squarely based on the principle that the beneficial co-owners were estopped from asserting rights against the mortgagee, proceed on a similar rationale. It has always been the case that the holder of a beneficial interest in land can be estopped from asserting that right against a purchaser. In such cases, however, the courts require that the person to be estopped has positively misled the purchaser.[42] Yet in these two cases, the mortgagees did not know of the existence of the two women and nor did they make enquiries as to their existence. There is a marked inconsistency between that line of authority and the approach taken in these two cases.

Limiting Boland   These two decisions limit the application of *Boland* to cases where the money is borrowed by the legal owner subsequent to the acquisition of the house and not to finance its purchase. This may indeed be a most desirable limitation but it is unfortunate that the result was achieved by what may, with respect, be described as somewhat dubious reasoning. It is nevertheless symptomatic of a judicial reluctance to extend the ambit of *Boland*[43] and, although these cases can be said to emasculate the approach of the House of Lords,[44] it is thought to be unlikely that they will be overturned.

---

[38] See M. P. Thompson (1986) 49 M.L.R. 245, [1986] Conv. 57; J. Martin (1986) 16 Fam. Law 315.
[39] [1971] A.C. 886.
[40] *Ibid.* at 904. See above p. 37.
[41] [1985] 1 W.L.R. 778 at 782.
[42] See *Abigail* v. *Lapin* [1934] A.C. 491; *Spiro* v. *Lintern* [1973] 1 W.L.R. 1002; *Wroth* v. *Tyler* [1974] Ch. 30; *Watts* v. *Spence* [1976] Ch. 115; *Midland Bank Ltd.* v. *Farmpride Hatcheries Ltd.* (1981) 260 E.G. 493. These cases were not cited in either *Henning* or *Mendelsohn*.
[43] See *e.g. Winkworth* v. *Edward Baron Development Co. Ltd.* [1986] 1 W.L.R. 1512 at 1515, *per* Lord Templeman.
[44] J. Martin (1986) 16 Fam. Law 315 at 316.

Unregistered land

Boland was a case where title to the land was registered. As such, the issue, once Mrs. Boland had established that she had a right in the property capable of adversely affecting a mortgagee, was whether she was in actual occupation of the land, within the meaning of section 70(1)(g) of the Land Registration Act 1925. Regarding this as a factual matter, the House of Lords held that she clearly was, despite the fact that the mortgagor also lived there. Had title to the land not been registered, the nature of her rights in the land would not have been affected. Their enforceability would, however, have been dependent on whether or not the bank had notice of her rights; whether they would have come to the bank's notice if such enquiries and inspections had been made as ought reasonably to have been made.[45]

Caunce v. Caunce

Constructive notice

Caunce v. *Caunce*[46] raised substantially the same issues as did *Boland*, but in this case the land was unregistered and so the issue was whether the mortgagee, which had made no enquiries of the wife, had constructive notice of her rights, she having been in occupation of the matrimonial home at all relevant times. Stamp J. held that it did not. He held in general terms that if the vendor or mortgagor is in occupation of the land himself, then a purchaser or mortgagee is not affected with notice of the equitable interests of any other person who might be resident there. In particular, this was so in this case as she could be seen to be in the house merely as the mortgagor's wife.[47]

Stamp J.'s approach was consistent with previous authorities as to the ambit of constructive notice,[48] but was nevertheless reflective of rather different social conditions. In *Hodgson* v. *Marks*,[49] the Court of Appeal accepted that the decision may have been correct in so far as the position of spouses were concerned but disapproved the wider dicta concerning other occupiers sharing accommodation with the legal owner. In *Boland*, the House of Lords went further and condemned the notion that a wife's occupation could be taken as a shadow of her husband's as "heavily obsolete,"[50] and *Caunce* was strongly disapproved.[51] Although this disapproval was technically *obiter*, it has been unrealistic to expect *Caunce* to be followed since *Boland*.

Kingsnorth Finance Co. Ltd. v. Tizard

In *Kingsnorth Finance Co. Ltd.* v. *Tizard*,[52] it was accepted that *Caunce* v. *Caunce* could not stand in the light of *Boland*. In this case, the matter was less straightforward, because the mortgagor's wife was not in permanent occupation of the house. She had recently left her husband, who was the sole legal owner of the house, and was staying with a friend who lived nearby. She did return to the matrimonial home on a daily basis to take the children to school and slept in the house occasionally, in a spare room where she kept some clothes and suitcases. Before granting

---

[45] L.P.A. 1925, s.199(1)(ii)(*b*).
[46] [1969] 1 W.L.R. 286.
[47] *Ibid.* at 293.
[48] See R. H. Maudsley (1973) 36 M.L.R. 25; M. P. Thompson [1984] Conv. 362 at 366–368.
[49] [1971] Ch. 892.
[50] [1981] A.C. 487 at 505, *per* Lord Wilberforce.
[51] *Ibid.* See also at 511, *per* Lord Scarman.
[52] [1986] 1 W.L.R. 783. See M. P. Thompson [1986] Conv. 283.

Mr. Tizard a mortgage, the plaintiffs' agents asked if he was married and he initially lied to them, stating that he was single. A man was sent around to inspect the house and he was suspicious that there might be a female occupant there but saw only a few suitcases. He drew the line at opening cupboards and drawers. From this inspection, it was concluded that he was a single man, sharing the house only with his children, and that the spare room was simply used for storage purposes. Nevertheless, Judge Finlay Q.C. sitting as a High Court judge, held that the plaintiffs had constructive notice that the wife was in actual occupation of the house, with the result that their mortgage was subject to her beneficial interest.

Extent of enquiries

It is submitted that while the result in this case can be justified, the reasoning employed is wrong. Judge Finlay laid great stress on the wife being in actual occupation. He also thought that the plaintiff should have discovered this fact and that the actual inspection of the house which was done did not exhaust the ambit of reasonable enquiries. As to this, the judge said:

What are reasonable enquiries?

> "Where, however, the object of the inspection (or one of the objects) is to ascertain who is in occupation, I cannot see that an inspection at a time pre-arranged with the vendor will necessarily attain that object. Such a pre-arranged inspection may achieve no more than an inquiry of the vendor or mortgagor and his answer to it."[53]

On this basis, it was held that an inspection on a Sunday afternoon at a time fixed with Mr. Tizard was not sufficient to class as having made reasonable enquiries and therefore the plaintiffs had constructive notice of the wife's beneficial interest.

Viewing by appointment

Judge Finlay clearly thought that a mortgagee should arrive unannounced at the property to check if the mortgagor is telling the truth when he states that he is single and lives in the house on his own. This, it is submitted, goes far beyond what are reasonable enquiries. It surely cannot be reasonable to adopt a practice which is based on the implicit assumption that one party to a business transaction is lying. Neither, it is submitted, should the mortgagee or his agent have to demand to see inside drawers and wardrobes to see if there are any clothes which would not be worn by the mortgagor. The purchaser is under a duty to make reasonable enquiries; he is not required to act as an over-enthusiastic private detective. It is, therefore, submitted that this aspect of the decision is wrong.

Occupation of unregistered land

In *Tizard*, the judge was concerned to see if the plaintiffs had constructive notice of the wife's occupation. This, with respect, is not the correct issue. The importance of occupation in unregistered land is that it puts a purchaser on notice that the occupier may have rights in that land. Notice can, however, be derived from other sources. In this case Mr. Tizard told the man who inspected the property that his wife had recently moved out of the house. The plaintiff's agent knew, therefore, of her existence. As it is by no means unlikely that she may have had a beneficial interest in the house, steps should have been taken to ascertain her whereabouts to ask her about this. In failing to do

Notice from other sources

---

[53] [1986] 1 W.L.R. 783 at 794–795.

so, the plaintiffs, it is submitted, failed to make reasonable enquiries. It should be remembered that in cases such as these, the beneficial co-owner is not always asserting a right to continue in occupation of the house; indeed, Mrs. Tizard was happy for the house to be sold. The issue was whether she had a prior claim to the proceeds of sale. If a mortgagee knows of a wife's existence, enquiries should be addressed to her. If this is not known, for example if the story had been that the children's mother had died, then on facts such as *Tizard*, a mortgagee should not be held to be affected with constructive notice of her rights.

Registered and unregistered land   Whether or not title to the land is registered can be significant in this type of case. If title to the land is registered, the issue of whether a beneficial co-owner has an overriding interest depends on whether or not that person is in actual occupation of the land. It is actual occupation which upgrades the minor interest into an overriding interest. Actual occupation is a factual matter and it is irrelevant whether or not its existence is discoverable by a purchaser. In unregistered land, however, the issue is whether a purchaser has made reasonable enquiries. If the beneficial co-owner is in fact in actual occupation, but this cannot be discovered by making reasonable enquiries, then a purchaser will take free from the occupier's rights. To that extent, there will be some difference between registered and unregistered land and the purchaser has slightly more security in the unregistered land system.

Establishing a right   In a number of the cases dealing with priorities, including *Boland* itself, the mortgagee has conceded that the person in occupation had acquired a beneficial interest in the house. This is an essential prerequisite if a possession action is to be resisted. It must be remembered that it is often in the interest of the legal owner to admit that there is beneficial co-ownership. This is because when, as in *Boland*, the marriage is continuing, the effect of holding that there is an overriding interest is that the mortgagor can continue to occupy the house with his wife, despite being in default on the mortgage. The courts are, therefore, quite rightly vigilant to see that the existence of a beneficial interest can be established on equitable principles and will not regard an admission by the sole legal owner as being in any way conclusive.[54]

Effect of finding overriding interest

Time of acquisition   A second, related point about the establishment of a beneficial interest in the house is that the acquisition of the interest must predate the mortgage. If a married couple are living in a house of which he is the sole legal and beneficial owner and he creates a mortgage, the mortgagee will have priority over any interest which the wife subsequently acquires under section 37 of the Matrimonial Proceedings and Property Act 1970 as a result of substantial improvements made to the house. Her interest takes effect against the equity of redemption.[55] The same principle applies to any estoppel rights acquired subsequent to the mortgage, whether by a spouse or any other occupier.[56]

---

[54] *Midland Bank plc* v. *Dobson* [1986] 1 F.L.R. 171; *Winkworth* v. *Edward Baron Developments Co. Ltd.* [1986] 1 W.L.R. 1512.
[55] See above pp. 45–46.
[56] For estoppel rights, see below pp. 136–139.

Undue influence

Where money is being loaned against the security of a house, it is clearly incumbent on the mortgagee, to protect its own interests, to ensure if there are other people with interests in the house, that they agree to their interests being postponed to the mortgagee. This is a task which must be undertaken with care as, otherwise, the consent may be voidable in equity. In particular, the mortgagee should not entrust the person seeking the loan with the task of obtaining the requisite consents.

Agency If the mortgagee used the borrower of the money as an agent, to obtain any necessary consents or signatures to the mortgage, any misconduct on the part of the agent will be imputed to the mortgagee. In *Avon Finance Co. Ltd.* v. *Bridger*[57] a son obtained a loan from a finance company to be secured against a house which was in his parents' names. He was entrusted to get their signatures to the mortgage deed and he represented to them that the document related to the building society mortgage taken out to finance the acquisition of the house. Because the company had used him as their agent, the undue influence and misrepresentation employed by him was imputed to them and the mortgage was set aside. Similarly, in *Kings North Trust Ltd.* v. *Bell*,[58] because the mortgagor's wife had a beneficial interest in the house, her consent was necessary to a second mortgage which was being taken out in favour of the finance company to secure a loan necessary to support his business, in which she was not involved. He obtained her signature by misrepresenting the purpose of the loan. This misrepresentation caused the Court of Appeal to set aside the consent form and her interest accordingly took effect as an overriding interest.

Imputed to the mortgagee

Independent advice In *Kings North Trust Ltd.* v. *Bell*, Dillon L.J. suggested that when a consent is necessary it would be prudent for the mortgagee to ensure that that person has independent legal advice.[59] Certainly the person should be advised to take advice[60] but the dangers for a mortgagee are considerably less if they deal directly with the person whose consent is required. If they do not use the person seeking the loan as their agent to obtain such consents, any undue influence actually employed by him will not be attributable to them.[61] The consent will then only be liable to be set aside if the mortgagee is guilty of undue influence in obtaining the consent. To establish this, the person seeking to have the consent set aside must show that the transaction was manifestly disadvantageous to her and that the mortgagee exerted undue pressure on her.[62] This will be difficult, particularly if she has been advised to get independent advice before signing. The

Setting aside consent

---

[57] [1985] 2 All E.R. 281 applying *Turnbull & Co.* v. *Duvall* [1902] A.C. 499; *Chaplin & Co. Ltd.* v. *Brammall* [1908] 1 K.B. 233. The case was actually decided in 1979.
[58] [1986] 1 W.L.R. 119. A similar argument failed on the facts in *Shephard* v. *Midland Bank plc* [1987] 2 F.L.R. 175.
[59] [1986] 1 W.L.R. 119 at 125.
[60] *Coldunell Ltd.* v. *Gallon* [1986] Q.B. 1184 at 1201, *per* Oliver L.J.
[61] *Ibid*. See J.E.M. [1986] Conv. 212.
[62] *National Westminster Bank plc* v. *Morgan* [1985] A.C. 686; *Cornish* v. *Midland Bank plc* [1985] 3 All E.R. 281.

Dispositions by two trustees

The heart of the problem in *Boland* was that, although there was a trust for sale, the mortgage had only been effected by one trustee for sale. It was generally assumed that had there been two trustees for sale, then the beneficial interests that existed behind that trust could not be asserted against a purchaser; the reason for this assumption being the overreaching provisions contained in Part I of the L.P.A. 1925.

The overreaching provisions

The principal overreaching provision in the L.P.A. 1925, is section 2. This provides that a conveyance[64] to a purchaser of a legal estate in land shall overreach any equitable interest or power affecting that estate, if the conveyance is made by trustees for sale. This is reinforced by section 26(3) which imposes an obligation upon the trustees for sale to consult the persons for the time being beneficially entitled in possession in the rents and profits until sale and, so far as is consistent with the general purposes of the trust, to give effect to those wishes but specifically provides that a purchaser is not to be concerned to see that this requirement has been complied with. Finally, section 27(1) provides that a purchaser of a legal estate from trustees for sale is not to be concerned with the trusts affecting the proceeds of sale of land subject to a trust for sale. Taken together, these sections clearly envisage that if the conveyance is executed by two trustees for sale,[65] then the purchaser is not to be concerned with th beneficial interests existing behind the trust for sale.

Interests behind a trust for sale

Although these statutory provisions seem to point clearly to the conclusion that the beneficial interests behind a trust for sale could not be enforced against a purchaser of a legal estate if the conveyance was executed by two trustees for sale, a counter-argument was raised. The gist of this argument was this.[66] Although conventionally, beneficial interests behind a trust for sale are seen, owing to the doctrine of conversion, to exist in the proceeds of sale, modern case law has established that, if the underlying purpose of the trust is to provide a home, then, in addition to their interest in the proceeds of sale, beneficiaries who are in actual occupation of the land have a number of other rights. These rights include a right not to be evicted by the trustees, a right to be consulted prior to a sale and a right to resist that sale taking place.[67] If these rights cease to exist after a conveyance by two trustees for sale, because of the overreaching provisions contained in Part I of the Act, then the

---

[63] This concept was introduced by Lord Denning M.R. in *Lloyds Bank* v. *Bundy* [1975] Q.B. 326, and was disapproved in *National Westminster Bank plc* v. *Morgan* [1985] A.C. 686 at 708 by Lord Scarman. See C. J. Barton and P. M. Rank [1985] Conv. 387.

[64] Conveyance is defined to include a mortgage: L.P.A. 1925, s.205(1)(ii).

[65] This assumes there are only two legal owners. If there are three or four legal owners, then all must execute the conveyance.

[66] For a full exposition of the argument, see M. P. Thompson (1986) 6 *Legal Studies* 140.

[67] These rights derive principally from *Bull* v. *Bull* [1955] 1 Q.B. 234, a decision approved in *Boland*. See Thompson (1986) 6 *Legal Studies* 140 at 143–146.

L.P.A. 1925, s.14	beneficiaries' position would seem to have been prejudiced. It was argued that they could not have this effect, because of section 14 which provides that:

> "This Part of this Act shall not prejudicially affect the interests of any person in possession or in actual occupation of land to which he may be entitled in right of such possession or occupation."

Flegg's Case	The argument that a conveyance by two trustees for sale would not necessarily overreach the beneficial interests behind a trust for sale was rejected by the House of Lords in *City of London Building Society* v. *Flegg*.[68] A property, aptly named Bleak House, was purchased in 1977 for £34,000. Mr. and Mrs. Flegg provided £18,000 and the balance was provided by the Hastings and Thanet Building Society. The Fleggs had no wish to be liable for the mortgage repayments, which were to be the responsibility of their daughter and son-in-law, the Maxwell-Browns. To achieve this result and, despite advice to the contrary, the property was conveyed to the Maxwell-Browns alone, as beneficial joint tenants. They were registered as sole proprietors and no restriction was entered on the proprietorship register. The Maxwell-Browns then borrowed various sums of money by way of mortgage, this being neither known to or approved of by the Fleggs. Finally, they borrowed £37,000 from the plaintiffs, executing a legal mortgage in their favour. This money was used to redeem all the subsisting mortgages, including the one in favour of the Hastings and Thanet Building Society, which had been approved by the Fleggs.[69] The issue in the case was whether the plaintiffs were entitled to possession or whether the Fleggs had an overriding interest binding upon them. The action for possession was upheld by Judge Thomas, sitting as a High Court judge, but this was reversed by the Court of Appeal.[70] That decision was in turn reversed by the House of Lords who restored the possession order.
Registration issues	Further facts, which are actually highly significant, but which received scant attention in either the House of Lords or the Court of Appeal, should also be related. These are that, before advancing the money, the plaintiffs obtained an official certificate of search which afforded them priority until January 14, 1982. The charge itself was executed on January 12, but was not lodged for registration, until January 26, outside the priority period. Meanwhile on December 7, the parents had lodged a caution against dealings and, as a result of the dispute, the plaintiffs had not, at the time of the hearing in the House of Lords, actually been registered as proprietors of the charge.
Non-registration	The significance of the plaintiffs not having been registered as proprietors of the charge is that, under section 26(1) of the Land Registration Act 1925, a charge is completed when the

---

[68] [1988] A.C. 54. For the provisional view that the decision should be reversed by legislation, see Law Commission (1988) W.P. No 106.
[69] It was common ground that this mortgage had priority over any interest that the Fleggs might have. It was conceded that the plaintiffs were not subrogated to the rights of that mortgagee: *Orakpo* v. *Manson Investments Ltd.* [1978] A.C. 95.
[70] [1986] Ch. 605.

registrar enters on the register the person in whose favour the charge is made as the proprietor of the charge and the particulars of the charge.[71] Although a legal mortgagee is treated as the purchaser of a legal estate, until he is registered as proprietor of the charge, he has only an equitable mortgage.[72] The significance of this is that the principal overreaching provisions, sections 2 and 27 of the L.P.A. 1925, operate to ensure that a purchaser of a legal estate shall overreach the interests behind a trust for sale if the conveyance is executed by two trustees for sale. As the plaintiffs in *Flegg* had only purchased an equitable estate, if overreaching had been effected by the mortgage itself, then it could not have occurred as a result of these statutory provisions and, therefore, section 14 could not have been relevant.

Overreaching under the general law Lord Oliver of Aylmerton, who gave the leading speech, took the view that it was not necessary to rely on the overreaching provisions contained in the L.P.A. 1925 to reach the conclusion that the mortgage itself had overreached the beneficial interest of the Fleggs, which was transferred to the equity of redemption.

Rights under a trust for sale Although Lord Oliver laid considerable stress on the doctrine of conversion, he did recognise that, by judicial construction, beneficial tenants in common who were in occupation of land retained some of the rights that legal tenants in common had enjoyed prior to 1925. These rights included the right to remain in occupation and to resist a sale. These rights, however, are "fathered by a trust for sale"[73] and cannot exist independently of it. Consequently, on the termination of the trust for sale, or the exercise of the trustees' powers, these rights must also either be terminated or modified.

This reasoning is not dependent on the statutory overreaching provisions and therefore conclusively meets the argument based upon section 14 of the L.P.A. 1925. Applying it to the facts, it meant that the execution of the mortgage

Transfer of beneficial interests document automatically transferred the beneficial interests to the equity of redemption. This would enable the Fleggs to retain possession as against the Maxwell-Browns, but would prevent them from asserting their interest against the mortgagee. When the mortgage came to be registered, the Fleggs would have no rights capable of existing as overriding interests.[74]

Distinguishing Boland The Fleggs had relied heavily on the decision in *Boland* to resist the possession action. That case was distinguished precisely on the basis that that mortgage had not been executed in the implementation of the powers of trustees for sale, whereas in this case it had. If the transactions had been sales rather than mortgages, this difference can be highlighted further. If the Maxwell-Browns had sold Bleak House, this would have

---

[71] See also Land Registration Act 1925, s.19(2). Section 27(3) does not operate to confer a retrospective legal charge back to the date of its creation: *Grace Raymer Investments Ltd.* v. *Waite* [1958] Ch. 831. See also *Lever Finance Ltd.* v. *Needleman's Trustees* [1956] Ch. 375 and *Emmet on Title* (19th ed.) para. 25.007.
[72] Ruoff and Roper, *Registered Conveyancing* (5th ed., 1986) p. 598.
[73] [1988] A.C. 54 at 83. For a similar analysis, see D. J. Hayton (1986) 130 New L.J. 208.
[74] *Cf.* the speech of Lord Templeman, where it is unclear if it is the mortgage or the registration that effected overreaching.

terminated any rights that the Fleggs had in the property as the trust for sale would have been performed. Pending registration of the purchaser as proprietor, the trustees would have held on a bare trust for him. If the house had been sold in *Boland*, however, this would not have been a purported execution of the trust for sale and the beneficiary in actual occupation could have asserted her rights against the purchaser.

Protecting the beneficial interest It will be recalled that in *Flegg*, the beneficiaries had lodged a caution against dealings. This registration occurred within the priority period conferred by the search and the mortgage was also executed within that period, albeit not registered. It is not apparent from the speeches in the House whether the fact that the mortgage was created in that period was regarded as significant. This raises the issue of whether, short of being registered as legal owners, there was any way that the Fleggs could have protected their interest.

Prior to the legal owners exercising their powers as trustees for sale, it would seem clear that the parents in *Flegg* had, as beneficial tenants in common, the right to be consulted and, so far as was consistent with the purpose of the trust, their wishes should have been given effect to.[75] In principle, these rights should be capable of protection by a restriction. Such a restriction is, in form, likely to be to the effect that no transfer or mortgage is to be registered without the consent of named beneficiaries.[76] It might be objected, in the light of Lord Oliver's speech, that such a restriction is inapposite as it is the mortgage or transfer itself that effects overreaching and that the restriction on registration is not protecting any enforceable right. Such an objection is considered to be unsound because section 58(1) of the Land Registration Act 1925 operates to prevent a transaction being effected unless the terms of the restriction are complied with. As a transfer or a mortgage is a transaction, this section would appear to curtail the trustees' power to overreach the beneficial interests without consulting the beneficiaries, if such a restriction is registered.

Restriction

L.R.A. 1925, s.58(1)

Cautions If a caution, as opposed to a restriction, is registered then the position is more doubtful. The consequence of registering a caution is that before any dealing with the property is registered, the registrar should serve notice on the cautioner to show cause why the dealing should not be registered.[77] At the hearing, the case for a restriction should be easy to establish. The normal principle with regard to registration is that it takes effect from the date when the application for registration is delivered.[78] By analogy, it is thought that the restriction should be operative from the date when the caution was registered, with the result that the mortgage or transfer would not overreach the beneficial interests.

As against this, in *Flegg* the registration of a caution was ineffective to protect the parents' beneficial interest. The

---

[75] L.P.A. 1925, s.26(3); Ruoff and Roper, above n. 72, pp. 861–862.
[76] *Ibid.* p. 872.
[77] Land Registration Act 1925, ss.54 and 55. To register a caution, it is sufficient if the cautioner is interested in any land. See also *ibid.* s.101(3). This includes a beneficiary under a trust for sale. *Elias* v. *Mitchell* [1972] Ch. 652.
[78] Land Registration Rules 1925, r. 83(1).

Priority period mortgage was, however, executed within the priority period afforded by the search, even though registration was not. As the mortgage itself was the overreaching event, it seems appropriate that the protection of the search should extend to it. If, however, the mortgage was created outside the priority period, it is hard to see any policy reason why the mortgagee should be protected and it is submitted that he would take subject to the cautioner's interest. In practice, no doubt a mortgagee who discovered the caution would not proceed with the transaction. If no search was effected, however, and the mortgage is created then this issue will arise. It is unfortunate that the House of Lords did not consider the registration issues more closely.

Unregistered land If title is unregistered, it would not appear that the holder of a beneficial interest behind a trust for sale could protect that interest by registration of a land charge. As any such a charge would only serve to give a purchaser notice of the matter that is registered, registration would in any event be ineffective as it is irrelevant if a purchaser has notice of interests that have been overreached. In contrast, registration in the registered title system can limit the powers of the proprietor to deal with the land. The only course open to people in the position of Mr. and Mrs. Flegg would appear to be to apply for an injunction to restrain unauthorised dealings with the land.

Conveying co-owned property after *Flegg* The decision in *City of London Building Society* v. *Flegg* is of major importance, confirming the effectiveness of the overreaching machinery when transactions are effected by two trustees for sale. It remains to consider the various situations when co-ownership of land may exist and the position of a purchaser[79] when the conveyance or transfer is, or is purported to be, executed by two legal owners. In so doing the situation where co-ownership exists from the outset can be distinguished from the situation where an additional trustee has been appointed some time after the land had been acquired.

Multiple beneficial ownership The first situation is where the legal title has been conveyed to two trustees but a number of other people are also co-owners in equity. These were the facts in *Flegg* and it is clear that a conveyance by the two trustees will overreach all the beneficial interests behind the trust for sale. The legal owners should contract to sell and convey the land as trustees.[80] If the sale or mortgage is wrongful, the trustees may be personally liable to the beneficiaries, and this is particularly so if the purchase money is misapplied. This is not a matter which concerns the purchaser.

Coincidence of legal and beneficial ownership A quite common situation is for land to be conveyed to two people who will hold the property upon trust for themselves. This will occur most frequently when the two people are a married couple. The conveyancing procedure in such a case is quite straightforward: both legal owners should be parties to the conveyance. Problems have arisen in practice, however, where one co-owner forges the other's signature so that it appears that the conveyance is by two trustees for sale, whereas in reality it is not.

---

[79] This term includes a mortgagee.
[80] They should not convey as beneficial owners, thereby giving wider covenants for title: *Emmet on Title* (19th ed.) paras. 14.01–14.03.

Forgery If title to the land is unregistered, it is quite clear that such a forged deed cannot be effective either to transfer the legal estate or to create a legal mortgage. It will not, however, be entirely ineffective. Assuming that the legal joint tenants are a husband and wife and the husband forges his wife's signature on a conveyance, the deed will be operative to transfer all his interest in the land.[81] The beneficial joint tenancy will be severed and his half share will pass to the purchaser.[82] The husband and wife will then hold the legal title on trust for sale for the wife and the purchaser. The purchaser should then petition the court for a sale under section 30 of the L.P.A. 1925. Unless the purchaser was aware of the forgery, it is thought likely that a sale will be ordered. If the transaction is a mortgage, this will operate on his own beneficial share and, in default, the mortgagee will bring proceedings under the Charging Orders Act 1979, having secured judgment for the debt.[83]

Joint tenancy severed

Registered land

If title to the land is registered and a forgery occurs, again assuming that the legal joint tenants are husband and wife, it is important to know, first whether the purchaser has been registered as a proprietor and secondly, whether or not the wife was in actual occupation of the land.

If the purchaser is registered as proprietor, he will acquire the legal title to the land, despite the conveyance or transfer being a forgery.[84] If the wife is in actual occupation, however, her beneficial interest will take effect as an overriding interest.[85] If, however, she is not in actual occupation of the land,[86] a purchaser registered as proprietor will take free from her rights. The wife should then apply to the court or to the registrar for the register to be rectified to give effect to her interest.[87] If, however, the purchaser has gone into possession of the land and has not himself substantially contributed to the error by fraud or lack of proper care, then it is unlikely that the register would be rectified to give effect to the wife's interest.[88] If that is the case then she will be entitled to an indemnity, the amount to be assessed in accordance with the value of the land when the registration occurred.[89]

Rectification

Indemnity

Powers of attorney[90] It is possible, where there is more than one legal owner of land, for one of them to confer on the other or others a power of attorney enabling them to perform the trustees' obligation. As this involves a delegation of a trustee's discretion, this must be done under section 25 of the Trustee Act 1925,[91] the effect of which is that the power cannot extend for more than 12

---

[81] L.P.A. 1925, s.63.
[82] *Ahmed* v. *Kendrick*, *The Times*, November 12, 1987. *Cedar Holdings Ltd.* v. *Green* [1981] Ch. 129, to the contrary, was overruled in *Williams & Glyn's Bank* v. *Boland* [1981] A.C. 487.
[83] *First National Securities Ltd.* v. *Hegerty* [1985] Q.B. 850. See above pp. 102–103.
[84] Land Registration Act 1925, ss.5, 20.
[85] *Ibid.* s.70(1)(*g*).
[86] See *Ahmed* v. *Kendrick*, *The Times*, November 12, 1987.
[87] Land Registration Act 1925, s.82(1)(*d*). The registered proprietor would if in good faith, be entitled to an indemnity: *ibid.* s.83(4).
[88] *Ibid.* s.82(3).
[89] *Ibid.* s.83(2)(ii).
[90] See generally, *Emmet on Title* (19th ed.) paras. 10.011–10.019.
[91] As amended by Powers of Attorney Act 1971, s.9.

months. This is so, even when the trustees themselves are the beneficial owners of the land.[92] The power of attorney must be signed and sealed by, or by direction and in the presence of, the donor of the power.[93]

Appointment of an additional trustee The final situation to be considered is when there is originally sole ownership at law but co-ownership in equity and the legal owner appoints a second trustee and then the two legal owners together execute a conveyance or mortgage of the property. The issues to be considered are first whether the legal owner can do this and, secondly, whether the purchaser will have priority over the competing beneficial interests. Put another way, had the husband in *Boland* appointed a second trustee before mortgaging the house to the bank, could his wife have asserted her rights in the house as an overriding interest?

Power to appoint   There seems no reason why the sole legal owner should not appoint an additional trustee.[94] Under section 36(6) of the Trustee Act 1925:

> "Where . . . there are not more than three trustees (none of them being a trust corporation) either original or substituted and whether appointed by the court or otherwise, then and in any such case—
> (a) the person or persons nominated for the purpose of appointing new trustees by the instrument, if any, creating the trust; or
> (b) if there is no such person . . . then the trustee or trustees for the time being;
> may by writing, appoint another person or other persons to be an additional trustee or additional trustees . . ."

Effect of appointment   If there is sole ownership at law but co-ownership in equity, then the holder of the legal title is a trustee. Accordingly, he would seem to be quite able to appoint an additional trustee. If this is done by deed, the deed is effective to vest the legal title in the person named and the existing trustee as joint tenants without further conveyance.[95] In the case of registered land, the appointment of a new trustee must be completed by registration.[96]

Conveyance by two trustees   If this practice, similar in effect to that which prevailed on the death of a joint tenant prior to the enactment of the Law of Property (Joint Tenants) Act 1964, is adopted then, as a result of *Flegg*, all beneficial interests behind the trust for sale will be overreached. In the scenario envisaged, where husband and wife are co-owners in equity but the husband is the sole owner at law, he can simply appoint a second trustee and any mortgage or conveyance that they execute will overreach the wife's interest. It

---

[92] *Walia* v. *Michael Naughton Ltd.* [1985] 1 W.L.R. 1115. For enduring powers, see Enduring Powers of Attorney Act 1985, s.3(3).
[93] Powers of Attorney Act 1971, s.1(1). If this is done by direction, two witnesses must be present and they must attest the power: s.1(2).
[94] See [1980] Conv. 315–316. *Cf.* A. M. Prichard [1980] Conv. 458.
[95] Trustee Act 1925, s.40(1)(2).
[96] Land Registration Act 1925, s.47. The registration fee is then reduced to one-half in respect of the registered title; Land Registration Fee Order 1986 (S.I. 1986 No. 1399) Sched. 6. See Ruoff and Roper, above n. 72, pp. 441–443.

should be remembered, however, that the trustees will be liable to account to the wife for the money that they receive and she will be able to sue either of them for breach of trust. This consideration may, in practice, dampen the enthusiasm of any associate of the husband, who is requested to act as a second trustee, to accept the invitation.

Estoppel interests

The strategem of appointing a second trustee to overreach a co-owner's beneficial interest will only be effective, if that person's interest takes effect behind a trust for sale. It may transpire, however, that the interest which is asserted against a purchaser is not a beneficial interest acquired under a resulting or constructive trust because of a direct contribution to the purchase price; instead, the claim to an interest may be based on proprietary estoppel.[97] If such a claim is made out, it is not at all clear that a purchaser who takes a conveyance from two legal owners will take free from this interest.

The nature of the interest

Where a person has made a direct financial contribution to the purchase of a house, the interest acquired will be under a resulting trust[98] and no difficulty arises in overreaching that interest, provided that the conveyance is by two trustees. Rather greater difficulty will arise when the person claiming an interest in land bases that claim on reliance on an expectation that she will have either an interest in it, or some indefinite right to occupy it. In such cases, although Sir Nicolas Browne-Wilkinson V.-C. has recently stated that the principles of proprietary estoppel are akin to the principles underlying the constructive trust,[99] it may become necessary to distinguish between them, if a purchaser is concerned.

Constructive trust

This is because if a constructive trust is imposed, the beneficiary acquires a beneficial interest in that property. The trustee will also have an interest and thus there will be beneficial co-ownership and an implied trust for sale. Overreaching will therefore be effected by a conveyance by the two legal owners of the land.

Proprietary estoppel

On the other hand, in estoppel cases, the court has a discretion as to how the equity that has arisen is to be satisfied. It may be that the court will conclude that the equity should be satisfied by giving the person a beneficial share in the property, but this is not a necessary conclusion. Thus in one case, the sole owner of a house was ordered to convey it to his erstwhile mistress to satisfy the estoppel.[1] Consideration must therefore be given to the differences between the constructive trust and estoppel and then to the issue of whether estoppel rights will bind a purchaser.

Constructive trusts and estoppel The basis of the constructive trust, as it operates in this area, is that the courts give effect to an agreement between the parties as to what the beneficial interests in a house should be. Such agreements are almost invariably oral

---

[97] Above pp. 46–50.
[98] Above pp. 41–46.
[99] *Grant* v. *Edwards* [1986] Ch. 638 at 656.
[1] *Pascoe* v. *Turner* [1979] 1 W.L.R. 431.

and, therefore, are not in themselves enforceable, in that a declaration of trust respecting any land must be proved in writing signed by some person who is able to declare such trust.[2] If a man and woman set up home together and agree that the house is to be jointly owned, but the house is conveyed into his name alone, that agreement will not be enforceable unless she can establish a constructive trust. This she can do by showing that she has contributed to the purchase of the house, either by financial contribution or in kind.[3] In that case, if the man was able to rely on the lack of writing to deny her beneficial entitlement, he would be unjustly enriched. To prevent this, a constructive trust is imposed to give effect to the agreement and co-ownership in equity will result.[4] If the man appoints a second trustee for sale and conveys to a purchaser, her interest will be overreached.

Principles of a constructive trust

Principles of estoppel

The basis upon which rights are gained through the medium of estoppel is similar but not entirely the same. In such cases, one party has the expectation of the right to indefinite occupation of the house. This may include the expectation of having a beneficial interest in the house but the nature of the expectation is often ill-defined. The person who has the expectation then relies upon it in circumstances where it would be inequitable for the sole owner of the house subsequently to evict her. This then gives rise to rights in estoppel which it is for the court to determine how best to satisfy. The essential differences between an estoppel case and one of constructive trust is the ill-defined nature of the initial understanding and the fact that there is reliance upon that understanding, rather than a contribution to the acquisition of the house.

Distinction

The distinction is best seen by an example. In *Maharaj (Sheila)* v. *Chand (Jai)*,[5] the plaintiff and defendant had an association and had a child. In reliance on his representation that a house into which they were moving would be a permanent home for her and her children, she gave up a flat and went to live with him in the house. She also used her earnings for household requirements and looking after the family. On the termination of the relationship, he sought possession but it was held by the Privy Council that she had, by virtue of the doctrine of proprietary estoppel, a personal right[6] as against him to stay in the house indefinitely. Although the Privy Council thought it possible that she might have been able to have claimed a beneficial interest in the house,[7] it was considered to be a much clearer case of estoppel. The thrust of her argument was the reliance on his representation, not her contribution to the purchase of the house.

---

[2] L.P.A. 1925, s.53(1)(*b*).
[3] See *e.g. Cooke* v. *Head* [1972] 1 W.L.R. 518.
[4] *Eves* v. *Eves* [1975] 1 W.L.R. 1338; *Re Densham, (A Bankrupt)* [1975] 1 W.L.R. 1519; *Grant* v. *Edwards* [1986] Ch. 638.
[5] [1986] A.C. 898. *Cf. Tanner* v. *Tanner* [1975] 1 W.L.R. 1346 where on similar facts, the Court of Appeal held that the women had a contractual right to remain in the house.
[6] *Maharaj (Sheila)* v. *Chand (Jai)* [1986] A.C. 898 at 903. It was not argued that she had a property right in the house, because of the provisions of the Fijian, Native Land Trust Act 1978 (c. 134).
[7] *Ibid.* at 907–908, *per* Sir Robin Cooke.

Enforcement of rights It is not at all clear whether interests generated by estoppel will bind purchasers, particularly if the land was conveyed as a purported exercise of a trust for sale. There are certainly dicta to the effect that estoppel rights will bind a purchaser[8] and in *E.R. Ives Investment Ltd.* v. *High*,[9] a purchaser who had bought land with actual notice of a right of way arising by estoppel was held to be bound by it. Similarly, in *Re Sharpe*,[10] a decision widely viewed as an estoppel case,[11] a trustee in bankruptcy was held to be bound by occupation rights. Despite these authorities, it is submitted that a purchaser will not necessarily be bound by estoppel rights, even if the holder of them is in actual occupation of the land at the time of the transaction.

The problem defined

The situation where difficulties might occur is where a man and a woman decide to cohabit and a house is purchased and conveyed into the man's name, he paying the deposit and the mortgage instalments. He leads her to believe that she will acquire an interest in the house, or that she will always be able to remain in it. Perhaps, at some later date, as their ways part, he even purports to give the house to her. She then relies on this expectation in circumstances whereby she acquires rights against him. The issue is whether those rights can be enforced against a purchaser.

Contract

It is possible that this situation will be seen as giving rise to a contractual relationship. Although such an analysis has been employed in a similar case,[12] it seems dubious both because it is difficult to see the necessary certainty in the dealings normally required for a contract and also that there is a problem finding consideration, as that doctrine is traditionally perceived. It now seems clear that such a contract cannot be enforced against a purchaser even with notice of it.[13]

Estoppel

If, as is far more likely, the woman gains rights through the medium of estoppel then it is possible that she will be able to assert those rights against a subsequent purchaser, if she was in occupation of the house when the transaction took place. Much will depend, it is suggested, on whether the transaction was effected by the man alone or whether he first appointed a second person as legal owner to effect the transaction.

Nature of estoppel rights

When rights have been acquired through estoppel, it is in the court's discretion as to how those rights should be satisfied and, in deciding that issue, the courts have regard to a wide variety of circumstances.[14] In the exercise of that discretion, the

---

[8] *Inwards* v. *Baker* [1965] 2 Q.B. 29 at 37, *per* Lord Denning M.R. Title had passed in this case by succession.
[9] [1967] 2 Q.B. 379. See also *Williams* v. *Staite* [1979] 2 Ch. 291.
[10] [1980] 1 W.L.R. 219. But see now *Ashburn Anstalt* v. *W.J. Arnold & Co.* (1987) 284 E.G. 1375.
[11] J. Martin [1980] Conv. 209 at 213–214; T. Bailey [1983] Conv. 99 at 101.
[12] *Tanner* v. *Tanner* [1975] 1 W.L.R. 1346. See also the somewhat different cases of *Hardwick* v. *Johnson* [1978] 1 W.L.R. 683 and *Chandler* v. *Kerley* [1978] 1 W.L.R. 693 where contracts were found to exist.
[13] *Ashburn Anstalt* v. *W.J. Arnold & Co.* (1987) 284 E.G. 1375 at 1384 disapproving dicta to the contrary by Lord Denning M.R. in *Errington* v. *Errington* [1952] 1 K.B. 290; *Binions* v. *Evans* [1972] Ch. 359 and *D.H.N. Food Distributors Ltd.* v. *Tower Hamlets London Borough Council* [1976] 1 W.L.R. 852.
[14] Above pp. 49–50.

court may award her a proprietary interest in the house, including an order that he convey the house to her,[15] or it may settle on some lesser remedy, such as allowing her to continue in occupation until compensated for her reliance.[16] There seems no reason in principle why the court should not satisfy the equity by declaring her to be a beneficial co-owner of the land. Because of the existence of this discretion, she has only a potential or inchoate right to an interest in land which must therefore be classified as an equity.[17]

Transaction by a single owner

Equities are quite capable of binding purchasers of land. They are capable of taking effect as an overriding interest[18] and, if title is unregistered, binding a purchaser with notice. If the man either sells or mortgages the house and the woman is in actual occupation at the relevant time then the purchaser will be bound by her equity. A court, in determining the extent of that equity should then, it is submitted, approach the exercise of the discretion in the same way as it would if the transaction had not occurred.

Transaction by two owners

If the man appoints a second legal owner and then effects the transaction, then it is suggested that the purchaser will take free from her rights. This result could be achieved by holding that the woman's equity should be satisfied by a declaration that she had a beneficial share in the house that has now been overreached by the trustees for sale and that her remedies lie against them. To hold that she had a continuing right of occupation against a purchaser through estoppel in these circumstances would lead to the strange result that a woman who has simply relied on an assurance that she could stay in a house would be in a stronger position than a woman who had contributed to its purchase. It is submitted, therefore, that estoppel rights, in the present context,[19] would be overreached by a conveyance executed by the legal owners, thereby equating the positions of occupying beneficiaries with interests under a constructive or resulting trust and occupiers with rights acquired through estoppel.

---

[15] *Pascoe* v. *Turner* [1979] 1 W.L.R. 431.
[16] *Dodsworth* v. *Dodsworth* (1973) 228 E.G. 1115; *Re Sharpe* [1980] 1 W.L.R. 219. See also the imaginative approach in *Griffiths* v. *Williams* (1978) 248 E.G. 947.
[17] See also T. Bailey [1983] Conv. 99.
[18] *Blacklocks* v. *J.B. Developments (Godalming) Ltd.* [1982] Ch. 183. See D. G. Barnsley [1983] Conv. 361.
[19] If the right claimed is in the nature of an easement, as in *E.R. Ives Investment Ltd.* v. *High* [1967] 2 Q.B. 379 and *Crabb* v. *Arun District Council* [1976] Ch. 179 then this argument will not apply.

INDEX

Acquiescence,
  estoppel, essence of, 47–48
Advancement,
  presumption of, 28
Agreement,
  family home, acquisition of interests in, 38–39
  licence. *See* Licence.
Agricultural Tenancy,
  security of tenure, 69
Alienation,
  severance by, 21–22
Arrears,
  mortgage possession action, 113
Arrest,
  domestic violence, in case of, 95–97
  ouster order, jurisdiction to make, 86–87, 93
Asset,
  family, 35
Attorney, powers of,
  dispositions by two trustees, 134–135

Bank Account. *See* Joint Bank Account.
Bankruptcy,
  co-owners, 107
  defrauding creditors, 104
  divorce settlement, 107–108
  joint property, 104
  matrimonial home,
    beneficial ownership, agreement as to, 105
    exceptions to statute, 105
    financial contribution, 105
    matrimonial orders, 106
    settlement, whether, 105
    valuable consideration, 105–106
  onus of proof, 107
  petition,
    five and seven years, lodged within, 107
    five years, lodged within, 107
  relevant time, 106–107
  setting transactions aside, 103–105
  settlement voidable not void, 105
  trustee in,
    petition for sale by,
      application after bankruptcy, 108

Bankruptcy—*cont.*
  trustee in—*cont.*
    petition for sale by—*cont.*
      beneficial interest, vesting of, 108
      conditional postponement, 112
      discretion to order sale, application within first year, 109
      child, 109–110
      cohabitees, 109, 110
      no presumptions, 109
      presumption after one year, 109
      statutory criteria, 108–109
      education, 111
      exceptional circumstances, 110–112
      homelessness, 111
      illness, 111
      legal title, vesting of, 108
      postponement, consequences of, 112
      trustee, presumption in favour of, 110–111
      spouse's right of occupation, 81
  undervalue, transactions at, 104, 106
Business,
  assistance in, 42–43
  tenancy, 68–69
Buy, right to. *See* Right to Buy.

Caution,
  dispositions by two trustees, 133
Charging Order,
  enforcement of charge,
    continuation of relationship, 103
    notice, 102
    postponement of sale, 102–103
  family home,
    balancing of interests, 101
    chronology of actions, 101
    difficulties, 99–100
    family considerations, 100–101
    outright transfer unusual, 101–102
    presumption in favour of order, 100

Charging Order—*cont.*
  family home—*cont.*
    principles to be applied, 101
    sale, factors in favour of, 102
    writ, timing of, 102
  jurisdiction, 98
  making absolute, 99
  procedure, 99
  property, 98
  purchaser, enforcement against, 98–99
  statutory provisions, 98
Child,
  ouster order,
    importance of needs, 91
    welfare paramount, 90
  trust for sale, underlying purpose of, 55–56
  trustee in bankruptcy, petition for sale by, 109–110
Co-owner,
  bankruptcy, effect of, 107
  different expectations of, 1
  petition for sale by. *See* Sale.
  spouse's right of occupation, 80
  surety, as, 116
Cohabitation,
  family member, who is, 76
  joint investments, joint account to finance, 30–31
  orders under Matrimonial Causes Act 1973, effect on, 58
  ouster order, jurisdiction to make, 88
  trustee in bankruptcy, petition for sale by, 109, 110
Common Law,
  agricultural tenancy, 69
Concurrent Interests,
  features of, 1
Conduct,
  reliance, change necessary in case of, 48
  severance by course of, 22–23
Consecutive Interests,
  features of, 1
Consents,
  trust for sale, 6
Constructive Trust,
  estoppel interests, 136, 137
  family home, acquisition of interests in, 37–38
  formalities, 38
Contract,
  beneficial interests sold behind trust for sale, 10
  estoppel interests, 138
Contribution,
  beneficial interest in land acquired by, 19

Contribution—*cont.*
  family home, acquisition of,
    business, assistance in, 42–43
    direct, 41
    indirect, 42
    interest, quantification of, 41–42
    mortgage instalments, 41
    proportion of payments, 41
    size of, 40
Conversion, doctrine of,
  contract to sell beneficial interests, 10
  overreaching, when occurring, 10
  real and personal property, 10
  restriction of, 10–11
  succession, 9–10
  trust for sale, rights of beneficiaries under, 9
Coparceny,
  virtual obsolescence of, 11
Council Housing. *See* Public Sector Tenant.
County Court,
  ouster order, procedure for making, 92–93
Court,
  consents, petition to dispense with, 6
  estoppel, discretion in case of, 49–50
Creditor,
  defrauding, 104

Death,
  contemporaneous, 11–12
  joint tenant, of, effect on succession, 74–75
  owner, of, possession action at retirement, 72
Dispute,
  joint ownership, as to, 1
  qualifying family members, between, 76
  sale, as to, 53
Distress,
  landlord and tenant rights, 65
Divorce Settlement,
  bankruptcy, effect of, 107–108
Domestic Violence. *See* Violence.

Education,
  trustee in bankruptcy, petition for sale by, 111
Employee,
  possession action, 71
Employment,
  giving up, 49
Entirety,
  tenancy by, abolition of, 11

INDEX

Equity,
  accounting. *See* Family Home.
  co-owner's rights in, 119–121
  deserted wife, of, 79
  exoneration, of, 116–117
  separation from legal position, 13
Estoppel,
  acquiescence, requirements of, 47–48
  conduct, change of, 48
  constructive trust, 136, 137
  distinction, 137
  enforcement of rights, 138–139
  establishment of, 47–49
  giving up employment, 49
  moving house, 48–49
  nature of interest, 136
  principles of, 137
  priorities, 136–139
  proprietary, 47, 136–137
  reliance, requirements of, 47–48
  remedies,
    discretion, 49–50
    expectation enforced in full, 49
    family law considerations, 50
    perfecting imperfect gift, 49
  unconscionability as basis of, 47
Exclusion Order,
  extended exclusion, 94
  period of, 93–94
  procedure, 93
  time limit usually imposed, 94
Exoneration,
  equity of, 116–117
Express Trust,
  creation of, 33
  family home, ownership of,
    declaration of interest, 34
    execution of deed, 34
    interests at acquisition, 35

Family Home,
  acquisition of interests in,
    agreement,
      actual, 38
      inferring, 38–39
    business, assistance in, 42–43
    contributions to acquisition,
      direct, 41
      indirect, 42
      mortgage instalments, 41
      proportion of payments, 41
      quantification of interest, 41–42
      resulting trust, giving rise to, 40
      size of, 40
    equitable interest, disposition of, 33–34

Family Home—*cont.*
  acquisition of interests in—*cont.*
    estoppel,
      acquiescence, requirements of, 47–48
      changed conduct, necessity for, 48
      establishment of, 47–49
      giving up employment, 48–49
      limitation of trusts, 47
      moving house, 48–49
      oral agreement, 46–47
      proprietary, 47
      reliance, requirements of, 47–48
      remedies,
        court's discretion, exercise of, 49–50
        expectation, enforcement in full, 49
        family law considerations, 50
        perfecting imperfect gift, 49
      unconscionability as basis of, 47
    express trust,
      declaration of interest, 34
      deed, execution of, 34
      interests at acquisition, 35
      rectification onus on person seeking, 34
    family asset, house as, 35–36
    formalities, 38
    House of Lords approach, 36–37
    household expenditure,
      Burns v. Burns, 44
      flexible approach, 43
      general discretionary approach, 43–44
      indirect contribution, 43
      reference to acquisition, 44
    improvements,
      cases outside Act, 46
      intentions of parties, 45
      statutory discretion, disregarded in exercising, 46
      substantial nature, must be of, 46
    intention at, 36, 37
    interest consensus, 39–40
    joint names, 40
    married couples, 44–45
    money consensus, 39–40
    presumptions, 36
    unmarried couples, 44–45
  bankruptcy, effect of. *See* Bankrupcy.

INDEX

Family Home—*cont.*
  beneficial interests in,
    agreement as to, 36–37
    ascertaining, 35
    problems of, 31
  charging order. *See* Charging Order.
  constructive trust, application of principles of, 35, 37–38
  implied trust, application of principles of, 35
  moving, 48–49
  ownership, relevance of,
    married couple, 32–33
    unmarried couple, 33
  resulting trust, application of principles of, 35, 37
  sale of,
    accounting,
      capital, 51
      endowment mortgage,
        deposit, initial contributions to, 52
        policy, joint payments of, 52
        sale prior to policy maturing, 52
      examples, 51–52
      interest, 51
    valuation,
      date of assessment, 50–51
      increases in value, 51–52
      proportions and, 50
      time of sale, 51
  separate ownership, 31
  separate property,
    consequences of, 31–32
    reallocation of, 32
Forfeiture,
  relief against, 65
Forgery,
  dispositions by two trustees, 134

Gift,
  imperfect, perfecting of, 49
  presumption of, 28

Hardship,
  possession action, 71
High Court,
  ouster order, procedure for making, 92
Home. *See* Family Home.
Homelessness,
  ouster order, effect of, 91–92
  trustee in bankruptcy, petition for sale by, 111
Homicide,
  severance by, 23–24
House of Lords,
  family home, approach to, 36–37

Household Expenditure,
  family home, acquisition of interest in, 43–44
Husband and Wife,
  deserted wife's equity, 79
  ouster order, jurisdiction to make, 85
  severance by, 21
  spouse's right of occupation. *See* Occupation.
  See also Family Home.

Illness,
  trustee in bankruptcy, petition for sale by, 111
Imperfect Settlement,
  creation of, 3–4
Improvements,
  family home, acquisition of interest in, 46
  substantial nature of, 46
Injunction,
  mandatory, application for new business tenancy, 69
  ouster order. *See* Occupation.
Insolvency,
  bankruptcy. *See* Bankruptcy.
  charging order. *See* Charging Order.
  exoneration, equity of, 116–117
  mortgage possession action. *See* Mortgage.
Interest,
  concurrent, 1
  consecutive, 1
  consensus distinguished from money consensus, 39–40
  unity of, 12
Investments,
  cohabitation, effect of, 30–31
  joint ownership, 30
  purchase of, 29–31

Joint Bank Account,
  beneficial co-ownership, 29
  convenience of, 29
  creation by individuals, 28–29
  investments, purchase of, 29–31
  joint tenancy, 29
  tenancy in common, 29
Joint Tenancy,
  advantages over tenancy in common, 13
  contemporaneous deaths, 11–12
  conveyance to joint tenants, 15
  essential nature of, 11
  fair rent, registration of, 62
  joint bank account, 29
  jus accrescendi, 11
  licence compared with, 61–64
  right to buy, 77

INDEX

Joint Tenancy—*cont.*
  severance. *See* Severance.
  shams, 63
  survivorship, right of, 11
  unities,
    interest, 12
    possession, 12
    time, 12
    title, 12
Jus Accrescendi,
  joint tenancy, 11
  unfairness of, 18

Land,
  maximum number of legal
    owners, 14
  problems of co-ownership, 1
  purchasing more, 7–8
  registered, severance in case of,
    26
  settled. *See* Settlement.
  trust for sale. *See* Trust for Sale.
  unregistered. *See* Unregistered
    Land.
Landlord and Tenant,
  general law, 65
  notice to quit,
    landlord, by, 65–66
    public sector tenant, 68
    tenant, by, 66
  possession action. *See*
    Possession.
  protected tenancy, 64
  single entity, co-owners
    comprising, 65
  termination of lease,
    break clause, 65
    distress, 65
    forfeiture, relief against, 65
Lease,
  joint tenancy. *See* Joint
    Tenancy.
  licence distinguished from, 62
  lodgings distinguished from,
    62–63
  notice to quit,
    landlord, by, 65–66
    tenant, by, 66
  termination of,
    break clause, 65
    distress, 65
    forfeiture, relief against, 65
  widow, given to, in case of trust
    for sale, 5
Leasehold Property,
  agricultural tenancy, 69
  business tenancy,
    Harris v. Black, 69
    mandatory injunction, 69
    new, application for, 68
    qualification to apply, 68–69

Leasehold Property—*cont.*
  business tenancy—*cont.*
    security of tenure, 68
  joint tenancy. *See* Joint
    Tenancy.
  ouster order, purpose of, 94
  possession. *See* Possession.
  rent control, 66
  right to buy. *See* Right to Buy.
  security of tenure, 66–67
  spouse's right of occupation,
    83–84
  succession. *See* Succession.
  tenants,
    private sector, 67
    public sector,
      joint tenants, provision for,
        68
      notice to quit, 68
      remaining joint tenant,
        position of, 68
      security of tenure, 67–68
Legal Aid,
  enforcement of charge, 60
  existence of charge, 59
  lump sums, 60
  preservation of property, 59–60
  recovery of property, 59–60
  types of proceeding, 60
Legal Position,
  separation from equitable
    position, 13
Licence,
  after *Street v. Mountford*, 63
  exclusive possession, no right to,
    61
  fair rent, registration of, 62
  joint tenancy compared with,
    61–64
  judicial response, 62
  lease distinguished from, 62
  rooms, separate tenancies of, 64
  shams, 63
  Somma v. Hazlehurst, 62
Living Together as Man and Wife.
  See Cohabitation.
Lodgings,
  lease distinguished from, 62–63
London,
  party walls, 26

Magistrates' Court,
  ouster order, jurisdiction to
    make, 86–87
Married Couple. *See* Husband and
  Wife.
Matrimonial Home. *See* Family
  Home.
Mesher Order,
  development of, 57
  drawbacks of, 58

Mesher Order—*cont.*
  popularity of, 57
Money,
  all estate clause not operating to convey beneficial interest, 10
  consensus distinguished from interest consensus, 39–40
Mortgage,
  acquisition, 115–116
  endowment, 52, 115
  instalment, 114–115
  instalments, acquisition of interests in family home, 41
  possession action,
    acquisition of interest, 113
    arrears, 113
    default clauses, 113
    deferred payments, 113–114
    discretion to postpone possession,
      acquisition mortgage, 115–116
      deferred payment, 115
      endowment mortgage, 115
      finance, 116
      instalment mortgage, 114–115
      length of postponement, 116
    instalments, 113–114
    Matrimonial Homes Act, rights under, 112–113
    notice of, 114
    registration, 114
    sole legal owner, 112
  right to buy, 78
  severance, 19
  spouse's right of occupation, 82–83
  undue influence, effect of, 128
  unregistered land, 125–127
  Williams & Glyn's Bank v. Boland, decision in,
    actual occupation, 121–122
    co-owner, rights of,
      equity, in, 119–121
      overriding interest, as, 121
    legal title, 119
    overriding interest, 118
    response to, 118–119
    time of occupation, 122–124
Mutual Agreement,
  severance by, 22–23
Mutual Easements,
  party walls, 26

Non-Molestation Order,
  procedure, 93

Occupation,
  actual, 121–122
  joint, underlying purpose of trust for sale, 55
ouster order,
  application for, 89
  arrest, power of, 86–87, 93, 95–97
  child,
    importance of needs of, 91
    welfare of, 90
  cohabitees, 88
  criteria for making, 89–92
  discretion, exercise of, 91–92
  Domestic Violence and Matrimonial Proceedings Act 1976, 87–88
  emergency procedure,
    ex parte applications, 94–95
    Practice Direction, 95
  exclusion of spouse, 84–85
  exclusion order, 89–90, 93
  expedited order, 95
  extended exclusion, 94
  jurisdiction to make,
    arrest, power of, 86–87
    magistrates' court, 86–87
    married couple, 85–86
    personal protection, 86
    violence, 86
  leasehold property,
    council housing, 94
    private sector, 94
  living together as man and wife, 88–89
  non-molestation order, 93
  period of exclusion, 93
  procedure, 92
  statutes, interrelation of, 92–95
  statutory criteria, 90
  time limit usually imposed, 94
owner-occupier, possession action by, 71–72
rent,
  jurisdiction to order, 56–57
  limitations of solution, 57
  ouster, 56
  undertakings to pay, 57
spouse's right of,
  co-owners, 80
  deserted wife's equity, 79
  leasehold property,
    council housing, 84
    security of tenure, 83–84
    termination of tenancy, 83
  non-registration, 83
  registration,
    effect of,
      precautions, 82
      Wroth v. Tyler, 82

Occupation—*cont.*
  spouse's right of—*cont.*
    registration—*cont.*
      methods of, 81
      mortgages, 82–83
      one house, 82
      third party, right enforceable aganist, 80–81
      trustee in bankruptcy, 81
      unregistered land, 81
      who can register, 81–82
    statutory, 79–80
    transfer of tenancy, 84
  time of, 122–124
  unregistered land, 126
Oral Declaration,
  severance by, 22
Order,
  charging. *See* Charging Order.
  Mesher. *See* Mesher Order.
Ouster,
  occupation rent, 56
  order. *See* Occupation.
Overreaching,
  conversion, doctrine of, 8, 9
  dispositions by two trustees, 129, 131–132
  implied trust for sale, 9
  two trustees, 8–9
Owner-Occupier,
  possession action, 71–72

Partnership,
  severance, 18
Party Walls,
  legal position with regard to, 26
  London, 26
  mutual easements, 26
Per Capita Agreement. *See* Licence.
Personal Property,
  advancement, presumption of, 28
  family home. *See* Family Home.
  gift, presumption of, 28
  investments, purchase of,
    cohabitation, effect of, 30–31
    joint bank account, use of, 29–30
    joint ownership, 30
  joint bank account,
    beneficial co-ownership, 29
    convenience, co-ownership for, 29
    joint tenancy, whether, 29
    problems of, 28
    tenancy in common, whether, 29
    when created, 28–29
  joint names, taken in, 27

Personal Property—*cont.*
  real property distinguished from, 10
  resulting trust, co-ownership arising by way of, 27–28
  trust,
    creation of, 27
    presumption of, 28
Personal Protection,
  ouster order, jurisdiction to make, 86
Petition,
  bankruptcy, 107
  consents, to dispense with, 6
  sale, for. *See* Sale.
  Section 30. *See* Sale.
Possession,
  action,
    discretionary grounds, 70
    dwelling-house reasonably required by landlord, 70–71
    employees, 71
    greater hardship provision, 71
    mortgage. *See* Mortgage.
    owner-occupiers, 71–72
    retirement,
      death of owner, 72
      joint landlords, 72
      landlord, intention of occupation by, 72
      tenant, conduct by, 73–74
      trustees, landlords as, 71
  exclusive, no right granted by licence, 61
  residential tenancy, 70
  unity of, 12
Precedent,
  severance by written declaration, 20
Priorities,
  dispositions by two trustees, 129–136
  estoppel interests, 136–139
  undue influence, 128–129
  unregistered land, 125–127
  Williams & Glyn's Bank v. Boland, decision in, 118–124
Private Sector Tenant,
  family member, who is, 76
  ouster order, purpose of, 94
  protective legislation, 67
  succession, 75, 76
Property,
  leasehold. *See* Leasehold Property.
  personal. *See* Personal Property.
Protected Tenancy,
  benefits of, 61
  landlord and tenant rights, 64

Public Sector Tenant,
  family member, who is, 75
  joint tenants, provision for, 68
  notice to quit, 68
  ouster order, purpose of, 94
  protective legislation, 67–68
  remaining joint tenant, position of, 68
  spouse's right of occupation, 84
  succession, 75
Purchaser,
  charging order, enforcement of, 98–99
  trust for sale, protection in case of, 6–7

Real Property,
  personal property distinguished from, 10
Registered Land,
  severance, 26
Registration,
  dispositions by two trustees, 130
  mortgage possession action, 114
  right to buy, 77
  spouse's right of occupation. *See* Occupation.
Reliance,
  estoppel, essence of, 47–48
Remedies,
  arrest. *See* Arrest.
  estoppel. *See* Estoppel.
Rent,
  control, 66
  fair, registration of, 62
  joint tenancy distinguished from licence, 62
  occupation, 56–57
Residential Tenancy,
  possession, grounds for, 70
Resulting Trust,
  personal property, application in sphere of, 27–28
Retirement,
  possession action on, 72
Right to Buy,
  discount,
    calculation of, 77–78
    length of residence, 77–78
    resale, covenant to repay on, 78
  joint tenancy, 76–77
  mortgage, right to,
    amounts to be borrowed, 78
    example, 78
    multipliers, 78
  one joint tenant, occupation by, 77
  purchase, joint tenancy after, 77
  registration of title, 77

Rooms,
  separate tenancies of, 64

Sale,
  charging order. *See* Charging Order.
  family home, of. *See* Family Home.
  overreaching. *See* Overreaching.
  petition for,
    dispute as to, 53
    legal aid,
      enforcement of charge, 60
      existence of charge, 59
      lump sums, 60
      preservation of property, 59–60
      recovery of property, 59–60
      types of proceeding, 60
    occupation rent,
      jurisdiction to order, 56–57
      limitations of solution, 57
      occupying co-owner ordered to pay, 56
      ouster, 56
      undertakings to pay, 57
    orders,
      cohabitation, effect of, 58
      flexible, 58
      mesher,
        development of, 57
        drawbacks of, 58
        popularity of, 57
      subsequent sale,
        county court jurisdiction, 59
        jurisdiction, 58–59
        original purpose of, 59
        premature sale, 59
    Section 30, 53, 54
    trustee in bankruptcy, by. *See* Bankruptcy.
    underlying purpose,
      child,
        general equitable approach, 55–56
        limitations of test, 55
        Rawlings v. Rawlings, 55
        relevant factors, 56
      implied agreement, 54
      joint occupation, 55
      test of, 54
  power of, 2–3
  right to buy. *See* Right to Buy.
  trust for. *See* Trust for Sale.
Security of Tenure,
  agricultural tenancy, 69
  business tenancy, 68–69
  implementation of, 66–67
  private sector tenants, 67

Index

Security of Tenure—*cont.*
  public sector tenants, 67–68
  spouse's right of occupation, 83–84
Settled Land Act 1925,
  power of sale, 2–3
  scheme of, 2–3
Settlement,
  co-ownership for life, 16
  divorce, 107–108
  drawbacks of, 3–4
  imperfect, 3–4
  power of sale, 2–3
  Settled Land Act, scheme of, 2–3
  strict,
    meaning, 2
    trust for sale distinguished from, 2, 7
  succession, 3
  two-deed system, 2
  voidable not void, 105
Severance,
  contributions,
    equal, 19
    unequal, 19
  course of conduct, by, 22–23
  effect of, 24–25
  homicide, by,
    constructive trust, whether, 24
    survivorship, possibility of, 23–24
    types of, 24
  husband and wife, by, 21
  implied, 18
  land,
    registered, 26
    unregistered, 25–26
  methods of, 19–20
  mortgages, 19
  mutual agreement, by, 19
    inferred, 23
    requisite intent, 23
    unenforceable contract, 22–23
  notice of, 20, 25–26
  partnership, by, 18
  procedure on, 25
  rebuttable presumption, 18–19
  statutory,
    Harris v. Goddard, 20–21
    notice indicating desire to sever, 20
    precedent, 20
    unequivocal intention, 20
  tenancy in common,
    conversion of beneficial joint tenancy to, 16
    express, 16–17
  unilateral action, by,
    alienation, 21–22
    oral declarations, 22

Severance—*cont.*
  words of,
    examples, 17
    general intention, 17
    inconsistent provisions, 18
Shams,
  meaning, 63
Spouse. *See* Husband and Wife.
Statutory Severance. *See* Severance.
Statutory Trust,
  imposition of, 14
  joint tenants, conveyance to, 15
  meaning, 14
  tenants in common, devise to, 14–15
  title, keeping beneficial interests off, 14
Strict Settlement. *See* Settlement.
Succession,
  conversion, doctrine of, 9–10
  death of joint tenant,
    contractual tenancy, suspension of, 75
    non-occupying joint tenants, 75
    private sector, 75
    public sector, 75
  member of family, person regarded as,
    cohabitees, 76
    platonic relationships, 76
    private sector, 76
    public sector, 75
    qualifying members, 76
  Settled Land Act, cumbersome structure imposed by, 3
  statutory, 74
Surety,
  co-owner as, 116
Survivorship,
  joint tenancy, concept of, 11
  tenancy in common, 13

Tenancy,
  agricultural, 69
  business, 68–69
  coparceny, 11
  entirety, by, 11
  in common. *See* Tenancy in Common.
  joint. *See* Joint Tenancy.
  protected, 61
  residential, grounds for possession, 70
  transfer of, 84
  See also Landlord and Tenant; Leasehold Property.
Tenancy in Common,
  abolition of, 13

Tenancy in Common—*cont.*
  advantages of joint tenancy over, 13
  express, 16–17
  joint bank account, 29
  joint tenancy, creation of, 63–64
  nature of, 12–13
  party walls, 26
  sole ownership at law but co-ownership involving, 15–16
  survivorship, no automatic right of, 13
  undivided shares, 13
Tenant in Common,
  devise to, 14–15
Third Party,
  spouse's right of occupation, 80–81
Time,
  unity of, 12
Title,
  fragmentation of, 18
  trustee in bankruptcy, petition for sale by, 108
  unity of, 12
Trust,
  constructive. *See* Constructive Trust.
  express. *See* Express Trust.
  resulting. *See* Resulting Trust.
  sale, for. *See* Trust for Sale.
  statutory. *See* Statutory Trust.
Trust for Sale,
  beneficiaries, rights under, 9
  co-ownership occurs primarily behind, 1
  consents,
    hindering sale, 6
    petition to court, 6
    sale not to take place without, 6
  contract to sell beneficial interests behind, 10
  creation of, 4
  dispositions by two trustees,
    additional trustee, appointment of, 135–136
    attorney, powers of, 134–135
    beneficial interest, protection of, 132–133
    conveying co-owned property, 133
    Flegg's case, 130
    forgery, 134
    interests behind, 129–130
    non-registration, 130–131
    overreaching provisions, 129, 131–132
    registration issues, 130
  implied, 9
  life, co-ownership for, 16

Trust for Sale—*cont.*
  meaning, 4
  overreaching,
    conversion, doctrine of, 8, 9
    implied trust for sale, 9
    interest in money, not land, 10
    other contexts, 10–11
    real and personal property, 10
    restricting conversion, 10–11
    succession, 9–10
    two trustees, 8–9
  petition for sale. *See* Sale.
  postponement of sale, 4–5, 5–6
  purchaser, protection of, 6–7
  residence provisions, 5
  strict settlement distinguished from, 2, 7
  trustees,
    legal title in, 4
    powers of,
      delegation, 8
      proceeds of sale, 7
      purchasing more land, 7–8
      restriction of, 7
    strict settlement distinguished from trust for sale, 7
  underlying purpose,
    child,
      general equitable approach, 55–56
      limitations of test, 55
      Rawlings v. Rawlings, 55
      relevant factors, 56
    implied agreement, 54
    joint occupation, 55
    test of, 54–55
  widow, non-assignable lease for life given to, 5
Trustee,
  additional, appointment of, 135–136
  bankruptcy, in. *See* Bankruptcy.
  overreaching, 8–9
  possession action, 71
  trust for sale. *See* Trust for Sale.

Unconscionability,
  estoppel, as basis of, 47
Underlying Purpose. *See* Trust for Sale.
Undue Influence,
  mortgage, effect on, 128–129
Unilateral Action,
  severance by, 21–22
Unmarried Couple,
  family home. *See* Family Home.
Unregistered Land,
  appointment, viewing by, 126
  constructive notice, 125
  dispositions by two trustees, 133

Index

Unregistered Land—*cont.*
  enquiries, extent of, 126
  establishing right, 127
  mortgage, 125–127
  notice from other sources, 126–127
  occupation, 126
  priorities, 125–127
  severance, 25–26
  spouse's right of occupation, 81

Valuation of Family Home. *See* Family Home.
Violence,
  arrest, powers of, 95–97

Violence—*cont.*
  ouster order, jurisdiction to make, 86

Walls. *See* Party Walls.
Widow,
  lease for life given to, 5
Will,
  real property distinguished from personal property, 10
Writ,
  charging order, timing as to, 102
Written Declaration,
  severance by, 20